P9-DZY-368

WEBSTER'S
NEW WORLD™

ROBERT'S RULES
of
ORDER

Simplified and Applied

WEBSTER'S NEW WORLD™

ROBERT'S RULES

of

ORDER

Simplified and Applied

Robert McConnell Productions

Webster's New World™
An Imprint of Simon & Schuster Macmillan
New York

Macmillan General Reference
A Simon & Schuster Macmillan Company
1633 Broadway
New York, NY 10019-6785

A Webster's New World™ book

MACMILLAN is a registered trademark of Macmillan, Inc.

Manufactured in the United States of America

02 01 00   — 5 4

Webster's New World Robert's rules of order : simplified and applied / Robert McConnell Productions.
p. cm.
"A Webster's New World book"—T.p. verso.
Includes index.
ISBN 0-02-862749-0 (pbk)
1. Parliamentary practice. I. Robert, Henry. M.
(Henry Martyn). 1837–1923. Robert's rules of order. II.
Robert McConnell Productions.
JF515.W42 1998
060.4'2—dc21   98-42343
CIP

ISBN: 0-02-862749-0

Contents

PART I: Meetings and Organizations

PART III: MEMBERSHIP

PART IV: MEETINGS AND STRATEGIES

PART V: APPENDICES

Preface and Acknowledgements

This book is dedicated to people who want a clear, simple explanation of the rules of parliamentary procedure and strategies for saving time at meetings while preserving the democratic process. Most people are familiar with the rules of parliamentary procedure as they are presented in *Robert's Rules of Order*. The goal of this book is to help you understand and apply these rules for more effective and efficient meetings. We explain the principles and concepts behind each rule in everyday language so that you can understand why a particular rule is important and what its role is in maintaining the democratic process. Then, we show you through scripts and everyday examples, how these rules can be applied in any meeting to bring order and help members get things done in a timely manner.

What makes this book unique? Several years ago an idea to produce videos to teach the basic rules of parliamentary procedure as exemplified in *Robert's Rules of Order* was born. These videos have sold thousands of copies worldwide. As technology progressed, we also created a website dedicated exclusively to helping people understand and apply the rules on a case by case basis and in an interactive way. This book takes the concept of teaching the rules through concise explanation of principles, everyday examples and cases from our videos and website and puts it into book form. See the final page of this book for more information about these videos and our website.

The authors would like to thank the following people for their help in preparing the final manuscript. Harold Corbin, Registered Parliamentarian, for reading the entire manuscript to ensure accuracy in conforming to *Robert's Rules of Order*. Jeanne Everett for reading the manuscript to ensure that it would make sense to the general reader and be free from errors in spelling, grammar, and punctuation. Sarah McConnell for reading the manuscript in its early stages and offering constructive suggestions. Faunette Johnston, Diana Francour, and the other editors at Macmillan Publishing for rendering the manuscript into its final form.

Introduction

There are some basic principles and procedures that apply to all decision making processes whether you are a family trying to plan an outing, a manager trying to lead a work team, or an officer in an organization trying to conduct a meeting. These principles and procedures are referred to formally as parliamentary procedure. Parliamentary procedures are the rules that help us maintain order and ensure fairness in all decision making processes. *Robert's Rules of Order* is one man's presentation and discussion of parliamentary procedure that has become the leading authority in most organizations today.

The basic principles behind all *Robert's Rules of Order* are:

1. Someone has to facilitate or direct the discussion and keep order.

2. All members of the group have the right to bring up ideas, discuss them, and come to a conclusion.

3. Members should come to an agreement about what to do.

4. Members should understand that the majority rules, but the rights of the minority are always protected by assuring them the right to speak and to vote.

The following chapters will first explain, in a simple way, the basic principles of *Robert's Rules of Order*. Then they will show you how and when to apply the rules so that you can expedite your business quickly and efficiently while ensuring fairness and due process.

Webster's New World Robert's Rules of Order: Simplified and Applied includes several tools that will help you in this step-by-step process. "Scripting" of exactly what to say and when to say it appears throughout the book. The scripts are structured like the dialogue found in a play and they begin by telling you who is to do the talking (in italics), followed by what should be said, and then any physical actions to be performed (in brackets), such as rising to obtain the floor, or rapping the gavel. Quick-reference boxes for each motion tell you at-a-glance the purpose of the motion, if it requires a second, is amendable, is debatable, what kind of vote is required to adopt it, and what the result will be if adopted. Easy-to-read charts provide a quick visual guide to the ranking of each motion so that you can quickly determine the correct order of proceedings. And finally, the appendices provide actual examples of minutes, officers' reports, scripts of an entire meeting, as well as a guide to correct terminology, and a short history of Henry Robert and the development of parliamentary procedure as it is practiced today.

PART I

MEETINGS AND ORGANIZATIONS

1

The Basics

In a democratic society there are many principles of conduct and self-government that we hold dear. When people come together in their organizations and governments to conduct business, certain rules, referred to collectively as parliamentary procedure, have been created and must be applied correctly to maintain these democratic principles.

Two mistakes are commonly made by organization members: not knowing parliamentary procedure at all, and misapplying it due to a lack of understanding the underlying democratic principles or to the desire to manipulate them. These mistakes invariably lead to confusion and, in the worst cases, can result in intimidation and the loss of members' rights. This chapter begins with an explanation of the fundamental democratic principles from which parliamentary procedure proceeds and how these principles affect and apply to the structure of an organization. Parliamentary procedure is then defined and a discussion of its importance and application in protecting basic democratic principles follows. It is imperative for all members and their organizations to understand these principles to ensure the preservation of the democratic process.

STRUCTURE OF AN ORGANIZATION

There are basically two ways to structure an organization. One way is based on the authoritarian model, which favors the concentration of power in a leader or a small group of people who may or may not be responsible to the members. In the extreme form of this model, one person or a small group (such as a board of directors) may make all the decisions with no input or final approval from the membership.

The second way to structure an organization is based on the democratic model, which is government by the people or the members. In the extreme form of this model, all decisions are made by the members and not by any elected representatives. However, in most organizations, there is an agreed upon balance of power that has been achieved between those who are elected to office and those who are the members.

The democratic style of government is founded upon laws and the rights and responsibilities of all the members, not the whims of an unaccountable leadership. Abraham Lincoln has defined democratic government as "government of the people, by the people, and for the people." The organization that has no rules or governing documents to establish a course of action will find itself in a state of anarchy. In the words of Henry M. Robert, who wrote what we know today as *Robert's Rules of Order,* "Where there is no law, but every man does what is right in his own eyes, there is the least of real liberty."

APPLYING DEMOCRATIC PRINCIPLES TO ORGANIZATIONS

For an organization to survive and grow, the democratic model has proved to be the best form of government because it makes use of the talent and abilities of all the members. Organizations are democratic to the extent that they conform in the following ways:

1. *The members rule through a decision-making process that they have established by a vote.* This process is embodied in the organization's governing documents—its constitution, bylaws, rules of order, standing rules, policy statements, and parliamentary authority, such as **Robert's Rules of Order**. This is government by the consent of the governed.

2. *Ideas come from the members and are presented to the assembly to decide upon.* Everyone gets the right to present ideas, to speak to them, and to vote on them.

3. *Leaders come from the people through an election process.* When the leader's term of office is ended, he or she returns to the people. There is no hierarchy of power; it is shared equally. All members have the right to be considered for office.

4. *There are checks and balances between the leadership and the members, as established in the governing documents.* As an example of checks and balances, officers and boards of directors have only the power assigned to them by the governing documents. Those powers not specifically given to officers and boards in the bylaws enable members to reverse decisions made by boards and officers. Another check and balance given in the bylaws is the right of the membership to remove ineffective or tyrannical leaders from office.

5. *All members are equal*—they have equal rights and responsibilities.

6. *There is impartiality and fairness.* The rule is by law and enactments, not by the whims of the leadership. The rules are applied equally, impartially, and fairly to all and not just a select few.

7. *There is equal justice under the law; members and officers have a right to a fair trial if accused.* There are written procedures for removing and replacing an officer when the officer is not fulfilling his or her duties.

8. *The majority rules, but the rights of the minority and absent members are protected.*

9. *Everything is accomplished in the spirit of openness, not secrecy.* Members have the right to know what is going on within the organization by attending meetings, by inspecting the official records, and by receiving notices and reports of committees, officers, and boards.

10. *Members have the right to resign from office or the organization.*

The rights and obligations of members and officers should be clearly stated in the governing documents. These documents consist of the corporate charter (if there is one), documents issued by the state for incorporation, bylaws (or the constitution), and any rules of order or standing rules. Each organization should adopt a parliamentary authority, which is a book of common parliamentary law that details the rules for conducting meetings, electing officers, and making and adopting motions. All members are entitled to have a copy of their governing rules.

For a democracy to succeed, the members must work harmoniously together. This is accomplished by each member knowing the purpose and goals of the organization, its rules, the rights of each individual member, and what each member is expected to do. One of the greatest threats to a democratic organization is for the members to become apathetic and let a small group of the membership do all the work. This creates schisms and promotes authoritarianism. Another threat is for a small group to work secretly behind the scenes to accomplish its own goals or its own agenda and then push this through without the rest of the membership having an input either through discussion or through the investigative process. Such actions cause mistrust and hostility.

If the *principles* of democracy are not upheld in the organization, knowing and following the *rules* of parliamentary procedure is valueless.

DEFINING PARLIAMENTARY PROCEDURE

Parliamentary procedure enables members to take care of business in an efficient manner and to maintain order while business is being conducted. It ensures that everyone gets the right to speak and to vote. Parliamentary procedure takes up business one thing at a time and promotes courtesy, justice, and impartiality. It ensures the rule of the majority while protecting the rights of the minority and absent members. Adhering to parliamentary procedure is democracy in action.

The procedures, or rules, are found in the organization's bylaws, standing rules, and in its adopted parliamentary authority. A *parliamentary authority* is a reference book that helps the members decide what to do when the group has no written rules concerning how certain things are done. The parliamentary authority most commonly used in North America, and the one this book is based upon, is *Robert's Rules of Order, Newly Revised.*

IMPORTANCE OF PARLIAMENTARY PROCEDURES

Parliamentary procedures provide proven, time-tested ways of determining action and carrying on an organization's business. One frequently asked question is: Why do I need to know these parliamentary rules—and what difference do they make? Knowing parliamentary procedures might be compared with knowing the "rules of the road." Because you have learned the rules of driving, you know which side of the road to drive on, who has the right of way at street corners, who goes first at a four-way stop, and the rules of turning left in front of oncoming traffic. Obeying these and other rules of the road keeps traffic flowing smoothly and accidents from happening. When everyone knows the parliamentary rules, meetings run smoothly, and the head-on collisions that can happen during the discussion of controversial motions can be prevented. If everyone in your group will learn the basics of parliamentary procedure, you will have more productive meetings, more members making and discussing motions, and more members willing to serve as officers and committee chairmen.

BASIC PRINCIPLES OF PARLIAMENTARY PROCEDURE

There are three fundamental principles of democracy and parliamentary procedure that everyone needs to know before learning the specific rules. If you can remember these principles, you will be able to solve problems that come up in your organization and meetings even if you can't remember the specific rules.

The first principle is: *business is taken up one thing at a time.* This maintains order, expedites business, and accomplishes the purpose of the organization.

The second principle is: *to promote courtesy, justice, impartiality, and equality.* This ensures that everyone is heard; that members treat each other with courtesy; and that everyone has the same rights, and no individual or special group is singled out for special favors.

The third principle is: *the rule of the majority while protecting the rights of the individual, minority, and absent members.* This principle ensures that, even though the majority rules, the minority has a right to be heard and its ideas are taken seriously. Similarly, the minority does not leave the organization because it did not win; it knows that it may win another day. Following this principle preserves the unity and harmony of the organization.

Applying These Basic Principles

The three fundamental principles of business being taken up one thing at a time; promoting courtesy, justice, impartiality, and equality; and the rule of the majority while protecting the rights of the individual, minority, and absent members can now be illustrated by individual rules. The following section takes each principle and then gives the individual rules that apply the principle.

Taking Up Business One Thing at a Time

Like most of us, members in a business meeting can do only one thing at a time. Thus comes into play the first and foremost rule of parliamentary procedure: taking up business one thing at a time.

1. The principle of taking up business one thing at a time establishes an order of business called an *agenda* or *order of business*. Everything on the agenda is taken

up in its proper order and disposed of before the members go on to the next item of the agenda.

2. Only one main motion can be pending at a time.

3. When a main motion is pending, members can make motions from a class of motions called secondary motions. And when these are taken up, they take precedence over the main motion. Any discussion is only on the secondary motion until it has been resolved or temporarily disposed of. Some examples of secondary motions are **amend**, **refer to a committee**, and **postpone**.

4. Only one member can be assigned the floor at a time.

5. Members take turns speaking.

6. No member speaks twice until all have had the opportunity to speak.

Promoting Courtesy

As children growing up, we were taught manners—or courtesies toward others. In our daily dealings and meetings with other people, courtesies are the necessities of life that promote harmony and unity.

Here are the ways courtesy is applied during meetings:

1. The chair or presiding officer calls the meeting to order on time. This is being courteous to those present. Why should they have to wait for the latecomers to arrive?

2. Members are seated promptly when the chair calls the meeting to order, and conversation stops.

3. Those members giving a report take a seat in front. This saves time.

4. Members rise to be recognized by the presiding officer and don't speak out of turn.

5. Members always refer to other members and officers in the third person. Officers are referred to by their title; for example, Mr. President or Madam President, Mr. Chairman or Madam Chairman. Members refer to each other by saying, for example, "the previous speaker" or "the delegate from District 2." This prevents personalizing and, in a worst case scenario, name-calling or personal attacks.

6. In debate, members do not "cross talk," or talk directly to each other, when another is speaking. All remarks are made through, and to, the chair.

7. Discussion is kept to the issues, not to personalities or other members motives.

8. When correcting a member, the presiding officer does not use the member's name but states: "Will the speaker keep his (or her) remarks to the issue at hand?"

   Or if a motion is out of order the chair states: "The motion is out of order," *not* "The member is out of order." (To tell a member that he or she is out of order is technically charging the member with an offense.)

9. Members speak clearly and loudly so all can hear, or members use a microphone if one is provided.

10. Members listen when others are speaking.

Justice, Impartiality, and Equality

Here is how justice, impartiality, and equality work in meetings:

1. The presiding officer does not take sides but allows all to be heard equally in debate. If the presiding

officer wants to voice an opinion about the issue under discussion, the presiding officer relinquishes the chair to another officer so that he or she can speak and vote.

2. The presiding officer and members should know the rules and apply them judiciously. Only major infractions are corrected. If members' rights are not being taken away and the infraction is minor, it isn't necessary to raise a **point of order** to correct the infraction.

3. The presiding officer ensures that all sides of an issue are heard and that the rules of debate are carefully followed. These measures prevent a small group from railroading something through.

4. Members have a right to move to take a vote by ballot during a controversial issue. A ballot vote preserves their privacy and prevents possible retaliation for the way they voted.

5. Members have a right to a trial when accused of wrongdoing.

The Rule of the Majority and Protection of the Minority

One of the most important rights that members have is the right to vote, knowing that the majority rules. At the same time, the majority never has the right to silence or take away rights from the minority. The principle of the rule of the majority while protecting the rights of the minority and absent members and the rights of the individual members, thus means:

1. Members have the right to be given notice of all meetings. Notice may be given by mail, phone, electronic communication, or announcement at a meeting.

2. Members have the right to know by previous notice when there is a proposal to rescind or to amend an action.

3. In any situation where rights may be taken away from members, there must be a two-thirds vote instead of a majority vote. Examples are amending the governing documents or removing someone from office or membership.

4. No one has the right to require a higher vote than a majority vote on issues unless specifically stated in the bylaws or the parliamentary authority.

5. Members have a right to be informed of the work of the organization. Reading the minutes of the prior meeting allows members to correct inaccurate information and informs the absent members of any action taken. Members have the right to hear reports of board action, committee work, and officers.

2

The Order of a Business Meeting

A business meeting provides members with the opportunity to propose ideas and to participate in forming the plans and actions of the organization. To do this in an orderly and efficient fashion, the business of the meeting is conducted according to the first principle of parliamentary procedure, which states that business is taken up one item at a time. The plan, or the established order, in which the items of business are taken up is called an *agenda*. This is a Latin word meaning "things to be done." Common parliamentary law over the years has arrived at an accepted order for a business meeting. Sometimes, however, an organization may wish to follow a different order of business. In that case, it must be written in the organization's own rules of order, which should be with, but not part of, the bylaws.

This chapter explains the accepted order of business, including how to plan and adopt an agenda and when special kinds of agendas are needed. It gives an overview of each aspect of the agenda, from determining a quorum to receiving reports from officers and committees, hearing new business, and adjourning the meeting.

ACCEPTED ORDER OF BUSINESS

After the president determines that a quorum (the required minimum number of members needed to have a meeting) is present, the president calls the meeting to order. He proceeds with the organization's established order of business. If an organization has no established order of business, the following is the customary order of business for organizations that have regular meetings within a quarterly time period.

1. **The minutes of the previous meeting are read and approved.** Often members want to dispense with the reading of the minutes because they do not feel that the minutes are important to hear. However, it must be remembered that the minutes are a legal document for the organization. By approving the minutes, the members are agreeing that "this is what happened at the meeting." Minutes are used in court when a legal action has been brought against the organization. Therefore, it is important that the minutes be approved by the assembly, or a committee named for the purpose of approving the minutes. There is no time limit on the correction of the minutes.

   The minutes also serve to inform members who were absent from the previous meeting of what happened at the meeting. The minutes provide an opportunity to correct oversights. For example, there may be motions that carry over business to the present meeting that are in the minutes but that are not on the agenda. Members who are alert while the minutes are being read can then ask that these motions be added to the agenda of the present meeting. Another important point concerning the minutes and placing items on the agenda is that the motion to lay on the table is recorded in the minutes but is not put on the agenda. It is a parliamentary rule that since the members voted to lay the motion on the table, only the members can take it from the table by making a motion to do so. By listening carefully when the minutes are read, members will take note of this and know the right course of action to take.

2. **The reports of officers, boards, and standing committees (those listed in the bylaws) are read and discussed.** It is not necessary for the officers and standing committees to give a report at every meeting. A report should be placed on the agenda only when there is something to report to the membership.

3. **The reports of special committees (if there are any) are heard.** These are committees that have been created for a special purpose and are not listed in the bylaws. They cease to exist when they have completed their work and have made their final report.

4. **Any special orders are presented.** These are motions postponed to this meeting and made a special order so that they come up before unfinished business (see Chapter 6).

5. **Unfinished business and general orders are discussed.** *Unfinished business* is a motion that was under discussion at the time the previous meeting adjourned. A *general order* is a motion that was postponed to the current meeting. These terms apply in meetings of groups that meet quarterly or more often.

6. **The members proceed to "new business."** *New business* proposes an issue that is new to this meeting. It may be something not discussed before or something that was defeated at a past meeting, or even at the last meeting, and it can be brought up again at this meeting.

7. **When the agenda items are finished and the assembly has no further business to propose, it's time to adjourn.**

PLANNING AND USING AGENDAS

The agenda, or order of business, described in the preceding section is a standard one. Depending on the needs of your organization, you can add items to the agenda and you can use special types of agenda. The following discussion will explain how to prepare an agenda in a logical manner and will also discuss adding optional agenda items, adopting an agenda, mailing an agenda, and streamlining an agenda.

Agenda Planning

In any kind of meeting, the person leading the meeting should preside from an *agenda*—an outline of items, listed in order of importance, that are to be accomplished at the meeting. Having an agenda keeps the meeting on track and saves time.

Agenda items come from the order of business as established either by the parliamentary authority or by the rules of the organization. After the general outline is prepared, the person preparing the agenda fills in the details.

The most important resource for filling in these details is the minutes of the previous meeting. From these minutes, the agenda planner should include any unfinished agenda items from the last meeting.

In agenda planning, look first for any special orders. These may be special orders made for the previous meeting but not disposed of before adjournment. They may be motions that were postponed to and made special orders for the current meeting. Special orders are of some priority or importance. This category has been created so members can complete more important tasks before they take up any other business. Items considered special orders, and therefore of high priority, are: nominations, elections of officers, and the voting of new members into membership.

After special orders, general orders and unfinished business. (The term "old business" is apt to be confusing and should not be used.) The first topic to be taken up under this category is *general orders*, which are any motion that was pending at the last meeting when the meeting adjourned. *Pending* means specifically that the motion had not been voted on but was still in the process of being discussed. Unfinished business is any motion that was on the agenda but which the members did not have time to take up before adjournment.

Third, look for motions that were postponed to the previous meeting but the members did not have time to discuss. These would be agenda items from the last meeting that are carried over to the current meeting.

Fourth, look for motions that were postponed to the present meeting. These are taken up in the order they were made at the previous meeting.

Once the minutes have been reviewed, the person preparing the agenda has a number of resources, mostly the members themselves. Consulting the board members or other officers ahead of time about the agenda items can save time. For example, when filling in the specifics under "reports of officers, boards, and committees," the president or whoever is preparing the agenda should ask the appropriate people whether they have anything to report. Only those who have reports to give are put on the agenda. Doing this saves time during the meeting because the president is calling on only those who have a report to give.

Under "new business," the person preparing the agenda should ask the board members or other officers if they have something that they want to put on the agenda before the meeting. Some organizations have a rule requiring members to submit any new business items to the secretary in writing before the items can be included in the agenda. However, in most organizations, when there is no new business on the agenda, the chair asks the members, "Is there any new business?" Members always have the right to present ideas to the assembly, and new business is the place to do it.

Other Possibilities for Agenda Topics

Most organizations incorporate some optional agenda items into their meetings. Examples of optional items are opening ceremonies, roll call, programs, announcements, and what has been called "for the good of the organization."

Opening ceremonies may be a pledge to the flag, a prayer or invocation, or any ritual that is unique to the organization and has nothing to do with business. This always comes immediately after the meeting is called to order. If there is a roll call of members to record attendance or establish a quorum, it follows the opening ceremonies. Then the minutes are read. Programs may include a special speaker or entertainment, and usually follow new business. Announcements come right before adjournment.

Some organizations take time right before adjournment for the "good of the order." This segment allows members to give suggestions for improvement or to give compliments concerning the work of the organization. However, no business can be brought up during this period of the meeting. Any ideas for new business that come from this segment should be brought up at another meeting.

Adopting the Agenda

Although the agenda may be adopted at the beginning of the meeting, it should not be used to tie the hands of the assembly, prevent members from bringing up business, or enable a small group to railroad through their pet projects. Agendas should have flexibility to provide for unseen things that may come up in a meeting. Some organizations want to adopt an agenda believing that no further items can be added as the meeting progresses, which, of course, is not true. If an agenda is adopted, changing it simply takes a two-thirds vote.

An organization can adopt an agenda only if its governing documents don't include rules of order dictating the order of a business meeting. (Rules of order unique to a particular organization are usually included with, but not part of, the bylaws.) Some organizations want to adopt the agenda believing that no further items can be added as the meeting progresses, which of course is not true.

There are some types of meetings in which it is most important to adopt the agenda: those that occur less than quarterly, conventions, or other sessions that may last for several days. Because these meetings take place infrequently, the advantage of adopting an agenda ensures that participants will accomplish the tasks on the agenda without getting sidetracked by other issues. An agenda is adopted by a majority vote. After it is adopted, it may be changed by a two-thirds vote, as mentioned, or by general consent.

Mailing an Agenda to the Members

Some organizations mail the agenda to the members before the meeting. The purpose is to provide members with information so that they can prepare for the meeting. However, the agenda can still be changed before the meeting. In other words, it is not binding on anyone. Items can be added before the meeting, and during the meeting by a motion, a second, and a two-thirds vote. It is important to remember that an agenda is just a suggested outline or structure for the meeting. Things can change between the time the agenda is mailed to the membership and the time the meeting takes place.

Consent and Priority Agendas

The *consent agenda* (or in some cases, the *consent calendar*) allows members to adopt a group of items *en bloc* without discussion. This is a good way to dispose of business that is noncontroversial, for example, approval of the minutes, paying the bills, and customary donations.

The consent agenda may be presented to the members at any time during the meeting. It is a list of items that can be disposed of *en bloc*, with a single vote and without discussion. Every member should have a printed copy of the consent agenda when the presiding officer presents it. When presenting it, the chair asks if any member wants to extract an item from the consent agenda.

To **extract an item**, a member need only rise and request, for example, that item 3 be removed from the agenda. This means that the member wants to discuss and vote on this issue separately. The request does not need a second and is not discussed, and no vote is taken to remove it from the consent agenda.

After the members have finished extracting items from the consent agenda, the presiding officer presents the modified consent agenda to the assembly once again and takes the vote by general consent. (See Chapter 5 on voting.)

The president could say it this way:

President: Are there items that the members want to
remove from the consent agenda? [*Pause;
if no one rises, then continue.*] If there is
no objection, the consent agenda will be
adopted. [*Pause; wait to see if anyone objects.*]
Hearing no objection, the following items as
published on your consent agenda are
adopted.

The items extracted can now be taken up or added
to the regular agenda under the proper categories for
bringing up such items.

The consent agenda is useful for streamlining action
on a group of items. Also useful, though in a different
way, is the *priority agenda*. This type of agenda is a list of
tasks to be accomplished, discussed, and voted on in the
order of importance. In committee meetings and in
groups or "work teams" that have informal meetings, a
priority agenda is a good way to organize the meeting.
This concept is also helpful in listing items under new
business. The most important or timely topics are placed
at the top of the agenda to ensure that they will be done
before the meeting ends.

QUORUM

Before any business can be legally transacted, a quorum
must be present. "Quorum" is a Latin word meaning
"of them," as in "do we have enough of them—the
members?"

A *quorum* is the minimum number of members
who must be present in order to conduct business. This
number should be in the organization's bylaws. If it is

not, then according to parliamentary law the quorum is a majority of the entire membership. The presiding officer should know what that number is and make sure a quorum is present before calling the meeting to order. To establish that a quorum is present the president can count those present, members can sign in, or a roll call can be taken. However, the officer does not have to state that there is a quorum present when he or she calls the meeting to order. If you are unsure whether there is a quorum present, you may ask the presiding officer after the meeting is called to order. To do this, you should stand and say:

Member: Mr. President, I rise to a parliamentary inquiry.

President: Please state your inquiry.

Member: Is there a quorum present?

If the president says yes, then you would say "Thank you" and sit down. If the president says no, then you could remind him or her:

Member: Mr. President, business cannot be conducted without a quorum. [*then sit down*]

Never conduct a business meeting without a quorum present. *If business is transacted without a quorum, it is null and void!* It is also important that a quorum be present throughout the entire time that business is being transacted. If you notice that people have left the meeting and there is no longer a quorum present, it is your duty to raise a **point of order** by informing the presiding officer that there is no longer a quorum present and any business transacted would now be null and void.

Member: [*rises*] Point of order.

President: Please state your point.

Member: Members have left and there is no longer a quorum. Any further business transacted would now be null and void.

President: Thank you. Your point is well taken. Since there is no longer a quorum present, this meeting is adjourned. [*raps the gavel once*]

What to Do When No Quorum Is Present

If no quorum is present and there appears to be no hope of getting one soon, the president can call the meeting to order to satisfy the bylaw requirement that the meeting be held and then announce that there is no quorum and adjourn the meeting. Or, the president can call the meeting to order, announce to the membership that there is no quorum, and entertain a motion to **recess** (which would enable members to try to obtain a quorum), or to **fix the time to which to adjourn** (which allows the membership to set another date and time to meet and which would be considered as a legal continuation of this meeting), or to **adjourn** (which means the meeting immediately ends).

These three motions: to recess, to fix the time to which to adjourn, and to adjourn are the only motions allowed when there is no quorum present.

CALLING THE MEETING TO ORDER

Every meeting must begin somewhere and have someone to lead it. The meeting begins when the president or chairman calls the meeting to order. The president does this by standing at the front of the room, where everyone can see him or her, and saying:

President: The meeting will come to order. [*one rap of the gavel*]

If the president doesn't have a gavel, he or she can get the members' attention by asking them to sit down because the meeting is going to begin. Or, a member of the organization can be assigned to encourage the members to sit down. Then the president calls the meeting to order.

President: [*no gavel*] Will the members please be seated? [*Pause and wait for them to be seated. Then say:*]

President: The meeting will come to order.

The members should immediately sit down and come to order by the request of the president.

READING AND APPROVING THE MINUTES

After the opening ceremonies, the first business in order is the reading of the minutes. The President asks the secretary to read the minutes of the previous meeting.

President: Will the secretary read the minutes of the previous meeting?

The secretary stands to read the minutes, and the president sits down while the secretary reads the minutes.

Secretary: The Santa Rosa Community Action League was called to order at 7:30 p.m., Tuesday, September 12, by the president. The secretary was present.

> The minutes were approved as read. The treasurer reported a balance of $500 in the bank account.
>
> John moved that we sponsor a public cleanup day on Saturday, October 2, at the park at noon. The motion was adopted. The president appointed John, Mary, and Mark to plan the event.
>
> The motion to sponsor a community breakfast was postponed to the next meeting.
>
> The meeting adjourned at 4 p.m.
>
> Julie Hayes
>
> Secretary

The secretary sits down and the president asks:

President: Are there any corrections?

The president then pauses and waits to see if there are corrections. If there are no corrections, the president says:

President: The minutes are approved as read.

If a member has a correction, the member rises, addresses the chair, and states:

Member: Mr. President, I believe that Margaret was also appointed to plan the cleanup day at the park.

The president should say:

President: If there is no objection, the minutes will be corrected by adding Margaret's name to the minutes. Are there further corrections?

[*pause*] Hearing none, the minutes are
approved as corrected.

If someone makes a motion to **dispense with the
reading of the minutes**, it means that the minutes will
not be read at this time but that they will be read at a
later time—at the next meeting or later in the present
meeting. This motion is not debatable and takes a
majority vote to adopt. If the members vote to dispense
with the reading of the minutes, the minutes can be
ordered read at any time later in the meeting when no
business is pending. Someone needs to make a motion
to have them read. This motion is not debatable, and
takes a majority vote to adopt.

REPORTS OF OFFICERS

After the secretary reads the minutes, the next business
in order is to hear the reports of the officers. Officers
give reports in the order listed in the bylaws. The most
common officer's report is that of the treasurer.

The president announces the next business in order
and calls on the first officer to give his or her report.

President: May we have the treasurer's report?

The treasurer stands to give the report, and the
president sits down during the report.

Treasurer: The report of the treasurer as of September 30:

Balance on hand	$500.00
Dues paid	$125.00
Expenditures	None

Balance on hand $625.00

Jody Parker

Treasurer

The treasurer steps aside, and the president assumes his or her place. Then the president asks:

President: Are there any questions?

If there are no questions, the treasurer gives the report to the secretary, and the President says:

President: The treasurer's report is filed.

If a member has a question to ask the treasurer, that person can rise, address the president, and ask:

Member: Mr. President, will the treasurer please tell us whether we are going to receive any funds from the school activity fund this year?

The president turns to the treasurer and says:

President: Will the treasurer please answer the member's question.

The president steps aside while the treasurer answers the question.

Treasurer: We will receive $100.00 dollars.

President: Are there further questions? [*pause*] If not, then the treasurer's report is filed.

The treasurer's report is always *filed* with the secretary. It is never *approved* or *adopted* by the assembly. When the treasurer's books are audited, then the auditor's report is adopted by the assembly.

Remember, it is important to keep order in the meeting, so members address all questions to the president. The president then can answer the question or ask another member to answer the question.

After all the reports of officers are given, the next business in order is the reports of the committees.

REPORTS OF COMMITTEES

There are two kinds of committee reports. The first kind gives information about what the committee has been doing. The second kind asks the members to decide a question and includes a motion at the end of the report.

President: The next business in order is to hear reports of the committees. Will the program committee report?

The president steps aside, and the committee chairman takes his or her place at the lectern.

Program Committee Chairman:

The programs for this year are a field trip to the area recycling plant, the Festival of Lights party in December, and the International Festival in April.

John Hamilton

Chairman

The chairman stands aside while the president asks:

President: Are there any questions?

Members can now ask questions. After questions, the committee's report is filed with the secretary.

President: The program committee's report is filed.

If a committee report includes a recommendation of action that it wants the organization to take, the report should include a motion at the end. Let's say that the program committee wants to bring in a speaker and charge admission to the general public as a way to raise money for the organization. The report could be given this way:

President: May we have the program committee's report.

Program Committee Chairman:

> The program committee would like to sponsor a workshop on parliamentary procedure to help us and other members of the community have more orderly meetings. We have found a parliamentarian who will give an all-day workshop for $200.00. We can charge an admission fee of $25 per person, pay for the parliamentarian, and make a profit of $500.
>
> Gloria Smith
>
> Chairman
>
> By direction of the committee, I move that we sponsor a parliamentary workshop on April 10, at the Community Center and charge $25.00 per person. [*The chairman sits down.*]

The president then repeats the motion and asks for discussion. A motion from a committee of more than one *does not need* a second because the committee has already voted to present the motion.

President: The question is on the adoption of the
             motion to sponsor a parliamentary workshop
             on April 10, at the Community Center and
             charge $25.00 per person. Is there any
             discussion?

The members discuss the motion and take a vote on it. If the motion is adopted, the action would be carried out.

UNFINISHED BUSINESS AND GENERAL ORDERS

After the committee reports, the next business in order is the unfinished business and general orders. This is business that was left undecided at the last meeting, or it is business that was delayed to this meeting by making the motion to postpone to the next meeting.

If there is unfinished business, it will be placed on the agenda and the president states it. The president does not ask for unfinished business.

President: The next business in order is unfinished
             business. At the last meeting, a motion to
             sponsor a community breakfast was post-
             poned to this meeting. Is there any discussion?

Members then discuss and vote on the motion.

NEW BUSINESS

If there is no unfinished business or general orders, the president goes on to the next business in order, which is new business. If there is no new business listed on the agenda, the president can ask:

President: Is there any new business?

If there is new business on the agenda, the president states what it is. Let's say the high school drama club has asked the president whether the Community Action League will make a $100.00 donation for stage sets. The president could say:

President: The next business in order is new business. The first item of new business is a request by the drama club that we donate $100.00 for stage-set materials. What are the members wishes?

If the members want to do this, then someone has to make a motion to do so. If no one wants to donate $100, the members remain silent. Then the president asks:

President: Is there any further business?

The members always have a right to bring forward ideas or business for the entire membership to discuss. This is done by making a main motion. Ideas are not discussed first and then a motion made, but rather a motion is made and then discussed. The principle of taking up one item of business at a time especially applies to main motions. Only one main motion can be presented at a time.

Members can keep bringing up new business by making motions, discussing them, and voting on them. After each motion is voted on, the president asks the members:

President: Is there any further business?

When no one has anything further to bring before the members, the chair does not have to ask for a motion to adjourn but can say:

President: Is there any further business?

The president pauses to look around the room to give any member the opportunity to rise and make a motion. If no one rises, the president says:

President: If there is no objection, the meeting will now adjourn. [*Pause to look around the room.*]

There are still five things members can do at this point (see Chapter 6, "The Motion to Adjourn").

President: Since there is no objection, the meeting is adjourned. [*one rap of the gavel*]

ADJOURNING THE MEETING

A motion to adjourn—or to end the meeting—can be made at any time during the meeting unless members have set a fixed time to adjourn. (See Chapter 6, "Fix the Time at Which to Adjourn".) To move to adjourn, a member must rise, address the president, be recognized by the presiding officer, and say:

Member 1: Mr. President,

President: [*recognizes member by either nodding at the person or by stating his or her name*]

Member 1: I move that the meeting adjourn.

Member 2: Second.

This motion needs a second; it is *not* debatable. The president takes a vote immediately:

President: It is moved and seconded that the meeting adjourn. All those in favor say "Aye." Those opposed say "No."

The ayes have it, and the meeting is adjourned. [*one rap of the gavel*]

3

Getting Business Before the Assembly

The most common way to get business before the members is to make a main motion. Ideas are not discussed first and then a motion made; instead, a motion is made and then the idea is discussed. This chapter explains the basic steps in presenting a motion, including how to make a main motion, how to discuss it, and how to take a vote on the motion. It also explains when a motion is out of order; for example, when it conflicts with the rules of the organization or the laws of the land, or when it proposes action outside the scope of the object of the organization.

BASIC STEPS IN PRESENTING A MOTION

Before you present a motion, make sure it contains all the pertinent information, including who, what, where, and when. The motion should be worded in the positive, not in the negative. Here is an example of a main motion:

> Madam President, I move that we have a picnic on Saturday, June 15, at 3 p.m. in the park.

This motion includes all the necessary information and states it in a positive manner. It is now ready to be presented.

37

1. A member stands and addresses the chair by saying:

    > Mr. President [or Madam President]

    or

    > Mr. Chairman [or Madam Chairman]

2. The chair assigns the member the floor by stating the member's name or nodding at the member.
    The member states the motion:

    > I move that . . .

    or

    > I move to . . .

    > I move to have a picnic on Saturday, June 15, at 3 p.m. in the park.

3. Another member seconds the motion by calling out:

    > I second the motion.

    or simply

    > Second.

4. The chair restates the motion and places it before the assembly by saying:

    > It is moved and seconded that . . . . Is there any discussion?

    > It is moved and seconded to have a picnic on Saturday, June 15, at 3 p.m. in the park. Is there any discussion?

5. The members now have the right to debate or discuss the motion.

6. When discussion is finished, the chair puts the motion to a vote by saying:

> All those in favor say "Aye." Those opposed
> say "No."

7. The chair announces the vote and who will carry
   out the action if it is adopted.

> The ayes have it, and the motion is carried.
> We will have a picnic on Saturday, June 15, at
> 3 p.m. in the park. The Social Committee will
> take care of the details.

or

> The noes have it, and the motion is lost. We
> will not have a picnic on Saturday, June 15, at
> 3 p.m. in the park. Is there further business?

Now let's look at these steps in detail.

MAKING A MAIN MOTION

To make a main motion, a member must obtain the floor.
The way to do this is to stand and address the president,
saying:

> Mr. President [or Madam President]

or

> Madam Chairman [or Mr. Chairman]

This is the correct parliamentary terminology. Many
people today want to say *chairwoman* or *chairperson*, but
these terms are incorrect. The English language does not
have feminine or masculine words, as do the Latin-based
languages. The word *chair* in English is the neuter
gender, neither masculine nor feminine. It refers
either to the person or the place (chair) occupied by
the person. The word *man* at the end does not mean a

masculine person but stands for the neuter gender *all mankind* including males and females. So in English, to acknowledge the gender of the person presiding in the *chair*, we use the honorifics Mr. or Madam, as follows: *Mr. Chairman* or *Madam Chairman.*

After the chair is addressed, the presiding officer recognizes the member by saying his or her name or by nodding at the member. The member has now been *assigned the floor* and can speak. No one else has the right to speak as long as the member has the floor.

The correct way to state a motion is:

I move that . . .

It helps to memorize and practice this phrase. Here's an example:

Member: Madam President, I move that we have a picnic on Saturday, June 15, at 3 p.m. in the park.

Write the motion on a piece of paper and give it to the president after you have stated it. This will help the chairman (or chair) repeat the motion to the assembly exactly the way it was moved. The way in which the presiding officer states the motion to the assembly is the official wording of the motion and is recorded in the minutes. Many times, presiding officers do not repeat the motion exactly as the member has stated it. If you put the motion in writing and give it to the presiding officer, the officer can repeat it exactly as you presented it, and the secretary can record it correctly in the minutes.

After you make the motion, sit down. The motion must be seconded by another member. A second simply means that another member thinks the motion should be discussed. It does not mean that the member is necessarily in favor of it.

The person who seconds the motion does not need to rise and address the president but can call out the second from where he or she is sitting. The member can say:

Member: Second.

or

I second the motion.

If no one seconds it, the president can ask:

President: Is there a second?

Member: I second it.

If the motion does not get a second, it cannot be discussed and the president goes on to the next business in order. The president can say:

President: Without a second, the motion will not be considered.

The phrase "dies for lack of a second" should be avoided.

If it is seconded, the president restates the motion to the members. This is called **placing the motion before the assembly**. The president must do this so that members can discuss the motion. The president says:

President: It is moved and seconded that we have a picnic on Saturday, June 15, at 3 p.m. in the park. Is there any discussion?

The president needs to memorize the following phrase in restating the motion:

It is moved and seconded that . . . . Is there any discussion?

DISCUSSING A MOTION

Members always have the right to debate or discuss a main motion. After the president asks for discussion, members can give reasons why they think having a picnic is a good idea or a bad idea.

The person who makes the motion has the first right to speak to the motion. To do that, the member rises, addresses the president, obtains the floor, and then speaks to the motion. After the member is done, he or she sits down so that someone else can speak to the motion—either for or against it. In discussing the motion, everyone gets to have a turn to talk, but everyone has to await his or her turn. A member can speak to a motion only when no one else has been assigned the floor. If two people stand to speak at the same time, the president will designate who should speak. The member not recognized sits down. When the other member finishes speaking, then the member who did not speak can stand to speak.

In debate, members address all remarks through the chair. Cross talk between members is not allowed, and mentioning other members' names is avoided as much as possible. All remarks are made in a courteous tone.

In most meetings, each member may speak two times on a debatable motion, but the member does not get the second turn as long as another member wants to speak for the first time. A member is not permitted to speak against his or her own motion. However, if the member changes his or her mind after hearing the motion discussed, the member may vote against it. (For more specific rules of debate, see Chapter 4.)

When speaking to a motion that you haven't made, a common courtesy before you begin your remarks is to say:

> I speak for the motion.

Or you could say:

> I speak against the motion.

In this way the assembly knows which side of the issue you are supporting. It also helps the president keep a balance in the debate. If there are more people speaking against the motion, the president might ask if anyone would like to speak for the motion.

In debate, everyone has the right to speak, and the president must be just and impartial in assigning the floor, allowing all sides of the issue to be heard.

Discussion continues until the president realizes that the membership is ready to vote and says:

> *President:* Hearing no further discussion, all those in favor of the motion say "Aye." Those opposed say "No."

TAKING THE VOTE

When no one rises to speak to the motion, the president calls for the vote. Most voting is taken by a voice vote. Main motions are adopted by a majority vote. That means more than half of those voting are in favor of the motion.

> *President:* Is there any further discussion? [*Pause and look around the room to see if anyone wants to speak.*] Hearing none, the question is on the adoption of the motion to have a picnic on Saturday, June 15, at 3 p.m. in the park. All those in favor say "Aye." Those opposed say "No."

The president always announces the result of the vote. If the affirmative wins, the vote is announced this way:

President: The ayes have it, and the motion is carried. We will have a picnic on Saturday, June 15, at 3 p.m. in the park.

If the negative wins, the vote is announced this way:

President: The noes have it, and the motion is lost. We won't be having a picnic on Saturday, June 15, at 3 p.m. in the park.

The president asks only for the "yes" and the "no" votes and does not ask for those who want to abstain. The president always takes the "no" vote even though the "yes" vote sounds unanimous.

The members must feel that any vote taken is a fair vote. If any member doubts the results of a voice vote, the member can call out:

Division.

or

I call for a division.

or

I doubt the result of the vote.

In this one instance, a member does not have to rise to obtain the floor but can call out "Division" from wherever he or she is sitting. It does not need a second.

The president immediately retakes the vote as a rising (but not counted) vote by asking the members to stand. The president says:

President: All those in favor please rise. Be seated. Those opposed please rise. Be seated. The affirmative has it, and the motion is carried.

Or, if more members were opposed, the president states:

President: The negative has it, and the motion is lost.

If the president is in doubt as to which side wins, he or she can retake the vote and have it counted. If a member wants the vote counted, the member makes a motion to have a counted vote. It takes a second, is not debatable, and a majority vote to adopt this motion.

The Ways a Vote Can Be Taken

In addition to a voice vote, the vote can be taken in other ways: by general consent, by a show of hands, by a rising vote, or by ballot. The chair can choose to take the vote by voice, show of hands, or rising. To take a ballot vote, a member must make a motion to do so. A ballot vote ensures the secrecy of each member's vote. If you do not want others to know how you voted, or if you want an accurate count of the vote, a ballot vote is the way to accomplish this. (For a more thorough explanation of these voting procedures, see Chapter 5.)

To ask for a ballot vote, a member must rise, address the chair, and move to take the vote by ballot. This motion needs a second, it is not debatable, and a majority of the members must vote in favor of taking a ballot vote.

Member: Mr. President, I move that this vote be taken by ballot.

Member: Second.

President: It is moved and seconded to take this vote by
          ballot. All those in favor, say "Aye." (aye)
          Those opposed say "No." The ayes have it,
          and we will take the vote by ballot.

If the members vote against the motion, the chair
would say:

President: The noes have it, and the vote will not be
          taken by ballot.

COMPLETING THE ACTION
OF THE MOTION

The action on the motion is completed when the president announces the result of the vote and how the action will be carried out. Members can expect the approved
action to be carried out as authorized unless they decide
to **reconsider the vote**, to **rescind the action**, or to
amend the adopted motion. (See Chapter 6, "Motions
that Bring a Question Again Before the Assembly.")

IMPORTANT POINTS TO REMEMBER
BEFORE MAKING A MOTION

Not every main motion is in order, and both the members and the presiding officer need to know when a presented motion violates the following rules. If a main
motion does violate the following rules, it is the presiding officer's duty to rule the motion out of order. If the
chair does not do this, then a member should call this to
the assembly's attention by raising a **point of order**.

1. *No motion is in order that conflicts with federal, state, or local law; or with the rules of a parent organization; or that conflicts with the organization's constitution or bylaws or other rules of the organization.* Even if the motion is adopted by a unanimous vote, it is null and void.

   For example, if someone makes a motion to expand the clubhouse and there are city or state zoning laws against it, then the motion is out of order; or if the school district has rules against having a student dance on a week night, a motion by a student group to have a dance on Tuesday evening is out of order.

2. *A motion that proposes action outside the scope of the object of the organization (the object should be written in the corporate charter or in the bylaws) is not in order unless the members vote to allow it to be considered.* This takes a two-thirds vote.

   For example, suppose an organization's object is to take care of stray animals and build a shelter for them. A member wants to include a soup kitchen for homeless people. This is outside the scope of the object of the organization.

   If the member makes the motion, the presiding officer would state:

   > The motion to have a soup kitchen for homeless people is outside the object of the organization. Is there any discussion about this being outside the scope of the object of the organization?

   Discussion can be only on whether the motion is or is not outside the scope of the organization. Any discussion about whether to have a soup kitchen is out of order. After discussion, the president should first explain what the effect of a "yes" or "no" vote will be on the consideration of this motion, then put it to a vote.

> For this motion to be considered, it takes a two-thirds vote. If you think this motion is within the scope of the object of the organization and want to consider it, vote "yes." If you think this motion is outside the scope of the organization, vote "no." We are only voting on considering the question. The vote taken does not adopt the motion. Are there any questions? All those in favor, please rise. [*members rise*]

> Be seated. [*members sit down*]

> Those opposed please rise. [*members rise*]

> Be seated. [*members sit down*]

> There is a two-thirds vote in the affirmative, and we will consider the question. It is moved and seconded that we have a soup kitchen for homeless people. Is there any discussion?

If the noes have it, the chair states:

> There is less than a two-thirds vote in the affirmative. The negative has it, and we will not be considering the motion to have a soup kitchen for homeless people.

The members always have a right to interpret their bylaws. This is an instance in which the bylaws are being interpreted.

3. *A main motion is not in order if it conflicts with a motion that was previously adopted by the assembly and that is still in force.* However, the assembly can decide to **rescind the action** or **amend something previously adopted**.

For example, let's say that the club has adopted a motion to give $100 yearly to the local Humane Society. If a member makes a motion to give $200 yearly to the Humane Society, the motion conflicts with what has already been adopted and is not in order. However, if it is phrased as the motion to *amend something previously adopted,* it is in order and it takes a two-thirds vote or a majority vote of the entire membership to adopt (if no previous notice has been given). With previous notice, it requires a majority vote to adopt. This protects the rights of the absent members.

4. *A main motion is not in order when it presents substantially the same question as a motion that has been rejected during the same session.* However, the motion can be brought up at another meeting, and this is known as **renewing the motion**.

   For example, suppose that the members vote down a motion to have a car wash to raise money for the dance fund. During discussion, it is made clear that the members do not want to have a car wash to raise money for anything. If later in the meeting a motion is made to have a car wash to raise money for the leadership training series, it is out of order. The motion can, however, be brought up at a later meeting. This is called **renewing the motion.**

   There is one way this motion can be brought up again at the same meeting, and that is if a member who voted on the prevailing side (in this case the negative) makes the motion to **reconsider the vote** on the motion to have a car wash. (See Chapter 6, "Motions That Bring a Question Again Before the Assembly.")

5. *A main motion is not in order if it conflicts with or presents substantially the same question as one that has*

been temporarily disposed of and is still within control of the assembly. Here are examples:

If a motion has been referred to a committee and the committee has not reported, the committee can be discharged and the assembly can take up the motion. (See Chapter 6, "Motions That Bring a Question Again Before the Assembly.")

If a motion has been postponed to later in the meeting or to another meeting, the rules can be suspended and the motion taken up at that time. (See Chapter 6, "Suspend the Rules.")

If a motion has been laid on the table, it can be taken from the table.

Members need to be alert to meeting tactics that refer a motion to a committee to bury it (don't investigate it), or lay it on the table to kill it. Or, while a motion is in the committee or laid on the table, someone presents another version of the motion. The members must realize that even though a motion is in committee or on the table, it is still under the control of the assembly and must be decided first.

4

Debating the Motion

It is the right of every member to debate or to discuss business that is introduced to the assembly in the form of a main motion. This right can be taken away or limited only by a motion to limit debate or to close debate (previous question), and either motion must have a two-thirds vote. (See Chapter 6, "To Limit or Extend the Limits of Debate" and "Previous Question.")

Only through discussion can the assembly make an informed decision from the facts and persuasive arguments that members present. Members should never be tempted to "gavel through" an issue (rush through a motion without any discussion) in an effort to save time or silence the opposition.

In his book *Parliamentary Law,* Henry Robert gives a word to the wise when he states, "Where there is radical difference of opinion in an organization, one side must yield. The great lesson for democracies to learn is for the majority to give the minority a full, free opportunity to present their side of the case, and then for the minority, having failed to win a majority to their views, gracefully to submit and to recognize the action as that of the entire organization, and cheerfully to assist in carrying it out, until they can secure its repeal."

This chapter explains the rules of debate and the circumstances under which debate can be limited. It also lists those motions that are debatable and those that are not.

RULES OF DEBATE

Even though members have the right to debate, there are established parliamentary rules concerning the privileges of debate.

1. A member must obtain the floor and be recognized by the presiding officer before beginning to speak. A member can't just start talking while seated. However, in small board meetings where rules of debate are less formal, this is allowed. (See Chapter 11, "Board Meetings.")

2. The member who made the motion has the first right to speak to the motion. He does this by rising and obtaining the floor after the chair places the motion before the assembly for discussion.

3. A member can speak twice to the motion, but the second turn can be taken only after everyone who wishes to speak the first time has spoken.

4. Each member can speak for ten minutes on each turn unless the assembly has adopted rules that state another amount of time.

5. Debate must be germane (related) to the motion.

6. Speakers must address all remarks to the chair; cross talk between members is not allowed.

    Speakers must be courteous and never attack other members or question the motives of the members. In controversial issues, the discussion is focused on the ideas, not on the personalities. Members must not use such inflammatory statements as "it's a lie," "it is a fraud," "he's a liar." However, a member might say,

> I believe there is strong evidence that the member's remarks are erroneous.

Profane language is also prohibited.

7. In debate, speakers refer to officers by title and avoid mentioning other members' names. Instead, they should refer to the members as

> the member who just spoke

or

> the delegate from Hawaii.

8. When speaking to a motion, it is important for the member to first let the assembly know which side of the issue he or she is on. If in favor of the motion, the member states:

> I speak for the motion.

and gives the reasons why. If opposed, the member states:

> I speak against the motion.

and gives the reasons why. This helps the chair alternate the debate.

In controversial issues, the presiding officer should alternate the debate between those who are speaking for and those speaking against the motion. After someone has spoken for the motion, the chair asks:

> Would anyone like to speak against the motion?

After someone speaks against the motion, the chair asks:

> Would someone like to speak in favor of the motion?

This ensures that all sides are represented, keeps tempers down, and prevents one side from dominating the discussion.

9. The member who makes the motion can't speak against his or her own motion, although he or she can vote against it. The person who seconds the motion, however, can speak against the motion because a second means "Let's discuss it," not "I agree." Sometimes a member will second a motion just so he or she can speak against it.

10. A member can't read, or have the secretary read, from part of a manuscript or book as part of his or her debate without the permission of the assembly. However, the member can read short, relevant printed extracts in debate to make a point.

11. During debate, a member can't talk against a previous action that is not pending, unless one of the motions to **rescind**, **reconsider**, or **amend something previously adopted** is pending; or unless the member concludes his or her remarks with one of these motions.

12. During debate, members should take care not to disturb the assembly by whispering, talking, walking across the floor, or causing other distractions.

13. During debate, the presiding officer sits down when a member has been assigned the floor to speak. Or, if the presiding officer can't be seen by the members when seated, the officer stands back from the lectern while the member is speaking. (Like the rule of one item of business at a time, this rule allows only one person at a time to have the floor.)

14. If at any time during debate the presiding officer needs to interrupt the speaker for a ruling (for example, if the chair is correcting something the speaker is doing) or needs to give information (for example, facts related to the discussion), the member should sit down until the presiding

officer has finished. Then the member can resume speaking.

15. In deliberative assemblies, members do not have the right to give some of their time to another member. If a member has not used his or her ten minutes, then the member forfeits the unused portion.

16. As the chairman, the presiding officer must remain impartial. As a *member*, the presiding officer has a right to debate. Thus, if the presiding officer does wish to speak to an issue, he or she relinquishes the chair to another officer (the vice president) who has not spoken and does not wish to speak. If no officer wishes to take the chair, a member who has not spoken and has received the assembly's approval can preside. The presiding officer resumes the chair when the motion has been either voted on by the assembly or temporarily put aside by a motion to **refer to a committee, postpone to another time**, or **lay on the table**.

17. In debating an issue, members also have the right to conclude their debate with a higher-ranking motion than the one pending. (See Appendix F for a chart on ranking motions.)

LIMITATIONS ON DEBATE

Members can put limits on debate and even stop the debate altogether. This must be done by making a motion. *The presiding officer cannot cut off the debate as long as one member wishes to rise and speak.* Neither can one member stop debate by yelling out "Question" or "It's time to take a vote."

Debate can be limited only by the motion to **limit debate**; and debate can be closed only by the motion **previous question** or **close debate**.

These motions need a second, are not debatable, and require a two-thirds vote to adopt. This vote must be taken by a rising (but not counted) vote. (For more details about these motions, see Chapter 6, "Subsidiary Motions.")

DEBATABLE MOTIONS AND UNDEBATABLE MOTIONS

Not all motions are debatable. Some motions are debatable in some situations and not in others. It is important to study the chapter on motions to see which are debatable and which aren't. (See Chapter 6.) The following is a list of debatable and nondebatable motions.

DEBATABLE MOTIONS

Main Motion

Postpone Indefinitely

Amend

Refer to a Committee

Postpone to a Certain Time

Appeal from the Decision of the Chair

Rescind

Amend Something Previously Adopted

Reconsider

Recess as an Incidental Main Motion

Fix the Time to Which to Adjourn (as an Incidental Main Motion)

UNDEBATABLE MOTIONS

Limit or Extend the Limits of Debate

Previous Questions (close debate)

Lay on the Table

Take from the Table

Call for the Orders of the Day

Raise a Question of Privilege

Recess (as a Privilege Motion)

Adjourn

Fix the Time to Which to Adjourn (as a Privilege Motion)

Point of Order

Withdraw a Motion

Suspend the Rules

Objection to Consideration of the Motion

Division of the Assembly

Division of the Question

Incidental Motions Relating to Voting, When the Subject is Pending

Dispense with the Reading of the Minutes

5

Voting

In democratic societies, the citizens have the right to assemble, the right to speak, and the right to vote. The right to assemble allows people of common interests to join together to accomplish some purpose. The right to speak allows members of that assembly to voice their opinions and concerns, and to persuade others that their opinions and concerns are valid and to take action. The right to vote is the assembly's way of allowing all members to decide an issue, in a democratic manner, after they have assembled and heard their fellow members' opinions and concerns.

The right to vote is essential in preserving democracy in organizations and elected bodies. There are three principles that need to be considered when the vote is taken:

1. Is the vote taken in a fair and impartial manner?

2. Does everyone who wants to vote get to vote?

3. Does the announced result represent the way the members voted?

These principles underlie the parliamentary procedures for voting; indeed, the specific rules of voting are designed to uphold them. This chapter explains those rules and the situations in which they are violated. It begins with the procedure for taking a vote and then discusses the idea of majority rule and defines majority vote. It also explains the numerous ways a vote can be taken and the appropriate actions to take when the result of a vote is doubted, and answers frequently asked questions about voting.

PROCEDURE FOR TAKING A VOTE

In taking a vote, the presiding officer or chair must follow an established general procedure:

1. The chair always asks for the affirmative vote first.

2. The chair always asks for the negative vote even if the affirmative vote seems unanimous.

3. The chair does not ask for abstentions.

4. The chair always announces the result of the vote and states what has just happened. If the affirmative has won, the chair also states who is responsible for carrying out the action. If the chair is in doubt about who should carry out the action, then the members need to make a motion about who should carry it out.

5. The chair must stay neutral in asking for the vote so as not to sway the membership. The chair does not say, for example:

   > All those in favor say "Aye." Contrary say "No."

6. The chair does not phrase the vote this way:

   > All those in favor say "Aye." Those opposed "same sign."

If the vote was taken this way , it would mean that both those in favor and those opposed would say Aye. So then who wins?

However, it is acceptable to phrase the vote this way:

> As many as are in favor say "Aye." Those opposed say "No."

Another accepted way is to say:

> All in favor say "Aye." Those opposed say "No."

7. It is understood that during all methods of voting a quorum must be present.

8. If the chair is in doubt about the result of the vote, the chair can retake the vote by a rising vote or by a rising and counted vote.

9. If a member doubts the result of the vote, the member should call out *"Division."* For an explanation of this action, see "Doubting the Result of the Vote," later in this chapter.

THE MAJORITY RULES

A fundamental principle in democratic societies is that the majority rules but that the rights of the minority and individual members are protected. Most business is adopted by a majority vote of members who are voting at a meeting where a quorum is present. However, to protect the rights of the minority and absent members, some motions require a two-thirds vote. The principle used in determining when to take a two-thirds vote is based on rights of the members or the assembly. When a proposed action takes away members' rights, a two-thirds vote is necessary. Motions to **limit** or **extend debate**, to

close debate, to make a motion a **special order**, **rescind** an action when no previous notice is given, and to **suspend the rules**, are some of the motions that need a two-thirds vote. Some actions are so important (for example, amending the bylaws and other governing documents, or removing a member from office or membership) that they require previous notice and a two-thirds vote.

If an organization wants the vote on certain issues to be greater than a majority or two-thirds vote, or wants to require that previous notice of a vote given, these qualifications should be clearly stated and defined in the bylaws. However, requiring a vote higher than a majority or two-thirds vote can allow a minority to rule instead of the majority, and a unanimous vote may end up allowing one person to rule. A vote requiring more than a majority should not be stated in terms of a "super majority," but should specify 80% of the members, or three-fourths of the members, or a majority of the entire membership.

Majority Vote Defined

A *majority vote* simply means more than half of those voting. More specifically, it means more than half of the votes cast by persons legally entitled to vote at a properly called meeting with a quorum present. Blank ballots or abstentions are not counted. By this definition, the majority is determined not by those present but by those voting. Here is an example:

If 20 people are present at the meeting and

15 members vote

the majority is 8

because the majority is determined by the number voting, not by the number present.

Modifications in Majority Vote

A majority vote can be qualified. Organizations can qualify a majority vote by adding these phrases to the word "voting" in their bylaws:

1. "a majority of those present"

2. "a majority of the entire membership"

These phrases change how the majority is figured. The more qualified the bylaws make a majority vote, the more difficult it is to adopt motions. Except for important issues and amending the bylaws, all actions should be adopted by a simple, unqualified majority vote.

A Majority of Those Present

If the bylaws state that a motion must be adopted by a **majority of those present**, then the majority is figured by the *number of members present*, not by the number of those voting. Here is an example:

A meeting has 20 members present.

A majority of those present would be 11 votes. This number does not change whether

15 people vote

10 members vote in the affirmative

5 members vote in the negative

5 members do not vote (abstain)

The motion fails because it takes 11 people voting in favor in order for a majority of those present to have adopted the motion. In this case, those not voting are said to support the negative rather than remain neutral. For that reason, this qualification is not recommended.

A Majority of the Entire Membership

If the bylaws state that a motion must be adopted by a **majority of the entire membership**, then the majority is determined by the number of the *entire membership,* not by the number who are present or who are voting. Here are some examples:

The membership of the organization is 40.

The majority is always 21 votes in the affirmative.

At a meeting 21 members attend. All would have to vote in favor of a motion in order for it to be adopted.

If only 20 attend the meeting, no motions can be adopted because it takes 21 votes to adopt.

30 members attend the meeting. The votes are

20 votes in the affirmative

7 in the negative

3 abstentions

The motion is lost because it takes 21 votes to adopt.

Requiring a majority of the entire membership is a helpful and useful qualification in one case: that is when the board is very small. Suppose an organization has an executive board of 5 members and the quorum is 3 members. If the bylaws state that all action must be adopted by a majority vote, and if only 3 members came to a meeting, 2 members are the majority and can make a decision. In this case, it is appropriate for the bylaws to require a majority vote of the entire membership of the board. This ensures that if only 3 members attend a meeting, all 3 have to agree before any action is adopted.

A TWO-THIRDS VOTE

In keeping with accepted parliamentary procedure, there are times when a two-thirds vote is required. This means that at a meeting where a quorum is present, it takes two-thirds of those voting in the affirmative for a motion to be adopted. Those who abstain are not counted.

To balance the rights of the individual member with the rights of the assembly, the following procedures require a two-thirds vote:

1. Limiting or closing debate

2. Suspending or modifying a rule or order previously adopted

3. Taking away membership or office

4. Anything that limits nominating or voting

5. Preventing the introduction of a motion

The two-thirds vote is taken by a rising vote. If the chair is uncertain whether there is a two-thirds vote in the affirmative, he or she should count those voting.

THE TIE VOTE

A *tie vote* occurs when 50% vote in favor and 50% vote against. No one has received a majority vote, or more than one-half. If there is no way to break the tie vote, then the motion is lost.

If the presiding officer has not voted and is a member of the assembly, he or she can vote to break the tie. He can also vote to make a two-thirds vote or can vote to reject a two-thirds vote. The presiding officer can also vote to make a tie vote. If 50 members vote for the motion and 49 members against the motion, the presiding officer could state that he or she is voting "no," making the vote a tie vote and the motion is therefore lost. The presiding officer cannot vote twice, however—once as a member and once as the presiding officer. For example, if the presiding officer votes in a ballot vote with the other members and the result is a tie, the officer can't break the tie as the presiding officer. In this case, the motion is lost because the vote is a tie vote.

WAYS THE VOTE CAN BE TAKEN

There are numerous ways a vote can be taken: by voice, by show of hands, by standing, by ballot, by roll call, and by general consent. The chair or presiding officer decides whether to take the vote by a voice, by show of hands, by standing, or by general consent. But the assembly must order a vote by ballot or roll call.

After members have discussed a motion, the chair puts it to a vote. The chair may ask,

> Are you ready for the question?

or

> Is there further discussion?

If no one rises to speak, the chair takes the vote, asking for the affirmative first and then the negative. The chair does not ask for abstentions.

In taking a vote by voice, the chair states:

> *Chair:* The question is on the adoption of the
> motion to buy a computer and a laser printer

for the office. All those in favor, say "Aye."
Those opposed say "No."

Then the chair repeats the outcome. If the ayes have it, the chair states:

> *Chair:* The ayes have it, and we will buy a computer and a laser printer for the office. The secretary will purchase it.

If the noes have it, the chair states:

> *Chair:* The noes have it, and we will not buy a computer and a laser printer for the office. Is there further business?

Taking a Vote by Show of Hands

In taking a vote by show of hands, the chair says:

> *Chair:* All those in favor, please raise your right hand. [*raise right hand*] Please lower them. Those opposed raise their right hand. [*raise hand*]
>
> Please lower them.

Then the chair announces the vote. If the affirmative has it, the chair states:

> *Chair:* The affirmative has it, and we will buy a computer and a laser printer for the office. The secretary will purchase it.

If the negative has it, the chair states:

> *Chair:* The negative has it, and we will not buy a computer and a laser printer for the office. Is there further business?

Taking a Vote by Rising (Standing)

The rising (or standing) method should be used in taking a two-thirds vote and when retaking a voice vote
when someone has called for a *division.*

In taking a rising vote, the chair says:

> *Chair:* All those in favor, please rise. [*members rise*]
>
> Be seated. [*members sit down*]
>
> Those opposed please rise. [*members rise*]
>
> Be seated. [*members sit down*]

Then the chair announces the vote. If the affirmative has it, the chair states:

> *Chair:* The affirmative has it, and we will buy a
> computer and a laser printer for the office.
> The secretary will purchase it.

If the negative has it, the chair states:

> *Chair:* The negative has it and we will not buy a
> computer and a laser printer for the office.
> Is there further business?

Taking a Vote by Ballot

In taking a ballot vote, everyone gets to vote, including
the presiding officer (if he is a member), unless the
organization has a rule that states differently. In this case,
the chair explains the procedure to the membership as it
happens:

> *Chair:* This vote will be taken by ballot. Will the
> tellers please give a ballot to each member.
> [*Pause while this happens.*]

> Does everyone have a ballot? [*Wait for a response. If someone doesn't have a ballot, direct a teller to give one to that member.*]

> If you are in favor of buying a computer and a laser printer for the office, write "yes" on the ballot. If you are opposed, write "no." Fold the paper in half, and the tellers' committee will collect the ballots.

If there is a ballot box, then the chair would instruct the members to rise and put the ballots in the box.

After it looks like everyone has voted, the chair can ask:

> *Chair:* Has everyone voted who wants to vote?

If there is a motion to close the polls at this time, it needs a second, and it requires a two-thirds vote to pass. If someone has not voted and wants to, this is the time to speak up. After the polls are closed a majority can reopen them for voting. The chair waits for a response, and if no one rises to hand in a ballot, then the chair states:

> *Chair:* The polls are closed, and the tellers will count the votes.

The tellers' committee then counts the ballots and puts the result on a teller's sheet.

The chairman of the tellers' committee reads the report to the membership but *does not announce the result of the vote.* He or she then hands the report to the presiding officer, who states:

> *Chair:* The teller's report reads:
>
> 22 ballots are cast.
>
> A majority to adopt is 12.

15 voted in the affirmative.

7 voted in the negative.

The affirmative has it, and the motion is adopted. We will buy a computer and a laser printer. The secretary will be responsible for purchasing it.

In taking a ballot vote:

1. The president (if a member) gets to vote with the other members.

2. The chairman of the tellers' committee reads the report but does not announce the vote.

3. The president repeats the teller's report and announces the vote. The teller's report is included in the minutes in its entirety.

4. Tellers should be appointed for their fairness and accuracy in counting the vote. If the issue is controversial, members from both sides should be appointed to count the ballots.

Taking a Vote by General or Unanimous Consent

General consent is a very effective way to take care of noncontroversial issues or motions for which it looks like there will be no objection. General consent does not mean everyone is in favor of the motion; it means that the opposition feels it is useless to discuss or vote on the issue and decides to keep silent, accepting the results. General consent should not be confused with a unanimous vote in which all the votes are the same, whether in favor of or in opposition to some issue.

The chair states it this way:

Is there any objection to . . .

Is there any objection to paying the bills?

Hearing none, the bills will be paid by the treasurer.

Is there any objection to taking a 5-minute recess?

Hearing none, the meeting stands in recess for 5 minutes.

Is there any objection to withdrawing the motion?

Hearing none, the motion is withdrawn.

Is there any objection to adjourning the meeting?

Hearing none, the meeting is adjourned.

If a member calls out *"I object!"* then the president puts the motion to a formal vote:

All those in favor of paying the bills, say "Aye." Those opposed say "No." The ayes have it, and the bills will be paid by the treasurer.

Another aspect of general consent is that the *chair can assume a motion*; he or she does not have to wait for someone else to make the motion. For example, after the treasurer or the secretary submits the amount of the bills to be paid, the chair assumes the motion to pay the bills and then asks if there is any objection to paying them.

Chair: Is there any objection to paying the bills for a total of $100? Hearing no objection, the bills will be paid.

If a member makes a motion to recess as a privileged motion, it is not debatable but is amendable. The chair can state:

> Is there any objection to taking a 5-minute recess?
>
> Hearing none, the meeting stands in recess for 5 minutes.

If a member objects, it does not necessarily mean that the member is against the action but that the member thinks it is wise to take a formal vote.

If a member objects, and no formal motion has been presented, then the chair must either ask for a motion or assume a motion, and ask for discussion and then take a formal vote.

> *Chair:* The question is on the adoption of paying the bills for $100. Is there any discussion? [*Pause and wait for discussion. If none, take the vote.*]
>
> Hearing none, all those in favor of paying the bills, say "Aye." Those opposed say "No." The ayes have it, and the motion is carried. The treasurer will pay the bills.

If a member is not sure about the effect of taking a vote by general consent, the member can call out, **"I reserve the right to object."** After a brief consultation, the member must either object or relinquish the right to object.

DOUBTING THE RESULT OF THE VOTE

It is the presiding officer's duty to announce the result of the vote, and the way he announces it determines the action to be taken. If the members do not immediately doubt the result of the vote, then the chair's declaration stands as the decision of the assembly. The members have the right to doubt the result of the vote until the chair states the question on another motion.

If a member thinks that the vote is too close to call or that the noes have it, and the chair announces the ayes have it, the member can call out

> Division.

or
> I doubt the result of the vote.

(This should not be used as a dilatory tactic to delay the proceedings when it is apparent which side has won).

A *division* is an **incidental motion**—it deals with a procedural question relating to a pending motion or business. It does not need a second and is not debatable. One member can ask for the vote to be retaken. The vote is never retaken in the same way. Thus, a voice vote that is doubted must be retaken visually—by a rising vote. In this way all the members can see how people are voting. The chair states:

> *Chair:* A division has been called for. All those in favor please rise. Be seated. Those opposed please rise. Be seated.

The chair then announces the vote.

If the vote still looks too close to call, the chair can retake it by having it counted. If a member wants the vote to be counted, he or she makes a motion to take a counted vote. The motion to take a counted vote needs a second, is not debatable, and takes a majority to adopt.

The chair then retakes the vote by first asking those in favor of the motion to stand and count off. Then the chair asks the negative to stand and count off. After all have voted, the chair announces the vote. The vote should be recorded in the minutes by saying how many have voted in the affirmative and how many have voted in the negative.

Doubting the Result of a Ballot Vote or Roll Call Vote

If the members doubt the result of a ballot vote or roll call vote, a member must make a motion to recount the teller's tabulation. This motion takes a majority to adopt it unless the organization has a rule that states differently. After a ballot vote, if there is no possibility that the assembly may order a recount, a motion should be made to destroy the ballots; or they can be filed for a specified time with the secretary and then destroyed.

The result of every ballot and roll call vote is recorded in the minutes.

OTHER VOTING PROCEDURES

There are other voting methods, such as proxy voting, a vote by mail, absentee voting, and preferential voting. If an organization wishes to use any of these methods, this fact should be so stated in the bylaws and the written procedures for carrying out the voting should be included.

FREQUENTLY ASKED QUESTIONS ABOUT VOTING

Q: Does a member have to vote?

A: *No. This is called "abstaining." Even though having each member vote is in the best interest of the member and the organization, no one can compel a member to vote.*

Q: Is an abstention counted as a "yes" vote or a "no" vote?

A: *To abstain means "not to vote." You can't count a "nonvote." Therefore, an abstention counts as a "zero."*

Q: Is there a time when an abstention could affect the result of a vote?

A: *Yes, when the vote is qualified in some way—a majority of those present or a majority of the entire membership. If the majority is determined by "those present," and 20 people are present, a majority is 11. If 10 vote in the affirmative, 9 vote in the negative, and 1 person abstains, the motion is lost because it takes 11 voting in the affirmative to adopt the motion. In this case the "abstention" helps those voting "no."*

Q: Is there a time when a member is not allowed to vote?

A: *Yes, when a motion is of direct personal or monetary interest to the member and to no one else, then the member should not vote.*

Q: Is there a time when a member can vote on a motion that directly affects him or her?

A: *Yes, when the member is named with other members in a motion, for example, when the member is a delegate to a convention or when the member is nominated for an office.*

Q: Can a member vote if his or her dues are not paid?

A: *If a member has not been dropped from the rolls, and is not under disciplinary action, then the member still has the full rights of membership, including the right to vote, unless the bylaws specifically address this situation.*

Q: Can a member change his or her vote?

A: *Yes, a member has the right to change his or her vote until the result is announced. After the result is announced, the member's vote can be changed only by permission of the assembly. Permission can be granted by general consent, or by a motion to grant permission which needs a second, is undebatable, and takes a majority vote to adopt.*

Q: Who makes the final decision on judging voting procedures?

A: *The assembly does unless the bylaws state differently. For example, if the tellers are unsure about how a ballot is marked, they can bring it to the assembly to decide.*

Q: What is an illegal vote and how is it counted?

A: *An illegal vote refers only to votes taken by ballot. An illegal vote is a ballot:*

1. *That is unreadable.*

2. *In which someone who is not a member of the organization has been voted for (for example, in an election if someone writes in "Mickey Mouse").*

3. *In which a person who is not eligible to run for office has been voted for.*

4. *In which two or more written ballots are folded together. However, if a blank ballot is folded inside a written ballot, it is not considered an illegal vote because blank ballots are not counted.*

5. *In which someone votes for too many candidates for a given office (this part of the ballot is considered illegal but not necessarily the entire ballot).*

6. *That has been cast by someone who is not eligible to vote.*

Q: **What happens to an illegal ballot?**

A: *An illegal ballot is not counted, but it is considered in the number for establishing the majority. It is listed on the teller's report as an "illegal ballot." For example, if 20 people vote, a majority would be 11. If 10 people vote for candidate X, 8 people vote for candidate Y, and 2 votes are illegal (one is unreadable; the other voted for Mickey Mouse), no one would win because no one received a majority vote. Another vote would need to be taken.*

Q: **How should a ballot vote be collected by the tellers?**

A: 1. *Members can come to the front and drop their ballots in a ballot box under the charge of two tellers.*

2. *Tellers can pass a receptacle to collect the ballots—one teller collecting the ballots, the other following to make sure that each member casts one ballot.*

3. *Members can hand their ballots to a teller who feels to see that only one ballot is cast; then the teller deposits the ballots in a container.*

PART II

MOTIONS SIMPLIFIED

6

Motions

Motions are tools that enable an organization to accomplish business efficiently and smoothly. They are the means of bringing business before the assembly, disposing of it quickly, and resolving matters of procedure and urgency. This chapter explains the five classes of motions and how each is used.

CLASSES OF MOTIONS

Motions help the members accomplish what they have come to the meeting to do. There are five classes of motions:

FIVE CLASSES OF MOTIONS		
I. Main	II. Subsidiary III. Privileged IV. Incidental (Secondary)	V. Motions that bring a question back before the assembly

The first class of motions—**main motions**—is used to present new business. The secondary motions—**subsidiary, privileged,** and **incidental motions**—can either help adopt the main motion or help business move forward according to the members' wishes. The last class of motions returns a motion to the assembly for reconsideration. Each class of motions has a certain purpose and has been assigned an order in which it can be brought up in a meeting. This assigned order is called *ranking motions* and follows the principle of taking up business one item at a time.

The better the members understand how to use motions correctly to expedite the organization's business, the shorter the meetings will be and the happier the members will be because they have accomplished their business in a minimum amount of time.

MAIN MOTIONS

A *main motion* brings new business before the assembly and is made while no business is pending. It needs a second, and is debatable, amendable, and takes a majority vote to adopt. Only one main motion can be pending at a time (*pending* refers to a motion placed before the assembly for discussion by the chair). A main motion is the lowest ranking of all the motions. This means that any secondary motion is discussed and voted on before a pending main motion is voted on.

An important point to remember in presenting business and making a main motion is that of *ownership*—who owns the main motion. When a member makes a main motion, it belongs to the maker of the motion until it is repeated by the chairman and placed before the assembly. Before the chair repeats the main motion, the person making the main motion can withdraw it or modify it without asking permission of the assembly.

After the chair places the main motion before the assembly, it belongs to the entire assembly, not to the maker of the motion. The assembly now decides what happens to the motion. It can be killed, delayed, or altered to suit the assembly's wishes. The assembly may make changes that the maker of the motion disapproves of. This is part of the democratic process: the right of the assembly to decide what affects it as a whole body. Therefore, after the motion is placed before the assembly, no one has to ask the maker of the motion for permission to make any changes.

Incidental Main Motions

There are two forms of a main motion. The first form introduces new business to the assembly. The other form is the incidental main motion which deals with procedural questions arising out of pending motions or business; it does not introduce a new topic and is also made while no businesss is pending. An example of a main motion is: "I move to buy a new computer and a laser printer." After this motion is adopted, an incidental main motion would be: "I move that the finance committee be in charge of purchasing the computer and the laser printer." This incidental main motion has been made when no business is pending, and is debatable and amendable. It is related to the main motion because it is concerned with who is going to carry out the adopted action of the main motion. Therefore, it is "incidental" to the motion from which it arises. Key words that can be used to identify incidental main motions include ratify, adopt, limit, and recess. For example, adopt proposals made in a committee report; limit the time of debate; ratify action taken in the absence of a quorum; make a motion to recess when no business is pending.

SECONDARY MOTIONS

In the five classes of motions, three of them are considered secondary motions—subsidiary, privileged, and incidental. The secondary motions enable more than one motion to be pending at a time but still follows the principle of taking up business one item at a time. In parliamentary terminology the word *pending* means: a motion that is stated by the chair and placed before the assembly for discussion and has not yet been disposed of by the assembly. While a main motion is pending, a member can propose a motion from the secondary motions. As each motion is proposed it is considered the immediately pending motion. The assembly now discusses it instead of the main motion or a previously pending secondary motion.

Secondary motions are not main motions, but motions that help the assembly to decide what to do with the main motion or how to get things done in the meeting. They are taken up in the order that they are made. They are assigned an order, called a *ranking of motions* (see "The Ladder of Motions," later in this chapter), in which they can be proposed, discussed, and voted on. The lowest-ranking motions must be proposed before one of higher ranking can be made. Motions of higher rank can be made while a motion of lower rank is pending; but a lower-ranking motion can't be made while a motion of higher rank is pending. As each higher-ranking motion is proposed, the members stop discussing the lower-ranking motion and immediately discuss the higher-ranking motion, which now becomes the pending motion. The following explains how the subsidiary, privileged, and incidental motions fit into this hierarchy of motions.

Subsidiary Motions

Subsidiary motions are the tools that help the assembly dispose of the main motion. Adopting a subsidiary motion always does something to the main motion. Subsidiary motions are assigned an order of precedence, or rank, so that business can be taken up one item at a time. The following list shows subsidiary motions ranked from top to bottom. The highest-ranking subsidiary motion is **to lay on the table**, and the lowest is **postpone indefinitely**.

TO LAY ON THE TABLE
(set aside temporarily)
PREVIOUS QUESTION
(stop debate)
LIMIT OR EXTEND LIMITS OF DEBATE
(shorten or lengthen debate)
POSTPONE TO A CERTAIN TIME
(put off to another time)
REFER TO A COMMITTEE
(let a committee investigate)
AMEND
(change a motion)
POSTPONE INDEFINITELY
(kill a motion)

LOWEST TO HIGHEST

Privileged Motions

Privileged motions do not relate to the pending motion but to special matters of immediate importance that may come up in the business meeting. Since these are usually urgent matters, they must be taken up immediately. Thus, privileged motions are of higher rank and take precedence over subsidiary motions. They are *undebatable* (but some are amendable). After they have been made and seconded, the chair takes a vote *without discussion*. Privileged motions, too, have been assigned an order in which they can be made and voted on. When a motion of lower rank is pending, only a higher-ranking motion can be made. As the following list shows, the highest-ranking privileged motion is **fix the time to which to adjourn**. In fact, it is the highest ranking of both privileged and subsidiary motions. If this motion is made while any other subsidiary or privileged motion is made, the members must vote on it *first*.

FIX THE TIME AT WHICH TO ADJOURN
(set another time
to continue the meeting)
ADJOURN
(end meeting now)
RECESS
(take a break)
RAISE A QUESTION OF PRIVILEGE
(welfare of individual/assembly)
CALL FOR THE ORDERS OF THE DAY
(stick to the agenda)

LOWEST TO HIGHEST

Incidental Motions

Incidental motions are secondary motions that deal with questions of procedure arising from the pending business but do not affect the pending business. Examples might be: raising a question about parliamentary procedure in the meeting; asking for more information relating to the motion under discussion; or pointing out that a very important rule has been broken or ignored. Incidental motions are usually undebatable, and must be decided upon immediately. They have no rank because they are taken up immediately when made. Here are some of the incidental motions:

POINT OF ORDER
(that's against the rules)
APPEAL
(disagree with chair's ruling)
DIVISION OF THE ASSEMBLY
(doubt the result of the vote)
REQUESTS AND INQUIRIES
(I have a question)
SUSPEND THE RULES
(put aside a rule temporarily)
DIVISION OF THE QUESTION
(divide a motion into two
or more questions)

MOTIONS THAT BRING A QUESTION AGAIN BEFORE THE ASSEMBLY

The purpose of the last class of motions is to bring a motion back before the assembly for its consideration. For example, a motion that was laid on the table (temporarily set aside) is brought back by the motion **to take from the table.** When members want to change their minds about a motion that was just voted on, they can **reconsider the vote.** If members are unhappy with action taken at a previous meeting, they can **rescind the action** or **amend something previously adopted.** One other motion in this category is **to discharge a committee.** This takes a motion out of committee before the committee has made its final report and puts it back into the hands of the assembly. All of these motions are made when no other business is pending. They need a second and are debatable except for **take from the table** which is not debatable. If no previous notice has been given, **rescind** and **amend something previously adopted** need a two-thirds vote to be adopted.

THE RANKING OF MOTIONS

As explained earlier, the principle of taking up one item of business at a time requires that the main motion, subsidiary motions, and privileged motions be assigned a rank.

If you think of this rank of motions as a ladder, the main motion is the bottom rung. This idea is illustrated in the following chart, "Ladder of Motions in Order of Rank." When the main motion is *pending* (being discussed), someone can make a motion of higher rank. For example, someone could make the motion to **amend**. If you look at the chart, you will notice we have now taken two steps up the ladder. **Amend** becomes the pending question because it is a higher-ranking motion than the main motion. Discussion is now on the motion to **amend** and not on the main motion. Someone could now make a higher-ranking motion than **amend**, but no one could make the motion to **postpone indefinitely** because it is a lower-ranking motion than **amend**. When making the motions, you go up the ladder, and when voting on the pending motions, you go backward down the ladder. Let's say the following motions have been made and are pending:

Recess

Postpone to a certain time

Amend

Main motion

In taking the vote, the president would start with the motion to **recess**. If adopted, the members would take a recess and when they returned they would begin discussing **postpone to a certain time**. Then they would vote on it. If adopted, the proposed amendment and main motion would be put off until a later time. When the time arrived to take up this main motion and amendment, the members would begin with discussing the amendment. After it had been voted on, the members would vote on the main motion.

LADDER OF MOTIONS IN ORDER OF RANK

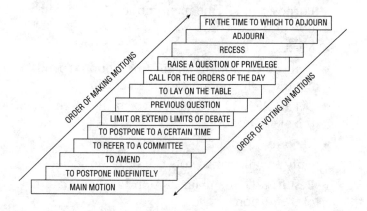

USING SUBSIDIARY MOTIONS TO HELP ADOPT A MAIN MOTION

Let's look at each subsidiary motion and how it can help move the main motion forward until the assembly arrives at its final decision. The discussion will begin with the lowest-ranking subsidiary motion, which is **postpone**

indefinitely, and will explain each motion in turn, through **lay on the table**, which is the highest-ranking motion. The purpose of each motion, its restrictions (whether it needs a second, is amendable, is debatable, etc.), and the result of that subsidiary motion on the main motion will be outlined at the beginning of each section. Then examples will show how to use the motion correctly. (See also Appendix B, "Correct Parliamentary Terminology.")

Postpone Indefinitely

- ♦ **Purpose:** To kill the main motion for the duration of the meeting.
- ♦ Needs a second.
- ♦ Is not amendable, but while this motion is pending the main motion can be amended.
- ♦ Debatable, and debate can go to the merits of the main motion.
- ♦ Majority to adopt.
- ♦ Only an affirmative vote can be reconsidered.
- ♦ **Result:** Kills the main motion for the duration of the session.

The motion to **postpone indefinitely** is the lowest ranking of the subsidiary motions, which means that a higher-ranking motion can be made while this motion is pending. In addition, the main motion can be **amended, referred to a committee, postponed to a certain time,** or **laid on the table.** If the main motion is **referred to a committee** while **postpone indefinitely** is pending, **postpone indefinitely** does not go to committee with the main motion.

Members can **close debate** or **limit** or **extend debate** on **postpone indefinitely** without affecting the main motion.

To make the motion, phrase it this way:

Member: I move to postpone the motion indefinitely.

or

Member: I move that the motion be postponed indefinitely.

Member: Second.

The President states it this way to the assembly:

President: It is moved and seconded to postpone the motion indefinitely. Is there any discussion on postponing indefinitely?

Amend

- ♦ **Purpose:** To change the motion; proposed amendments must be germane to the main motion.
- ♦ Needs a second.
- ♦ Is amendable, but it must be germane or related to the amendment.
- ♦ Debatable. Debate goes only to the amendment.
- ♦ Majority vote to adopt. If amending a motion or document that takes a two-thirds vote to adopt, the proposed amendment takes only a majority vote.
- ♦ Can be reconsidered.
- ♦ **Result:** If adopted, the proposed change becomes part of the main motion.

The purpose of this motion is to change the main motion. There are three ways to amend:

1. Insert words or add words

2. Strike out words

3. Strike out and insert words

Anyone can make the motion to amend. It must be germane, or related, to what it is amending. In the House of Representatives, members are allowed to attach anything to a bill, but this is not the case in deliberative assemblies, who follow adopted parliamentary authorities. For example, in a deliberative assembly, if the members are discussing a motion "to paint the clubhouse," a member can't propose an amendment by adding at the end of the motion "to sponsor a dance on July 4th." This is not germane to painting the clubhouse. It is really a new main motion. Anytime there is a question about whether an amendment is germane, the president can let the members decide by a vote.

An amendment can be amended. The first amendment is called a *primary amendment*, and it applies to the main motion. Its amendment is called a *secondary amendment* and applies only to the primary amendment. The secondary amendment must be germane to the primary amendment. It needs a second and is debatable. Debate is on the merits of the secondary amendment. An amendment to the third degree is not allowed. Only one set of primary and secondary amendments can be pending at the same time.

The motion to amend can be applied to any motion that has a variable. This includes some subsidiary motions and some privileged motions.

Here's an example of each of the ways to amend a main motion. A member has made the main motion to buy a computer and a laser printer.

Member: I move to buy a computer and a laser printer.

The following illustrations show examples of wording the various forms of amending.

1. *To amend by inserting words* ("inserting" means to add words within the motion):

   Member: I move to amend the motion by inserting "brand X" before the word "computer."

   Member: Second.

   The presiding officer repeats it this way:

   President: It is moved and seconded to amend the motion by inserting "brand X" before the word "computer." If adopted, the motion would read, "to buy a brand X computer and laser printer." Is there any discussion on the proposed amendment? [*Discussion is only on whether to buy "brand X," not on whether to buy a computer and laser printer.*]

2. *To amend by adding words* (this is a form of inserting words but the words are added at the end of the motion instead of in the middle):

   Member: I move to amend the motion by adding at the end "not to exceed the cost of $1,000."

   Member: Second.

   President: It is moved and seconded to amend the motion by adding at the end "not to exceed the cost of $1,000." If adopted, the motion would read, "to buy a computer and laser printer not to exceed the cost of $1,000." Is there any discussion on the proposed amendment? [*Discussion is only on "the cost of $1,000," not on buying the computer and laser printer.*]

3. *To amend by striking out words* (this means deleting something in the motion):

Member: I move to amend the motion by striking out "and laser printer."

Member: Second.

President: It is moved and seconded to amend the motion by striking out "and a laser printer." If adopted the motion would read, "to buy a computer." Is there any discussion on the proposed amendment?

4. *To amend by striking out and inserting words* (this means deleting something in the motion and replacing it with something else):

Member: I move to amend the motion by striking out "and laser printer" and inserting "an ink jet printer."

Member: Second.

President: It is moved and seconded to amend the motion by striking out "and a laser printer" and inserting "an ink jet printer." If adopted, the motion would read, "to buy a computer and ink jet printer." Is there any discussion on the proposed amendment?

Voting on Amendments to the Main Motion

Many people get lost in the amendment process. If you are presiding, it is important to write down the amendments as they are proposed, so that you don't get lost. It is also helpful for the secretary to follow the procedure carefully and write down the amendments as well, so that if the president asks, "where are we?," the secretary will be able to provide that information.

The following section takes you through the entire process of voting on amendments and how they are incorporated into the motion if adopted.

Begin with the following as the main motion:

> To buy a computer and a laser printer not to exceed the cost of $1,500.

After some discussion, the following **primary** amendment is proposed:

Member 2: I move to amend the motion by striking out $1,500 and inserting $2,000.

Member 3: Second.

President: It is moved and seconded to amend the motion by striking out $1,500 and inserting $2,000. If adopted the motion would read, "to buy a computer and a laser printer not to exceed the cost of $2,000." Is there any discussion on the proposed amendment?

There is now a main motion and primary amendment pending. After some discussion another amendment is proposed. This is called a secondary amendment.

Member 4: I move to amend the amendment by striking out $2,000 and inserting $2,500.

Member 5: Second.

President: It is moved and seconded to amend the amendment by striking out $2,000 and

inserting $2,500. If adopted the motion
would read, "to buy a computer and a laser
printer not to exceed the cost of $2,500."
Is there any discussion on the proposed
amendment?

At this point discussion goes only to the secondary
amendment. There are now three motions pending.

Secondary Amendment

Primary Amendment

Main Motion

In voting, the chair begins by taking a vote on the
secondary amendment. This is similar to ranking of
motions. The secondary amendment is the highest ranking motion in this series of motions.

President: The question is on the adoption of the
proposed amendment to strike out $2,000
and insert $2,500. If adopted, the motion
would read, "to buy a computer and laser
printer not to exceed the cost of $2,500."
All those in favor of striking out $2,000 and
inserting $2,500 say "aye." Those opposed
say "no." The ayes have it and $2,500
replaces $2,000.

The effect of this vote now makes the secondary
amendment the primary amendment. So the members
still need to vote on whether "$2,500" should replace
the "$1,000" that was stated in the original main
motion. The president continues:

President: The question is on the adoption of the
proposed amendment to strike out $1,000
and insert $2,500. If adopted, the motion

would read, "to buy a computer and laser printer not to exceed $2,500." Is there further discussion?

Members now have the opportunity to discuss whether they want to pay $2,500 for a computer and laser printer or pay $1,000.

President: All those in favor of striking out $1,000 and inserting $2,500 say "aye." Those opposed, say "no." The ayes have it and $2,500 replaces $1, 000. The question is now on the adoption of the main motion as amended, "to buy a computer and laser printer not to exceed the cost of $2,500." Is there any discussion?

Adopting the amendment, does not adopt the main motion. All it did was say that a majority of the membership thinks $2,500 is enough money to buy a computer and laser printer. Now the main motion *as amended* needs to be adopted.

President: The question is on the adoption of the motion as amended, "to buy a computer and laser printer not to exceed the cost of $2,500." All those in favor say "aye." Those opposed, say "no." The ayes have it, and the motion is carried. We will buy a computer and laser printer not to exceed the cost of $2,500. The secretary and treasurer will be in charge of buying it.

The key point to remember when voting on amendments is to follow the correct order of amendments back to the original main motion. The presiding officer always begins voting with the secondary amendment, then the primary amendment, and finally takes the vote on the main motion.

This is what happens if the secondary amendment is defeated.

President: The question is on adopting the proposed amendment by striking out $2,000 and inserting $2,500. If adopted the motion would read "to buy a computer and a laser printer not to exceed the cost of $2,500." All those in favor of striking $2,000 and inserting $2,500, say "aye." Those opposed say "no." The noes have it and the proposed amendment is lost."

Since the secondary amendment was defeated, the president now asks for the vote on the primary amendment.

President: The question is on the adoption of the proposed amendment to strike out $1,000 and insert $2,000. If adopted, the motion would read "to buy a computer and a laser printer not to exceed the cost of $2,000." Is there any discussion on the proposed amendment? Hearing none, all those in favor say "aye." Those opposed say "no." The ayes have it and $2,000 replaces $1,000."

Now the vote is taken on the main motion as amended.

President: The question is on the adoption of the main motion as amended, "to buy a computer and laser printer not to exceed the cost of $2,000." Is there further discussion? Hearing none, all those in favor say "aye." Those opposed say "no." The ayes have it and the motion is carried. We will buy a computer and a laser printer not to exceed the cost of $2,000."

If the proposed amendment to strike out $1,000 and insert $2,000 had been defeated, then the members would vote on the main motion as originally presented, "**to buy a computer and laser printer not to exceed the cost of $1,000.**"

After the members finish voting on the secondary amendment, primary amendment, but before the main motion *as amended* is voted on, the members could still amend the motion further. They could strike out "laser" and insert "ink jet" or "dot matrix." They could also insert a brand name before "computer" if they so desired.

The most important rule to remember in amending motions, is that the secondary motion must be germane to the primary motion or it is not in order. For example, with the primary amendment pending to strike out "$1,000" and insert "$2,000" pending, it would be out of order to propose an amendment to strike out "laser" and insert "ink jet"—the type of printer is not germane to the cost. Replacing "ink jet" with "laser" would be considered the beginning of another group of amendments. Once the members begin with amending the cost, they must follow all of the steps of the amending process in order until the cost issue has been decided by the assembly. After this is done, they can amend another part of the motion.

Refer to a Committee

- ♦ **Purpose:** Have a small group investigate a proposal.
- ♦ Needs a second.
- ♦ Any variable in the motion is amendable.
- ♦ Debatable. Debate goes only to the merits of referring the motion to a committee.

- ◆ Majority vote to adopt.
- ◆ Can be reconsidered if the committee hasn't begun discussion of the motion.
- ◆ **Result:** If adopted, the motion goes to the committee to investigate and does not return to the membership until the committee is ready to report or until the membership has adopted a time for the committee to report back to the assembly.

The purpose of the motion **refer to a committee** is to obtain information by referring the motion to a small, selected group of members for investigation. When making the motion to refer to a committee, state *which committee, what it is to do, and when it is to report back to the membership.* If you do not put a date when the committee is to report, the motion might die in committee. To make the motion to **refer to a committee**, state it this way:

Member: I move to refer the motion to the finance committee to investigate which is the best kind of computer and laser printer and what the cost is, and to report back to us at the next meeting.

Member: Second.

President: It is moved and seconded that we refer the motion to the finance committee to investigate which is the best kind of computer and laser printer and what the cost is, and to report back to us at the next meeting. Is there any discussion about referring the motion?

Another form of this motion, is to move that the assembly act as the committee. In small assemblies (those under fifty), the motion is to **consider informally**.

Consider Informally

- ♦ **Purpose:** Have the assembly act as a committee.
- ♦ Needs a second.
- ♦ Is debatable. Debate is on the merits of informal consideration.
- ♦ Majority vote to adopt.
- ♦ Only a negative vote can be reconsidered.
- ♦ **Result:** If adopted, this motion enables the assembly to act as the committee. Its effect is to take away the restrictions on debating the main motion and any proposed amendments. Any other motions made are under the regular rules of debate. By a two-thirds vote, members can limit the length or number of speeches or can close debate.

The motion to **consider informally** is another form of the motion to **refer to a committee**. The assembly acts as the committee. In small assemblies (those having fewer than 50 members), the motion is to **consider informally**. In large assemblies it is the motion to go into a **committee of the whole**. To make the motion, state:

Member: I move that the motion be considered informally.

Member: Second.

President: It is moved and seconded to consider the
motion informally. Is there any discussion?

Anytime the members want to end **informal
consideration**, someone can move that **the regular rules
of debate be enforced** or that **the question be considered formally**. This takes a majority vote to adopt.

As soon as the motion is disposed of temporarily or
finally, informal consideration ends. Business conducted
while under informal consideration is recorded in the
minutes of the meeting.

Postpone to a Certain Time

♦ **Purpose:** To put off or delay a decision.

♦ Needs a second.

♦ The time element is amendable.

♦ Debatable. Debate goes only to the merits of
   postponing.

♦ Majority vote to adopt.

♦ Can be reconsidered.

♦ **Result:** Discussion and decision are put off until
   later in the meeting or until the next meeting
   when no business is pending.

The motion **postpone to a certain time** should not
be confused with **to lay on the table**.

In many groups, it is common to hear, "let's table
the motion to the next meeting." This is an incorrect
usage of **lay on the table** and does not accomplish what
the member actually intends. If such a motion is made,
the chair should restate the motion as **postpone to the
next meeting** and ask for discussion.

When the motion to **postpone to the next meeting** is adopted, it appears under unfinished business and general orders at the next meeting. If a motion is made "to postpone to the next meeting until 8 p.m.," the motion is taken up at approximately that time. If other business is being discussed at 8 p.m., the members finish with that business and then take up the motion that was postponed until 8 p.m. When members want a motion to come up at an exact time in the meeting, even if it interrupts business under discussion, it needs to be made a **special order** for that time.

Postpone to a Certain Time Made into a Special Order

- ♦ **Purpose:** To ensure that a motion will be taken up at a specified time.
- ♦ Needs a second.
- ♦ Debatable.
- ♦ Time is amendable.
- ♦ A two-thirds vote to adopt.
- ♦ Can be reconsidered.
- ♦ **Result:** If adopted, it must be taken up at the specified time even if business is pending. (To set aside the special order, see the discussion "Call for the Orders of the Day" later in the chapter.)

The motion to **postpone** has certain time limits. It can't be postponed beyond a quarterly time interval or the next regular business meeting (whichever comes first). It can't be used as a motion to kill. If the motion to **postpone to the next meeting** is adopted, it appears on the agenda under unfinished business and general orders. To make the motion to **postpone to a certain time**, say:

Member: I move to postpone the motion to the next meeting.

Member: Second.

President: It is moved and seconded to postpone the motion to the next meeting. Is there any discussion on postponing the motion?

To postpone the motion and make it a **special order**, say:

Member: I move to postpone the motion to the next meeting, and make it a special order for 8 p.m.

Member: Second.

President: It is moved and seconded to postpone the motion to the next meeting, and make it a special order for 8 p.m. This motion is amendable and takes a two-thirds vote to adopt since it provides for a suspension of a rule. Is there any discussion on postponing the motion?

The chair takes the vote as a rising vote.

To Limit or Extend the Limits of Debate

♦ **Purpose:** To limit or extend the time of debate or the number of times a person can speak in debate; or to put a time limit on a particular motion. For example: to limit the entire debate to 30 minutes.

- ◆ Needs a second.
- ◆ Time element is amendable.
- ◆ Not debatable.
- ◆ Takes a two-thirds vote to adopt.
- ◆ Only an affirmative vote can be reconsidered **without** debate before the time limit expires. If partially carried out, only the time remaining can be reconsidered.
- ◆ If the motion has been voted down, it can be made again after there has been some progress in the debate.
- ◆ **Result:** It changes the standard rules of debate.

If an assembly has no special rule of order about how long a member can speak in debate or how many times, a member may speak twice to a motion and up to 10 minutes each time. If a member wishes to extend or limit the debate, he or she makes this motion. Conventions have standing rules that regulate how long each motion or topic is to be considered. If this is the case, when the time has arrived to go on to the next business in order, a member can make the motion to **extend the limits of debate**. A two-thirds vote is needed to adopt because the motion is altering the rights of the individual members.

There are several ways this motion can be used. One way is to reduce the number of speeches or the time allowed for members to speak to an issue:

Member: I move to limit debate to 5 minutes per person.

Member: Second.

President: It is moved and seconded to limit debate to 5 minutes per person. This motion is not debatable but is amendable. Are you ready for the question? All those in favor please rise. Be seated. Those opposed please rise. Be seated. The affirmative has it, and debate will be limited to 5 minutes per person.

or

The negative has it, and debate will not be limited. Each person can speak 10 minutes to the question. Is there any discussion?

Another way is to extend debate that has been set for a certain time. For example, a convention may have a rule that debate stops at a certain time; then a motion could be made to extend this time.

Member: I move to extend the debate 5 more minutes.

Member: Second.

President: It is moved and seconded to extend the debate 5 more minutes. This motion is not debatable but is amendable. Are you ready for the question? All in favor please rise. Be seated. Those opposed please rise. Be seated. The affirmative has it, and debate will be extended 5 more minutes.

or

The negative has it, and the debate will not be extended. It is time to take a vote on the motion to . . . . All those in favor say "Aye." Those opposed say "No." [*Then announce the vote.*]

The motion to limit or extend debate can also be used to **fix the hour for closing debate and taking the vote**.

Member: I move that at 3 p.m. debate be closed and the vote be taken.

Member: Second.

President: It is moved and seconded that at 3 p.m. debate be closed and the vote be taken. This motion is not debatable but is amendable. Are you ready for the question? All those in favor please rise. Be seated. Those opposed please rise. Be seated. The affirmative has it, and debate will be closed at 3 p.m. and the vote taken.

or

The negative has it, and debate will not end at 3 p.m. Is there further discussion?

Previous Question

- ♦ **Purpose:** To stop debate and immediately take the vote.
- ♦ Needs a second.
- ♦ Not amendable.
- ♦ Not debatable.
- ♦ Two-thirds vote to adopt.
- ♦ Can be reconsidered without debate before any vote has been taken under the order of the previous question.

♦ **Result:** If adopted, the members take a vote on the immediate pending question. If the previous question is called on all pending questions, then the vote is taken on all pending questions.

The motion **previous question** is the most misunderstood and misused motion in meetings. There is only one way to stop debate, and that is to make this motion. Since it takes members' rights away, it requires a two-thirds vote to close debate.

Many people do not understand the **previous question**. They think that they can just yell out "Question!" and the chair should stop debate and take a vote on the motion. The chairman *never* has the authority to close debate as long as one person wants to discuss the motion—or the **previous question** is adopted.

The time to make a motion for the **previous question** is when a member thinks the debate on the motion has become tedious. The member wants to close debate and take a vote so that the membership can proceed to other business. The member must rise, address the chair, and move the previous question:

Member: I move the Previous Question.

   or

              I move to close debate and take the vote immediately.

Member: Second.

The president should handle it this way:

President: The question is on adopting the previous question on the pending motion. If adopted, this will stop debate and we will vote immediately. All those in favor please rise. Be seated.

> Those opposed please rise. Be seated.
> [*Announce the vote.*]

If the affirmative has it:

President: There are two-thirds in the affirmative, and the previous question is adopted. Debate is stopped. All those in favor of buying a computer and a laser printer say "Aye." Those opposed say "No." [*Announce the result of the vote.*]

If the negative has it:

President: There are less than two-thirds in the affirmative. The previous question is lost. Is there further discussion?

In its unqualified form, this motion applies only to the immediate pending motion. If adopted, debate ceases and the vote is taken immediately on the pending question. The **previous question** may be made on all pending questions or on consecutive pending questions.

Note: Even though this is one of the highest-ranking subsidiary motions, it is not proper to make this motion before anyone has had the right to debate. If a controversial issue is presented to the membership, it is unfair to close debate before someone in the opposition has the right to speak. Henry Robert, in his book *Parliamentary Law*, says:

> Where there is radical difference of opinion in an organization, one side must yield. The great lesson for democracies to learn is for the majority to give to the minority a full, free opportunity to present their side of the case, and then for the minority, having failed to win a majority of their views, gracefully to submit and to recognize the action as that of the entire organization, and cheerfully to assist in carrying it out, until they can secure its repeal.

To Lay on the Table

♦ **Purpose:** To set the main motion aside temporarily in order to take up something of immediate urgency. The intent is not to kill the motion or to put it off to the next meeting.

♦ Needs a second.

♦ Not amendable.

♦ Not debatable.

♦ Takes a majority to adopt.

♦ Can't be reconsidered. If adopted, it can be taken from the table; and if it is defeated, it can be made again after debate has progressed and something more urgent comes up again.

♦ **Result:** If adopted, it places the main motion and any of its adhering motions on the table or in the hands of the secretary. It stays on the table until someone moves to take it from the table.

The motion to **lay on the table** is the second most misused motion in meetings. Members either "table it" to kill a motion or "table it" to postpone a motion. In essence, the motion to **lay on the table** takes away the members' right to debate with a majority vote.

When **lay on the table** has been adopted, it allows a majority of the members to immediately halt consideration of the motion without debate. When a motion has been laid on the table, and if the meeting adjourns before it is taken from the table, it is not put on the agenda for the next meeting. A member must take it from the table at the next meeting before it can again be discussed. Since the members moved to lay it on the table, only the members can take it from the table. That is why this motion is reserved for an immediate urgency only. When a member makes this motion and does not state the reason for making the motion, the chair should ask the member to state his or her reason for making the motion. If it is apparent that the member wants to kill the motion, the chair should rule the motion out of order and explain to the member that the proper motion would be to **postpone the motion indefinitely** if it is in order at that time; or the chair can take the liberty to place the motion before the assembly, as "to postpone it indefinitely," and ask for discussion. (See "Ranking of Motions" at the beginning of this chapter.)

A member should state the reasons for making this motion. A member cannot lay a motion on the table and then make another motion that conflicts with the motion laid on the table. If the motion is not used correctly, the chair should rule it out of order and should state the proper procedure. If the chair does not do this, a member should rise to a **point of order** and explain the correct procedure.

When a main motion is laid on the table, all adhering subsidiary motions go with it. For example, if a main motion and its subsidiary motions to amend and to refer to a committee are pending, these go to the table with the main motion.

This motion is recorded in the minutes but it is not put on the agenda. A member must remember to make the motion **to take from the table**. If the motion is laid on the table and is not taken from the table by the end of the next meeting, it dies. After it dies, a member would have to present it as a "new" main motion.

To make this motion a member states:

Member: I move to lay the motion on the table.

Member: Second.

President: It is moved and seconded to lay the motion on the table. All those in favor say "Aye." Those opposed say "No." [*Announce the vote.*]

Legitimate Uses of the Motion to Lay on the Table

As explained earlier, the motion to **lay on the table** cannot be used to kill a motion or to put it off to a later time. It is reserved for an urgent matter that can't wait.

The chair is allowed to rule whether the matter is urgent and whether the motion will be entertained.

Examples of urgent situations are:

1. The speaker for the program has arrived and needs to leave early, so a member can move to lay the pending business aside as a courtesy to the speaker.

2. Something on the agenda needs to be resolved during the current meeting. It is getting late, and the member is concerned that the meeting will adjourn without resolving the important business. A member can move to lay the pending business on the table to take up this important matter.

This motion should be used sparingly in meetings, if at all.

USING PRIVILEGED MOTIONS

Here we look at *privileged motions,* those motions that do not relate to the pending motion but that are special matters of immediate importance arising in the meeting. The discussion will begin with the lowest-ranking privileged motion—**call for the orders of the day**—and proceed to the highest-ranking one—**fix the time to**

which to adjourn. The purpose of each motion, its restrictions (whether it needs a second, is amendable, etc.), and the result of that privileged motion will be outlined at the beginning of each section. Then examples will show how to use the motion correctly.

Call for the Orders of the Day

- ♦ **Purpose:** Make the assembly conform to the agenda or order of business, or make the assembly take up a general order or special order.
- ♦ One member can call for the orders of the day.
- ♦ Does not require a second.
- ♦ Not amendable.
- ♦ Not debatable.
- ♦ No vote is taken unless the members want to set aside the orders of the day, which takes a two-thirds vote.
- ♦ Cannot be reconsidered.
- ♦ **Result:** Stop whatever the assembly is doing and go to the orders of the day.

When the agenda isn't being followed, or a motion that was made a **special order** is not being taken up at the right time, one member can **call for the orders of the day**. This motion does not require a second. It is not debatable. The chair must immediately go to the orders of the day or take a vote to set aside the orders of the day. If the chair assumes a motion to set aside the orders of the day, it must be adopted by a two-thirds vote in the *negative*. If a member moves to set aside the orders of the day, it takes a two-thirds vote in the *affirmative*.

Let's say the members are debating the motion to buy a computer. The chair either has forgotten that the time has arrived to take up a special order or has decided to ignore it. A member calls for the orders of the day. The chair can do one of two things. The chair can stop the discussion and go to the orders of the day. Or, if the chair feels that the members are almost ready to vote on the computer and would like to set aside the orders of the day to finish the business at hand, the chair can take a vote on the motion to **call for the orders of the day**.

Member: I call for the orders of the day.

Chairman: The orders of the day are called for. The order of the day is the motion to give $1,000 to the Environmental Club. The question is: Will the members proceed to the orders of the day? As many as are in favor please rise. [*a few members rise*] Be seated. Those opposed please rise. [*many members rise*] Be seated. There is a two-thirds vote in the negative, and we will not proceed to the orders of the day. Is there any further discussion about buying a computer and a laser printer?

If the vote is less than two-thirds in the negative, the chair would state:

Chairman: There is less than a two-thirds vote in the negative, and we will now proceed to the orders of the day. The question is on the motion to give $1,000 to the Environmental Club. Is there any discussion?

When this motion has been disposed of, the members return to the motion to buy a computer and a laser printer.

If a member wants to set aside the orders of the day he can state, **"I move that the time for considering the pending question be extended."** This motion takes a two-thirds vote in the *affirmative* to adopt.

Raise a Question of Privilege

- ♦ **Purpose:** Permits a member to make a request or a main motion relating to the rights and privileges of the assembly or a member and to consider it immediately, because of its urgency, while other business is pending.
- ♦ It does not need a second.
- ♦ Not debatable.
- ♦ Chair rules on the request.
- ♦ **Result:** The chair's ruling determines the outcome.

A common question of privilege has to do with noise or temperature in the assembly room. There are **questions of privilege concerning the assembly** and **questions of privilege concerning the individual**. Of the two, privilege of the assembly has a higher priority. To raise a question of privilege, a member would usually state it this way:

Member: Madam President, I rise to a question of privilege concerning the assembly.

President: Please state the question.

Member: It is too hot in here. Could we have the heat turned down?

The chair then makes a ruling.

President: Is there any objection to turning down the heat? Hearing none, will member X turn down the thermostat.

An example of a motion that is considered a question of privilege is the motion to go into "executive session," during which time the proceedings are kept secret.

To make a motion to go into executive session, a member would state:

Member: Madam President, I rise to a question of privilege to make a motion.

President: Please state your motion.

Member: I move that we go into executive session to discuss this issue.

President: The chair rules that the question is one of privilege to be entertained immediately. Is there a second?

Member: Second.

President: It is moved and seconded to go into executive session. Is there any discussion?

Debate follows on whether to go into executive session; this motion is amendable; then a vote is taken. If the motion is adopted, those who are not members must leave and the meeting goes into a secret session. The minutes of this portion of the meeting can be approved only at an executive session.

Recess

♦ **Purpose:** To take a short intermission and then resume business where the members left off. As a privileged motion, a motion to recess is made when other business is pending.

♦ Needs a second.

♦ Length of recess is amendable.

♦ Not debatable.

♦ Majority vote to adopt.

♦ Can't be reconsidered.

♦ **Result:** Members take a short break.

To make the motion, a member says:

Member: I move to take a ——— minute recess.

Member: Second.

President: It is moved and seconded to take a ——— minute recess. All those in favor say "Aye." Those opposed say "No." The ayes have it, and we will take a ——— minute recess. This meeting stands in recess for ——— minutes. [*one rap of the gavel*]

When the recess is finished, the president calls the meeting to order with one rap of the gavel.

A recess is generally short in duration, though it may last several hours, but it is never for more than a day. Organizations do not take long recesses like Congress. If members want to take a longer recess, they should set an adjourned meeting. (See the motion **to fix the time to which to adjourn.** Also see "Adjourned Meetings" in Chapter 11.)

Note that it is also possible to recess when no business is pending. This motion to recess is an incidental main motion. (See the next section.)

Recess as an Incidental Main Motion

When no other business is pending, a motion to **recess as an incidental main motion** can be made. The difference between this motion and **recess as a privileged motion**, described in the preceding section, is that **recess as an incidental main motion** is debatable and the previous use of recess is not debatable.

Adjourn

♦ **Purpose:** To end the meeting NOW!

♦ Needs a second.

♦ Not amendable.

♦ Not debatable.

♦ A majority vote to adopt.

♦ Can't be reconsidered but can be made again after some progress in the meeting.

♦ **Result:** It ends the meeting, and the business halts at the point where the members adjourned. If the members are in the middle of discussing a motion, this motion will come up at the next meeting under unfinished business and general orders.

As a privileged motion one made when other motions are pending, **adjourn** takes precedence over all other motions, except the motion **to fix the time to which to adjourn**. If adopted, and before the chair announces the adjournment, members can rise to make announcements, give previous notice about a motion to be made at the next meeting, and make a motion to **reconsider, reconsider and enter on the minutes**, or **fix the time to which to adjourn**. If the meeting adjourns while business is pending, this business carries over to the next meeting and appears on the agenda under *unfinished business and general orders*. For example:

Member: I move to adjourn.

Member: Second.

President: It is moved and seconded that we adjourn. All those in favor say "Aye." Those opposed say "No." The ayes have it, the motion is carried, and the meeting is adjourned.

or

The noes have it, the motion is lost, and the meeting will not adjourn. Is there further business?

Fix the Time to Which to Adjourn

- ◆ **Purpose:** To set a later time to continue this meeting before the next regular meeting. In parliamentary terminology, it sets the time for an adjourned meeting.
- ◆ Needs a second.
- ◆ The time and date of the adjourned meeting are amendable.
- ◆ Not debatable.
- ◆ A majority vote adopts.
- ◆ Can be reconsidered.
- ◆ **Result:** Sets the date, place, and time for the meeting to continue.

As a privileged motion, **fix the time to which to adjourn** is the highest-ranking motion. An adjourned meeting is a legal continuation of the present meeting. This motion never adjourns the meeting; it sets the time and date for another meeting. (See Chapter 11, "Meetings," for information about an adjourned meeting.)

When no business is pending, this is an incidental main motion. The only difference between the motion as an incidental main motion and as a privileged one is that it is debatable when no business is pending. To make the motion privileged, a member states:

Member: I move that when this meeting adjourns, it adjourn to meet tomorrow at 8 p.m.

Member: Second.

President: It is moved and seconded that when this meeting adjourns, it adjourn to meet tomorrow at 8 p.m. All those in favor say "Aye." Those opposed say "No." The ayes have it, and when this meeting adjourns, it will meet tomorrow at 8 p.m.

The chair goes back to whatever business was pending. If the noes have it, the chair states:

The noes have it, and the motion is lost. We won't be having an adjourned meeting.

Fix the Time <u>at</u> which to Adjourn

- ♦ **Purpose:** To set the time to adjourn the meeting.
- ♦ Needs a second.
- ♦ Amendable.

- ◆ Is debatable because it is an incidental main motion.
- ◆ Takes a majority to adopt.
- ◆ Can't be reconsidered.
- ◆ **Result:** The members must adjourn at the time they have now set for adjournment. When that time comes, the presiding officer must announce that the time for adjournment has arrived and then adjourn the meeting. If members want to continue the meeting at this point, they must move to **suspend the rules** in order to continue the meeting. (See the discussion of the motion **suspend the rules** in the next section "Using Incidental Motions.")

Since this is an incidental main motion, it is made when no other business is pending. To fix the time at which to adjourn, a member states:

Member: I move that the meeting adjourn at 9 p.m.

Member: Second.

President: It is moved and seconded that the meeting adjourn at 9 p.m. Is there any discussion? (The time for adjournment is amendable.)

After the vote is taken, the chair announces it this way if the affirmative wins:

President: The ayes have it, the motion is carried, and the meeting will adjourn at 9 p.m.

If the negative has it, the chair announces it this way:

President: The noes have it, and the motion is lost.

and members can now make the motion to adjourn at any time during the meeting, or even at 9 p.m. by making the motion **to adjourn**. If adopted the meeting will adjourn.

Fix the time **at** which to adjourn is helpful if someone has to leave the meeting at a certain time and does not want to miss any important business. If this motion is adopted, it ensures that no further business will be considered by ending the meeting.

USING INCIDENTAL MOTIONS

Here we look at *incidental motions,* those motions that concern questions of procedure related to the pending business. These motions are not ranked because they are taken up immediately when made. The purpose of each motion, its restrictions (whether it needs a second, is amendable, is debatable, etc.), and the result of that incidental motion will be outlined at the beginning of each section. Then examples will show how to use the motion correctly.

Point of Order

- ♦ **Purpose:** To correct a breach in the rules.
- ♦ No second
- ♦ Not debatable.
- ♦ Presiding officer rules on the point.
- ♦ Cannot be reconsidered.
- ♦ **Result:** The chair's ruling stands unless someone appeals it.

The purpose of a **point of order** is to correct a breach in the rules when the presiding officer does not correct it, or when the presiding officer makes a breach of the rules. **Point of order** should not be used for *minor* infractions. It does not need a second, can interrupt a speaker, and is ruled upon by the chair. It is made at the time of the infraction. If the infraction is of a continuing nature, a point of order can be made at any time. If a member does not agree with the chair's ruling, the member can **appeal from the decision of the chair**.

To make a point of order, the member says:

Member: I rise to a point of order.

or

Member: Point of order.

President: Please state your point.

Member: There is no longer a quorum present, and any business transacted will be null and void.

President: Your point is well taken. Since there is no longer a quorum present, this meeting is adjourned. [*one rap of the gavel*]

The president could rule against the point of order by stating:

President: Your point is not well taken, and the meeting will continue.

Appeal from the Decision of the Chair or Appeal

- ◆ **Purpose:** To disagree with the chair's ruling and let the members decide the disagreement by taking a vote.
- ◆ Needs a second.
- ◆ Must be made at the time the ruling was made.
- ◆ Debatable. However, it is not debatable if it relates to rules of speaking, relates to the priority of business (order of business), or applies to a ruling on an undebatable motion.
- ◆ Not amendable.
- ◆ Majority or tie vote sustains the decision of the chair.
- ◆ Can be reconsidered.
- ◆ **Result:** If adopted, it upholds the chair's ruling.

An **appeal** is made immediately after the ruling of the chair. This motion needs a second and is debatable *unless* it is made while an undebatable motion is pending or relates to the priority of business. The chair has the first opportunity to speak to the appeal. After members of the assembly have spoken to the appeal, the chair has the last right to speak before taking the vote. A majority vote is needed to sustain the decision of the chair.

Let's say the members are discussing a motion to send delegates to the state convention. A member makes the motion to amend by adding at the end "and to build tennis courts." The presiding officer rules the proposed amendment out of order because it is not related to the motion. The member proposing the amendment then makes the motion to **appeal from the decision of the chair**. He states:

Member: I appeal from the decision of the chair.

President: It is moved and seconded to appeal from the decision of the chair. The question before the assembly is, "Shall the decision of the chair be sustained?" Is there any discussion?

If the chair wants to speak first—which he or she is entitled to do—the chair states:

President: The chair ruled that the amendment was not germane because building the tennis courts is not related to sending delegates to the convention. Is there further discussion?

Then each member has the right to speak *once* to the appeal. After everyone has spoken who wishes to speak, the chair can give his or her reason for the ruling. Then the chair takes the vote. The correct phrasing for the vote is:

President: The question is, "Shall the decision of the chair be sustained?" All those in favor say "Aye." Those opposed say "No."

The chair announces the vote and whether the decision is sustained or not sustained.

If the members vote for the decision of the chair, then business continues in accordance with the chair's ruling. In this case the proposed amendment to add "tennis courts" to the motion is not in order. The members will only consider sending delegates to the convention.

If the members vote against the decision of the chair, then the proposed amendment "to build tennis courts" will be considered a valid amendment and the members will discuss and vote on the proposed amendment.

Requests and Inquiries

This procedure is a way to obtain information. One way is to ask for parliamentary information. This is called a **parliamentary inquiry**. The chair answers the inquiry. Another way is to ask for information about the subject being discussed. This is called a **point of information**. These are always directed to, or through, the chair, for example:

Member: I rise to parliamentary inquiry.

President: Please state your inquiry.

Member: Is it appropriate to lay this business on the table so that we can take up the item on the agenda to send delegates to the state convention?

President: [*gives an opinion*]

This is just an opinion, not a ruling, and is not subject to an appeal. The member can follow the chair's advice or ignore it. To make a **point of information**, a member states:

Member: I rise to a point of information.

President: Please state your point.

Member: Do we have enough money in the treasury to send four delegates to the convention?

President: [*If the chair does not know the answer, he or she can ask someone who does.*] Will the treasurer please answer the member's question?

Treasurer: We have allotted $1,000 to send delegates.

President: Does that answer the member's question?

Member: [*answers either yes or no*]

Request for Permission to Withdraw or Modify a Motion

- ♦ **Purpose:** Withdraw or modify a motion without taking a vote.
- ♦ Does not need a second if asking permission to withdraw. Needs a second if modifying the motion.
- ♦ Not debatable.
- ♦ Vote by general consent when asking permission to withdraw.
- ♦ The vote to modify can be reconsidered. Only the negative vote in withdrawing the motion can be reconsidered.
- ♦ **Result:** When withdrawn, it is as if the motion had never been made. If modified, then it is presented to the assembly in the modified form.

Before the chair states the motion, it belongs to the maker of the motion and he or she can withdraw it or modify it without the permission of the assembly. After the motion is stated by the chair, it belongs to the assembly and the maker must ask permission to modify or withdraw it.

Note: There is some misunderstanding about this procedure. If the chair has not stated the motion, the member can withdraw it without permission of the person who seconded it. If the member modifies the motion and the seconder withdraws his or her second, then someone else must second the motion.

Remember, after the motion has been stated by the chair, the motion belongs to the assembly and not to the maker of the motion. The assembly, not the person who seconded the motion, must give permission to withdraw the motion or to modify it.

After a motion has been seconded but not repeated by the presiding officer, the maker of the motion can quickly rise and say:

Member: Madam President, I wish to modify my
          motion by adding at the end "not to
          exceed the cost of $1,000."

or

          Madam President, I wish to withdraw the
          motion.

The president either states that the motion is withdrawn or repeats it in the modified version. If the seconder withdraws his or her second from the modified form, the president can ask for a second.

Before the chair states the motion, another member can rise and ask the president if the maker of the motion would accept a change in it. The maker can either accept or reject the proposed change. If the maker rejects the proposed change, the member suggesting the change can propose an amendment after it has been placed before the assembly. If the change is accepted by the maker, the changed motion becomes pending. This is referred to by some authorities as a "friendly amendment."

After the motion is under discussion and the maker of the motion wants to withdraw the motion, he or she has to ask permission of the assembly. The member states:

Member: Mr. President, I ask permission to withdraw
          the motion.

This request should be handled by general consent:

President: Is there any objection to withdrawing the motion? Hearing none, the motion is withdrawn.

If there is an objection, the presiding officer puts it to a vote.

A withdrawn motion is not recorded in the minutes unless the motion has carried over from another meeting. Then it is recorded in the minutes.

Object to Consideration of a Question

- **Purpose:** To prevent the main motion from being considered.
- No second.
- Not debatable.
- Takes a two-thirds vote in the negative not to consider.
- Only a negative vote, not an affirmative vote, can be reconsidered.
- **Result:** If two-thirds of the members vote in the negative, then the motion cannot be considered for the duration of the meeting. It can be proposed again at another meeting.

The purpose of **object to consideration of a question** is to prevent a motion from being considered. This motion should not be used as a dilatory tactic. Only when a member feels that it would be divisive for the motion to come before the assembly should this objection be made. Anyone can object to consideration, including the presiding officer. This motion does not need a second and is not debatable or amendable. A vote must be taken immediately on whether the motion should be considered. The objection must be made before any discussion has begun on the motion. It takes a two-thirds vote against consideration to sustain the objection.

To make this motion, a member must rise immediately after the motion is stated by the chair and say:

Member: Mr. President (or Madam President), I object to consideration of the question.

The chair immediately takes a vote. In taking a vote, the chair should phrase it this way:

Chair: The consideration of the question is objected to. Shall the question be considered? Those in favor of considering the question rise. [*pause*]

Be seated. [*pause*]

Those opposed to considering the question rise. [pause]

Be seated. [*pause*]

If more than a third of the membership is in favor of considering the question, the chair announces the vote this way:

Chair: There are less than two-thirds opposed, and the objection is not sustained. The question is on the motion . . . .

If two-thirds of the membership vote against considering the question, the chair announces the vote this way:

Chair: There are two-thirds opposed, and the question will not be considered. Is there further business?

In putting the question to the membership, the chair states:

Chair: Shall the question be considered?

Those who want to prevent consideration must vote in the negative.

Division of the Assembly

- ♦ **Purpose:** To doubt the result of the vote.
- ♦ No second.
- ♦ Not debatable.
- ♦ **Result:** The vote is immediately retaken in a different way than it was originally taken.

For examples of using this motion, see "Taking the Vote" in Chapter 3 and "Doubting the Result of the Vote" in Chapter 5.

Suspend the Rules

- ♦ **Purpose:** To set aside a rule of the assembly (except bylaws or the corporate charter).
- ♦ Needs a second.
- ♦ Not debatable.
- ♦ Not amendable.
- ♦ Takes a two-thirds vote.
- ♦ Cannot be reconsidered.
- ♦ **Result:** Rules are set aside so that members can do something contrary to the rules.

The motion to suspend the rules is used primarily to take up a particular item of business in the order of business out of its regular order, to set aside a procedural rule, or an ordinary standing rule. Here are examples of how to apply this motion:

1. To enable the assembly to take up something out of its proper order in the agenda; for example, to take up something under new business before taking up unfinished business. To move to suspend the rules, a member would say:

   Member: I move to suspend the rules and take up the topic "to repair the clubhouse."

   Member: Second.

2. To suspend the rules of debate and amendment, and vote immediately, a member would say:

   Member: I move to suspend the rules and agree to the resolution . . . .

   Member: Second.

   Any rule that suspends a parliamentary rule or order of business takes a two-thirds vote. If it is not controversial, then the vote can be taken by general (unanimous) consent. ("Without objection . . . ") The presiding officer takes the vote this way:

   President: It is moved and seconded to suspend the rules and take up "the repairs to the clubhouse." All those in favor please rise. Be seated. Those opposed please rise. Be seated. The affirmative has it, and the rules are suspended. We will proceed to the item about repairing the clubhouse.

At this point the member who suspended the rules should rise and make a motion about repairing the clubhouse.

To take the vote by general (unanimous) consent, the chair states the motion this way:

President: Is there any objection to suspending the rules and taking up the item to repair the clubhouse? [*pause*] Hearing none, the rules are suspended, and the next item of business is repairing the clubhouse.

When the members dispose of the motion to repair the clubhouse, they return to the place in the agenda where they left off.

3. To suspend an ordinary *standing rule* of the society. These are rules that do not have to do with parliamentary procedure but with the policies of the society, time of the meetings, or something of an administrative nature. These rules can be suspended by majority vote because they do not involve the protection of a minority. The rules are suspended only for the duration of the meeting. Suspending the rules does not bind any future meetings. The rules that can't be suspended are bylaws (unless their suspension is provided for) and rules protecting absent members or the basic rights of individual members or to dispense with an entire established order of business.

USING MOTIONS THAT BRING A QUESTION AGAIN BEFORE THE ASSEMBLY

The motions that follow are ones that return a question to the assembly for reconsideration. These motions are made when no other business is pending. The purpose of each motion, its restrictions (whether it needs a second, is debatable, can be reconsidered, etc.), and the result of the motion will be outlined at the beginning of each section. Then examples will show how to use the motion correctly.

To Take from the Table

♦ **Purpose:** To take a motion from the table.

♦ Needs a second.

♦ Not debatable.

♦ Needs a majority to adopt.

♦ Cannot be reconsidered.

♦ **Result:** Takes a motion from the table, and it now becomes the immediate pending business.

When a motion is **laid on the table** (set aside temporarily), it must be **taken from the table** by the end of the next meeting, or it dies. This motion must be made when no other business is pending. Anyone can make this motion. It needs a second and is not debatable. The vote is taken immediately, and a majority vote is needed to adopt. If adopted, the motion that was tabled is now before the assembly, as when it was laid on the table. For example, if several motions were pending when it was laid on the table—a main motion, an amendment, and refer to a committee—the chair begins discussion with the last motion made, which was refer to a committee. To make the motion, a member says:

Member: I move to take from the table the motion relating to the computer.

Member: Second.

President: It is moved and seconded to take from the table the motion relating to the computer. All those in favor say "Aye." Those opposed say "No." The ayes have it, and the motion to buy a computer and a laser printer is taken from the table. The last pending motion was refer to a committee. Is there any further discussion on referring to a committee?

Renewal of Main Motions

If a main motion is defeated, it can't be brought before the assembly again at the same meeting unless it is a substantially new question, by a change in wording, or a difference in time or conditions, or through special procedures of **reconsider the vote**. It can be brought up again at another meeting as if it were a new motion.

Reconsider

- ◆ **Purpose:** To reconsider the vote on a motion.
- ◆ Only a member who voted on the prevailing side can make the motion.
- ◆ Needs a second.
- ◆ Debatable if the motion it reconsiders is debatable.
- ◆ Majority vote to adopt.

- Cannot be reconsidered.
- Can be made but not considered when other business is pending.
- **Result:** If adopted, the motion is again before the assembly as if it had not been voted on.

Reconsider allows the assembly to change its mind about how the membership voted on a motion. In a group whose meetings last one day, this motion must be made at the same meeting in which the vote was taken. In conventions or sessions of more than one day, a motion voted on at one meeting can be reconsidered the next day. If the time has run out on the motion to reconsider, the members can offer the motion to **rescind** the action or **amend something previously adopted**. If the action was defeated at the previous meeting, a member can re-introduce it as new business. This is called **renewing the motion**.

Reconsider is also an unusual motion because by making the motion to reconsider, it suspends all action until the motion to reconsider is taken up or terminates. Therefore, to prevent its dilatory use by the losing side, only a member that voted on the prevailing side can make the motion, although anyone can second it. It is debatable if the motion to be reconsidered is debatable, and debate can go to the merits of the main motion. It is not amendable and requires a majority vote to be adopted.

A member who makes this motion should state that he or she voted on the prevailing side. If the member doesn't state this, it is the chair's duty to ask the member whether he or she voted on the prevailing side. If there is no business pending, the motion is taken up immediately. If business is pending, the chair tells the secretary to make a note that the motion to reconsider has been made, and it isn't taken up until a member calls up the motion to **reconsider the vote** when no other business is pending, which could be at another meeting.

If the motion to **reconsider the vote** is carried, the motion being reconsidered is before the assembly as if it had never been voted on. And if a member has exhausted his or her right to debate the motion, the member can't debate it again unless it is taken up at another meeting.

A motion cannot be reconsidered in these cases: when the provisions of the motion have been partially carried out; when a vote has caused something to be done that can't be undone; when a contract has been made and the other party has been notified of the vote; or when the same result can be obtained by some other parliamentary motion.

To make the motion, a member states:

Member: I move to reconsider the vote on the motion to buy a computer and a laser printer. I voted on the prevailing side.

Member: Second.

President: It is moved and seconded to reconsider the vote on the motion to buy a computer and a laser printer. Is there any discussion on reconsidering the vote?

Members can discuss the merits of the main motion. The members must remember that this is a two-step process. They first vote on *whether to reconsider the vote*. If this motion is adopted, then the motion that was reconsidered is again under discussion and they take another vote on it.

Because the motion to reconsider suspends action until it is taken up, it has been assigned a time requirement. If the assembly's next meeting is within a quarterly time interval, it must be taken up before the end of the next meeting. If it isn't taken up, then the members can proceed with the action. If the next meeting is more than a quarterly time interval, then the motion to reconsider must be taken up at the current meeting. If it isn't taken up, then the members proceed with the action.

To Call Up the Motion to Reconsider

If business is pending when the motion to reconsider is made, then it must be "called up" when no business is pending. To call up the motion to reconsider, a member rises, addresses the chair, and states:

Member: I call up the motion to reconsider.

Since it was seconded when it was originally proposed, the chair immediately states it this way:

Chair: It is moved and seconded to reconsider the vote on the motion to buy a computer and a laser printer. Is there any discussion on the motion to reconsider the vote?

Rescind and Amend Something Previously Adopted

♦ **Purpose:** To change something previously adopted either by striking out the entire action or by changing part of it.

♦ Needs a second.

♦ Is debatable.

♦ Majority vote with previous notice.

♦ Negative vote only can be reconsidered.

♦ Two-thirds vote or majority vote of the entire membership without previous notice. The reason for such a high vote is to protect the rights of the absent members.

♦ **Result:** If this motion is adopted, the previously adopted motion is reversed or changed.

The rules concerning the two motions to **rescind** and to **amend something previously adopted** are very similar. The purpose is to reverse or to change something previously adopted by the assembly. These are considered incidental main motions. They need a second and are debatable. They are not in order if the action has already been carried out and is impossible to undo. Debate can go to the merits of the original motion.

A motion can't be rescinded or amended :

1. If someone has made the motion to reconsider the vote and it can be called up.

2. If something has been done, and it is impossible to undo.

3. If the members have voted to enter into a contract and the other party has been notified.

4. When a resignation has been acted upon and the person notified. When a person has been elected to membership or expelled from membership and notified. (If expelled from membership, then this person would have to reapply according to the bylaws.) When an officer has been elected to or removed from office and notified. (If a person has been elected to office and the members want to "rescind" the action, they can do so if the bylaws permit this.)

The vote requirement:

1. With previous notice, it takes a majority vote.

2. Without previous notice, it takes a two-thirds vote or a majority vote of the entire membership.

To give previous notice, a member can request that the notice be included in the letter sent to the membership notifying them of the meeting; or it can be given orally at the previous meeting.

To give previous notice at a meeting, a member states:

Member: Mr. President, I rise to give previous notice that at the next meeting I will make a motion to rescind the action we give a donation to the Fourth Annual President's Night banquet.

Previous notice is *never* seconded. When the member makes the motion at the next meeting, then it will need a second. The secretary records the previous notice in the minutes.

At the next meeting the member rises and states the motion.

Member: I move to rescind the action that we give a donation to the Fourth Annual President's Night banquet.

Member: Second.

President: It is moved and seconded to rescind the action that we give a donation to the Fourth Annual President's Night banquet. Since previous notice has been given, it will take a majority to adopt. Is there any discussion?

If the member did not give previous notice, the chair states:

> Since no previous notice has been given, it will take a two-thirds vote to adopt (or a majority of the entire membership, whichever is the easiest to obtain).

To phrase a motion to amend something previously adopted, a member says:

Member: I move to amend the motion that was adopted to give $100 to Habitat for Humanity, by striking out $100 and inserting $200.

Member: Second.

President: It is moved and seconded to amend the motion that was adopted to give $100 to Habitat for Humanity, by striking out $100 and inserting $200. If adopted, we will give $200 to Habitat for Humanity. Is there any discussion on the proposed amendment?

Discharge a Committee

- ♦ **Purpose:** To take a matter out of the hands of the committee before its report is given so that the assembly can decide.
- ♦ Needs a second.
- ♦ Is amendable.
- ♦ Is debatable. Debate can go to the merits of the question in the committee.

◆ Vote required: If no previous notice has been given, either a two-thirds vote or a majority of the entire membership is needed, whichever is more practical to obtain. If previous notice has been given, a majority vote is needed.

◆ **Result:** If adopted and if a motion was referred to the committee by a subsidiary motion, then the motion is immediately before the assembly for discussion.

Note: If the committee fails to report at the time specified, then it takes only a majority vote. Or, if the committee is giving a partial report, the members can discharge the committee by a majority vote.

The motion to **discharge a committee** is an incidental main motion and can be made only when no other business is pending. This motion should be used only when a committee has failed to report at the specified time or when something urgent has come up and the assembly needs to decide now. This is a useful motion to prevent something from dying in committee.

RESOLUTIONS

A resolution is a formal way of presenting a motion. It is a main motion, needs a second, and is handled like any other main motion except that it is always presented in writing. The name of the organization is mentioned in the resolution, and the word "resolved" is always in italics. A resolution can be as simple as:

> *Resolved,* That the Glee Club sponsor
> a "Day of Singing" on April 25 to honor
> Glee Clubs in our state.

If a resolution is proposed at a mass meeting, it can be worded in the following way:

> *Resolved,* That in the sense of this meeting,
> we form a Neighborhood Watch program and
> send letters to all the homes between Martin
> and Smith streets inviting homeowners to
> participate.

Sometimes a resolution will include a preamble. This enables members to give background information and to state the reasons why the motion should be adopted. However, a preamble to a resolution is usually not necessary. In fact, a preamble should be used only when the maker of the resolution wants to give little-known information or wants to present important points regarding the adoption of the motion if there's some doubt about whether or not it will pass. A preamble contains "whereas" clauses that communicate the important background information to the assembly; the actual resolution then follows. A resolution with a preamble should contain only as many "whereas" clauses as necessary. For example,

> *Whereas,* A study done by the city com-
> mission reveals that there are 100 stray dogs
> and 250 stray cats in Center City;

> *Resolved,* That the Morningside City
> Improvement Corporation form a committee
> of five to be appointed by the board to
> investigate the cost of establishing a feeding
> program, as well as establishing a shelter for

these animals, and report its findings at the next meeting.

If the resolution has more than one "whereas" clause, it is written this way:

> *Whereas,* A study done by the city commission reveals that there are 100 stray dogs and 250 stray cats in Center City;
>
> *Whereas,* These hungry animals are wreaking havoc with garbage; *and*
>
> *Whereas,* They are having kittens and puppies every two to three months; *now, therefore, be it*
>
> *Resolved,* That the Morningside City Improvement Corporation form a committee of five to be appointed by the board to investigate the cost of establishing a feeding program, as well as establishing a shelter for these animals and report its findings at the next meeting.

PART III

MEMBERSHIP

7

Officers

The bylaws of every organization should include a provision for officers. Each organization has the right to determine the number of officers, their duties, how they are elected, the term of office, and whether they can be removed from office, along with the reason and the stated procedure for removal.

This chapter looks in detail at the two offices that are essential to an efficient organization: those of the president and the secretary. It examines their duties, responsibilities, and limitations. Other topics in this chapter include the purpose and content of the minutes, the roles of the treasurer and the board, and steps to ensure the vitality and long-life of the organization.

AN OVERVIEW

Officers are usually selected from the membership. However, in some legislative bodies, the United States Senate for example, the president comes from outside the membership. In certain circumstances where a controversial issue is being discussed, members may want to have the ability to hire the services of a nonmember—a professional presiding officer—to conduct the meeting.

When members become officers, they still retain all the rights that they had as regular members: the right to make motions, to debate, and to vote. However, those serving as president must remain impartial. For this reason, there are rules governing when the president can make a motion, participate in the debate, and vote.

Those who are elected to office or appointed to a committee chairmanship are responsible for keeping records of their assignments and then giving those records to their successors. If an organization has a permanent facility, the permanent records of the society, the minutes, the treasurer's books, checkbooks, and records of any investments should be kept at the facility and should not be taken home with the officers. The secretary and the treasurer should be provided with a place at the facility to do their work. In a small organization, where the officers frequently keep the records of the society in their homes, provision should be made to have these records returned to someone in the organization if that member is not re-elected to his or her office or if the member resigns membership or should die. A common problem in small organizations is getting the checkbook back from the treasurer, or the minutes book back from the secretary if he or she is not re-elected to office or stops attending meetings.

When electing officers, the membership needs to take into consideration the reliability of the people being considered for office. Those who are elected to office need to seriously consider the obligations and duties of that office before accepting the responsibilities of the office. If, during a term, an officer realizes that he or she cannot keep up with the demands of the office, the officer should either arrange for help with his or her duties or resign. If the officer resigns, all the documents entrusted to him or her should be returned at the same time as the officer's resignation letter. Should the officer be unable to return the documents in person, they should be mailed to the secretary, by certified mail with a "return receipt." This will ensure that the records of the organization arrive safely.

Organizations need a minimum of two officers: a president and a secretary. The president presides at the meeting, and the secretary records the transactions of the meeting in the minutes.

THE PRESIDENT

The office of president and its duties will vary according to how the organization is structured in the bylaws. In some social or professional organizations, the president is the most important officer for determining the focus and action of the organization. Those running for the office of president may actually run on "platforms," with members voting for the candidate based on the philosophy, goals, or plans for the organization presented in the platform. In other organizations, the primary responsibility of the president is presiding at meetings, with much of the administrative duties invested in committees and the legislative power vested in an executive board.

Whatever the structure of the organization, the president has authority to do only the things that are assigned to that office by the bylaws. Often, those elected to the office of president misunderstand their role in the organization and believe that the members have given them free reign to run the organization anyway they please, thus setting up a dictatorship. Primarily the office of president includes fulfilling a leadership role by setting goals or a specific tone for the organization during the term of office, presiding at the meetings, and performing administrative duties as assigned by the bylaws.

Administrative Duties of the President

The chief administrative duty of the president is to represent the organization. The president signs all legal documents; supervises the employees and the activities of the organization; represents, or speaks for, the organization; and presides at meetings. These duties will vary with organizations and should be stated in the bylaws.

The following discussion focuses on the president's responsibilities as a presiding officer and the rules the president must follow when presiding at meetings.

Presiding Duties of the President

The key duties of the presiding officer are to:

1. Keep order.

2. Be fair and impartial.

3. Protect the rights of all the members.

It is the presiding officer's responsibility to uphold and enforce these principles. Let's look at each of them individually.

Keeping Order

To keep order in a meeting, the president should be thoroughly familiar with the bylaws, other rules of the organization, parliamentary procedure in general, and the organization's selected parliamentary authority in particular.

1. The president should be familiar with the the basic rules of calling a meeting to order; establishing and following an agenda or order of business; the proper steps in making, debating, and voting on motions; and the different classes or types of motions and how

they are ranked. (These basics are covered in Part II, "Motions Simplified," of this book.)

2. The president and the secretary should prepare the agenda together. The president should be familiar with any unfinished business and any new business that will be appearing on the agenda. If the proposed business is controversial, the president can plan ahead for problems that may arise during the meeting and consult with a parliamentarian beforehand to learn how to handle the situation.

3. If standing committees are to give reports, the president should call these committee members prior to the meeting to see if they have a report to give. The president should call on only those people at the meeting who have indicated in advance that they have reports.

4. The president should come to the meeting with paper and pencil to write down the motions as the members make them. At the meeting, the president or the secretary should have a copy of the organization's bylaws, standing rules, rules of order, and the parliamentary authority. The president should have a thorough working knowledge of these governing documents.

5. The president should call the meeting to order on time and determine that a quorum is present before proceeding with the meeting. The president does not have to announce that a quorum is present.

6. The president should announce all business in the proper sequence and entertain every motion that is in order. If in doubt why a member is rising, the president can ask:

For what purpose does the member rise?

If the member is rising to do something that is not in order at that time, this question allows the president to stop the incorrect procedure immediately without wasting the assembly's time. If it is in order, then the president allows the member to proceed. This phrase keeps business going in the right direction.

7. The president must state each legitimate motion for the purpose of discussion and for taking a vote. The president ensures the rights of the members to debate the motion by allowing each side fair representation during controversial issues, and by keeping debate to its time limits. The president takes the vote on motions and knows the proper type of vote required for the different classes of motions. He or she announces the result of the vote so that all members know what action is taken and, if adopted, who will be responsible for carrying out the action.

8. The president should rule on any procedure that does not follow correct procedures; for example, motions that are not in order at a certain time, debate that gets off the subject, and any effort by members to deprive others of their rights to debate and make motions. The president must entertain all appeals to his or her rulings, and let the members vote on the appeal. The president has an obligation to answer any member's questions about the business being discussed or any parliamentary inquiries about procedure.

9. The president declares the meeting adjourned by vote of the assembly at the end of the program, or in cases where an uncontrollable situation such as a riot is taking place or when the health or safety of the members is in danger.

Ensuring Fairness and Impartiality

The most important principle that all presiding officers must remember is that the presiding officer represents all the members, not just a select few and not just those with whom he or she agrees. The duty of the presiding officer is to keep control of the meeting, but more than that it is to see that during debate all the facts—pros and cons—come out in the discussion so that the assembly can make an informed decision. No member should feel that the presiding officer is taking sides, but rather that the officer is allowing the assembly through the democratic process to arrive at the will of the majority.

1. In a business meeting, the president cannot make motions or enter into debate.

    The president can enter into debate only if he or she leaves the chair; that is, if the officer gives up his or her function of presiding over the meeting. If the presiding officer steps down and enters debate, he or she must stay out of the chair, (not return to presiding) until the motion has been disposed of either temporarily or finally.

    The president also steps down from the chair and lets the vice president or another officer preside when a motion has direct personal or monetary interest, or when he or she is being censured. (However, the presiding officer can stay in the chair during nominations and elections when he or she is a candidate for office or is being considered in a motion with others.)

2. The president does not vote unless it is to break a tie vote or create a tie vote. However, the president can vote with other members when the vote is by ballot. (See Chapter 5, "Voting.")

3. The president can give information, correct misinformation, and help members with parliamentary procedures. The president is obligated to help the

members phrase motions, even when he is opposed to the motion.

4. The president must remember to sit down when a member has been assigned the floor. If there is no place to sit, or if the president cannot be seen by the members when he or she is seated, the president should stand back from the lectern.

5. The president is responsible for enforcing the rules and decorum of debate, and alternates between the pros and cons in a controversial situation. (See Chapter 4, "Debating the Motion.")

6. The presiding officer always refers to himself as the "chair" when talking to the members. For example, the presiding officer might say,

> The chair rules the discussion is out of order at this time.

Protecting the Rights of the Members

A truly effective president protects the rights of the members by following the laws himself. The president upholds the bylaws and other rules of the organization, and enforces them by informing the members when bylaws are being ignored or disobeyed. The president rules out of order all motions that conflict with the bylaws and other governing documents of the organization, and any motions that violate local, state, or national government. If members propose a motion that conflicts with the bylaws, the president should rule the motion out of order and explain the procedure for amending the bylaws, if that is possible. If members propose a motion that violates parliamentary rules, the president should rule it out of order and then explain the proper procedure that helps the members accomplish their goals.

1. It is the president's duty to protect the assembly from frivolous or dilatory motions (undemocratic ways of delaying business) and from any attempt by a few members to push an action through without following the democratic process. (See "Important Points to Remember Before Making a Motion," in Chapter 3.)

2. Dilatory practices that a president should look for are:

   - Calling for a division when it is very clear which side has won, or calling for a division after every vote that is taken.

   - Continually making the motion to adjourn for the purpose of obstructing business.

   - Making absurd motions or amendments.

   - Several members raising "points of order" for no reason.

3. If members are using dilatory practices to obstruct the meeting, the chair needs to remain calm and courteous, but firm. The chair can do one of two things: not recognize the members or rule the motions out of order. However, the chair must not do either of these two things to speed up a meeting. These are strictly measures to be taken if a member is clearly being dilatory. The president is there to serve the wishes of the entire assembly and should not allow any personal feelings to affect his or her judgment.

4. The chair should know the procedures for calling to order a member who has become unruly and disruptive. To call a member to order, the chair can say:

> The member is out of order and will be
> seated.

Should the member continue to misbehave, the president can ask the secretary to record in the minutes the
objectional behavior or language. If the member does
not quiet down or apologize for his or her behavior,
the next step is to "name the offender," which is
preferring charges. This should be done only as a last
resort. If the president prefers charges, the president
should state what the member has done. It is then up
to the assembly as to what action should be taken.
If the members are not readily coming forth with a
motion that sets a penalty, the president can ask:

> What penalty shall be imposed on the
> member?

It is now up to the membership to propose a penalty. The motion is debatable, and the member has a
right to speak to the motion. This motion takes a
majority vote unless the motion would take away
rights of membership, in which case a two-thirds vote
is needed.

The members should resolve such issues without resorting to this procedure. If the conduct of a
member gets out of hand, the president can always
declare a recess and talk with the member during
the recess to try to resolve the problem.

Necessary Qualities of an Effective Presiding Officer

The discussion so far has concerned the responsibilities
of a president when presiding. However, there are times
when others may have to conduct the meeting, for

example, when the president is absent or when a committee meeting or board meeting needs a member to preside. It is useful for every member of an organization to cultivate the following qualities.

- Good judgment—knowing when to strictly enforce the rules and when strict enforcement would impede the flow of business.

- Teachablility—the willingness to learn the correct procedures and to use them fairly and judiciously.

- Good listening skills—what are the members saying and what signals are they giving to the presiding officer to help the officer expedite business?

- Calmness—the ability to keep peace if the meeting becomes turbulent.

- Humility—not taking offense if the members correct what the presiding officer is doing or if they appeal from the decision of the chair.

- Firmness—staying the course and following proper procedures when necessary and not allowing members to take shortcuts when it impedes the rights of a member of the assembly.

Legal and Ethical Considerations

Although the president has been given the power to sign legal documents and represent the society, he or she should never bind the society to contracts that the members have not agreed to by a vote; nor should the president speak to an issue in public without the permission of the society. By taking such actions without the society's permission, the president is inviting the members to begin proceedings for removal from office.

THE VICE PRESIDENT

The office of vice president might be called "president in training." The specific parliamentary duties of the vice president are to preside when the president is unable to be at the meeting or when the president has to step down from the chair because he or she wishes to debate an issue. Other situations calling for the vice president to preside would be if the president were being censured or when a motion was being made that concerned only the president.

Normally, the vice president takes over if the office of president is vacated for any reason. If there is more than one vice president, the offices should be numbered in the bylaws. The bylaws should also state the order of succession if the office of president is declared vacant.

When the vice president is presiding, he or she is addressed by the members as "Mr. President" or "Madam President." When the vice president and the president are both on the platform, the vice president is addressed as "Mr. Vice President" or "Madam Vice President." If in doubt, "Mr." or "Madam Chairman" is also correct.

If the bylaws specifically say that the president is to appoint all committees, and the vice president is presiding when a member makes a motion to form a special committee, the vice president cannot appoint the committee members, unless the bylaws provide for this particular rule's suspension. (Note that no other presiding member can make the appointments either.)

THE SECRETARY

At the beginning of this chapter, the overview stated that organizations need a minimum of two officers to conduct a meeting and to keep the organization together:

the president and the secretary. Many people think that the president is the most important member of the organization. Others argue that the secretary is, since this officer is responsible for keeping all the records of the organization, preparing the agenda, handling correspondence, sending notices of meetings to members, taking and recording the minutes, and performing other administrative duties that may be assigned by the organization.

In general, the secretary is responsible for:

1. Keeping all the records of the organization, including committee reports, on file and keeping an up-to-date list of all the members.

2. Notifying members of their election to office, appointment to committees, and furnishing them with the proper documents.

3. Notifying members of election or of appointment as a delegate at a convention, and furnishing them with credentials.

4. Signing all the minutes and other certified acts of the organization, unless the bylaws specify differently.

5. Maintaining the official documents of the organization, including the bylaws, rules of order, standing rules, correspondence, and minutes. Keeping the bylaws and other governing documents up-to-date with any changes made through the amendment process, and bringing these documents to the meeting.

6. Mailing to members a notice for each forthcoming meeting.

7. Taking minutes at all business and board meetings, handling the correspondence, and preparing the agenda for the meetings unless the president prefers to do this. (See the next section, "Minutes.")

The secretary must know how to call a meeting to order if the president and vice president are absent and know how to preside until a temporary chairman is elected by the assembly.

8. Bringing to each meeting: the minutes book, bylaws, rules, the membership list, a list of committees and their membership, the agenda, records, ballots, and any supplies that may be needed.

If the secretary or any of the officers have duties other than those listed in the adopted parliamentary authority, the additional duties should be written in the bylaws or standing rules.

Minutes

The most frequently asked question by those who have just been elected or appointed to the office of secretary is, "What do I put in the minutes?" If a person asks enough parliamentarians, reads enough books on the subject, and consults various parliamentary authorities, he or she will find many viewpoints on this subject. The answer is to follow the recommendations of the organization's parliamentary authority and the wishes of the organization itself regarding the contents of the minutes. If the secretary is recording minutes for a legislative body, for example a city government, there may be state codes governing the content of those minutes.

The minutes should contain a record of what is done, not what is said. Minutes do not contain interjected personal comments or someone's opinion about what has happened. It is the assembly's responsibility to approve and correct the minutes. What the assembly approves is considered the final wording of the minutes. If a mistake is found in the minutes at any later time, it can be corrected by bringing it to the attention of the assembly. This is done by making the motion to amend something previously adopted, or the mistake can be fixed by general or unanimous consent. Many times, the presiding officer, together with the secretary, will review the minutes for accuracy and wording before the secretary puts them into final form. However, the president should not insist on a particular wording merely to make himself or herself look good or to change the outcome of decisions made.

If the minutes are to be published (for example, when minutes of public meetings are sent to all the members), the minutes should contain in addition to the standard information a list of speakers on each side of the question, with an abstract text of each address. Also, committee reports and the action taken on them are printed in full. At such a meeting, it would be wise to record the meeting.

When writing the minutes, a good technique is to write so that anyone else reading the minutes would be able to visualize what was done at the meeting. Write the minutes as soon as possible after the meeting while it is fresh in your mind!

Taking the Minutes

The secretary may ask, Why do I need a thorough knowledge of parliamentary procedure simply to take the minutes? If the secretary does not understand, for example, the ranking of motions or other key procedures, the minutes will not be accurate. For example, all secondary motions (subsidiary, privileged, and incidental) that are adopted must be recorded in the minutes. (See Appendix D, "Sample Minutes.") The secretary who has a thorough knowledge of parliamentary procedure can also be of great help to the presiding officer when there is no parliamentarian present. The following sections explain the contents of each part of the minutes, including how to correct mistakes, how to organize and group material, and the form for signing the minutes.

The Opening Paragraph

The opening paragraph includes the following items:

Call to Order

- The name of the organization, the date and time, the place of meeting if different from the usual, and the kind of meeting—regular, special, or adjourned.

- The fact that the regular presiding officer and the secretary were present—or the names of their substitutes.

- The roll call (if required by the rules of order): those who are present and those absent, and whether any member comes late or leaves early. In board minutes, it is a good idea to name those present and those absent.

Approval of the Minutes of Previous Meeting(s)

- What action was taken on the minutes of the previous meeting ("approved as read" or "corrected"). Corrections should be recorded in the minutes of both meetings; that is, in the minutes where the mistake was found, and in the minutes of the meeting where it was read.

For example, the minutes for the meeting on August 3 would read:

> The minutes of the meeting on July 3 were corrected to read "the balance in the treasury is $500."
>
> The minutes were approved as corrected.

The secretary then corrects the minutes for July 3 by drawing a line through the mistake, writing above the mistake "$500," and initialing it.

The Body of the Minutes

The following items are included in the body of the minutes, with or without headings:

Reports of Officers and Committees

- The fact that the reports of officers, boards, and standing and special committees were given, and what action was taken, if any. Some minutes include a brief summary of committee reports. Some minutes give the entire treasurer's report, and some just give beginning and ending balances. The members should decide how much of the treasurer's report they want in the minutes. If the members receive a copy of the treasurer's report, then perhaps only the beginning balance, total income, total expenditures, and the ending balance need to go into the minutes.

Special Orders—Election of Officers

- When nominations and elections are being recorded, the names presented by the nominating committee are recorded first, then the names of those nominated from the floor. In reporting the vote, the secretary includes the tellers' committee report, which is a record of all the candidates and how many votes each received. Then the chair's declaration of each member elected is recorded. (For an example of a teller's report and how the president handles it, see Chapter 8, "Election by Ballot Vote", and "Teller's Sheet and Report.") The number of votes each nominee received is also recorded in the minutes, as well as a statement of the term of office.

Here's an example of problems that arise when details are left out of the minutes. An organization elected board members for a three-year term. It elected two board members in odd years, and three members in even years. The organization went through a period of people moving away, which left vacancies that had to be filled. Because the organization hadn't recorded in the minutes which members were elected at which time, the members didn't know if they were electing members to fill a full three-year term or a shorter remaining term. The lesson here is obviously to be specific in recording elections in the minutes.

Unfinished Business

- The minutes should include unfinished business only if there was unfinished business on the agenda. The minutes should state what action was taken on business that carried over from the previous meeting.

New Business

- The name of the maker of a motion but not the person who seconds it—unless it is customary or the group desires it.

- The final wording of all main motions* (with amendments incorporated) and all motions that bring a question back before the assembly. Also, what happened to each motion—whether it was adopted, lost, or temporarily disposed of. However, if the motion was withdrawn,** it is not recorded. If a motion was laid on the table and not taken from the table at the same meeting, this fact should be recorded in the minutes. Also, the motions to postpone and to refer to a committee should be included in the minutes, if they were adopted.

- Secondary motions that are adopted. If the motion to recess is adopted, the minutes should state what time the members recessed and what time the meeting was called back to order.

*Special Note: When an assembly adopts a motion that is of a continuing nature (for example, time of the meeting, buying plaques for outgoing officers, giving money to an organization on a yearly basis, having a yearly dance, or a set function at a certain time), such motions should also be recorded in a notebook called standing rules. Since these motions are ongoing and can be rescinded or amended only by previous notice and a majority vote, or by a two-thirds vote without notice, they are easier to find if kept in a separate document because the secretary does not have to go through all the minutes to find the original motion. These motions are numbered when put in the standing rules.

**Special Note: If a motion has been postponed to another meeting and then withdrawn, this fact should be noted in the minutes so that there is some record of the disposition of the motion.

Program and Announcements

The following items are grouped together in separate paragraphs and come at the end of the minutes:

Speaker

- The name of the guest speaker and the program, if there is one. No effort should be made to summarize points given by the speaker.

Previous notice

- All previous notice of motions and their content. For example, if someone gives "previous notice" to rescind or amend a previous action, the minutes should record that "Member X gave previous notice that, at the next meeting, she will rescind . . . (include here the approximate wording of what the member proposes to rescind)." (See "Rescind and Amend Something Previously Adopted" in Chapter 6.)

Announcements

- Any important announcements. For example, if the meeting place and the time are different for each meeting, the chair's announcement of the time and the location is recorded in the minutes.

Other Important Items to Be Included

These items are included in the minutes as they occur:

- The results of a counted or a balloted vote. If a counted vote is ordered or if a ballot vote is taken during the meeting, the votes on each side should be recorded in the minutes. However, the votes are not recorded if the organization has a rule or tradition that they are not. If a roll call vote is taken, the names of those voting on each side and those answering "present" should be recorded.

- The fact that the assembly has gone into a committee of the whole or quasi committee of the whole, and its report. (For further information, see "Committee of the Whole" and "Quasi Committee of the Whole" in Chapter 11.)

- All points of order and the chair's ruling. Also recorded are all appeals and whether they were sustained or lost.

Adjournment and Signature of the Secretary

- The last paragraph contains the hour of adjournment.

- The signature and title of the person who took the minutes. The president signs if customary or desired by the assembly. (Omit the traditional phrase, "respectfully submitted," however.)

Approval and Corrections of the Minutes

- The minutes are read immediately after the call to order and the opening ceremonies. They are approved as read or as corrected. They are usually approved by general consent.

  If an assembly meets quarterly, the minutes of an annual meeting are approved at the next regular meeting or by a committee appointed to approve the minutes.

- Minutes may be corrected whenever an error is found, regardless of the time that has elapsed. To correct the minutes after they have been approved requires a two-thirds vote, unless previous notice has been given.

- Nothing is ever erased from the minutes. Corrections are made in the margin. (If the minutes are double-spaced, the correction can be written above what is corrected.) When material is expunged, a line is drawn through the words that are to be expunged. Crossed out material should still be readable.

- When minutes are approved, the word "approved" and the secretary's initials and date of the approval are written next to the signature of the secretary. Alternatively, a line can be provided at the bottom of the page that says "approval date."

(For an example of minutes in finished form, see Appendix D, "Sample Minutes.")

Form of the Minutes

With today's computer technology, very few secretaries are writing the minutes by hand in a bound ledger book with numbered pages. If the pen has given way to the computer, then the organization needs to find a way to keep its minutes on consecutively numbered pages, and have them bound yearly.

When writing the minutes, each subject is a separate paragraph. Some parliamentarians recommend putting headings at the top of each new paragraph. Examples would be "Reports of Officers and Committees," "Reports," "Unfinished Business," "New Business," etc. Some secretaries leave a wide margin and then put a short summary of the paragraph in the margin. This enables those looking at the minutes months or years later to easily find the item they are searching for. Whichever way you choose, be consistent.

It is a good idea to have the minutes carefully reviewed for accuracy, spelling, and grammar before putting them in their final form—either handwritten into a bound, page-numbered book, or printed by computer and compiled into a notebook.

THE TREASURER

The treasurer is responsible for receiving and disbursing the money of the organization. The treasurer's general duties and responsibilities should be stated in the bylaws; administrative duties should be stated in the standing rules.

Depending on the complexity of the organization, the treasurer's duties will vary.

The Treasurer's Duty in Small Clubs

In small clubs where the dues are the source of income and where there are not many expenditures, the treasurer's job is relatively simple. These duties may include:

1. Receiving and depositing dues in the club's bank account. (A treasurer should never keep club monies in his or her personal account!)

2. Giving members receipts for their dues.

3. Paying the bills that the club has voted to pay (for example, writing a check), or if the organization has set up another way to pay bills, following that process.

4. Giving a report at the meetings.

5. Recording which members have paid their dues, when bills are paid and the check number, and other items that will be necessary in order for a committee to audit the books at the end of the fiscal year.

6. Balancing and reconciling the checking account.

The Treasurer's Report in Small Clubs

In a small club the treasurer's report is usually given orally and can be very simple. Here are examples of two ways the treasurer's report could be written; the second itemizes all expenditures:

TREASURER'S REPORT

Balance on hand April 1, 1998	$350.00.
Total receipts (income)	$15.00
Total disbursements	$5.00
Balance on hand April 31, 1998	$360.00.

Or the treasurer could itemize the disbursements (expenditures).

TREASURER'S REPORT

Balance on hand April 1, 1998	450.00
Income/Receipts	165.00
Dues	15.00
Fundraising	150.00
Disbursements/Expenditures	30.00
Postage	15.00
Printing	12.00
Telephone	3.00
Balance on hand April 30, 1998	585.00

(Signed)_____

Treasurer

The Treasurer's report is not approved by the assembly but is filed for audit. The auditor's report is then approved.

(See Chapter 2, "Calling the Meeting to Order," "Reports of Officers.")

The Treasurer's Duty in Larger Organizations

In larger organizations with employees, the treasurer will be responsible for payroll, including deducting social security and income taxes. If the organization is incorporated and owns property, the treasurer will be required to file applicable local, state, and federal taxes.

In this case the treasurer should be versed in bookkeeping and/or accounting practices. The treasurer's reports will probably be more detailed than those in a small organization.

Duties may also include preparing and submitting a budget for approval. If the treasurer is to handle large sums of money, he or she should be bonded to protect the organization from loss.

The Budget

Many organizations work from a yearly budget. Usually the treasurer prepares the budget with the help of the financial committee, the committee chairmen, and perhaps the executive board. The budget is then submitted to the governing body for approval. A budget is a guide for spending; it is not set in stone. When it is presented to the membership, it can be amended by the members anytime, even after it is adopted.

When a bill is received that is within the budget, the person responsible for that budget item, such as a committee chairman, signs the bill as approved and gives it to the treasurer for payment. For example: The Buildings and Grounds Committee has a budget of

$2,000 for painting. When bids were taken for painting, the lowest bid was $1,950. A contract was signed and when the job was completed, a bill was received for $1,950. The chairman of the Building and Grounds Committee approves the bill, by signing his name and writing the words "approved for payment," and sends it to the treasurer who then pays the bill. However, some organizations may still require membership approval for the expenditure to be paid even though it is within a budgeted amount.

If the budget has not allotted enough for painting, and the lowest bid is for $2,050, then the chairman of the Building and Grounds Committee must get membership approval for the additional expense before contracting for the printing.

If an organization does not work from a budget, then each expenditure must have prior approval by the membership unless they have a rule stating differently. In this situation, the Builing and Grounds committee, gets estimates on painting and submits them to the membership for a vote. After the membership has decided on which bid to accept, then the Building and Grounds Committee chairman can enter into a contract with the company, and the work can be done. When the bill is received, and the committee is satisfied with the work done, the treasurer pays the bill.

The Audit

An audit of the treasurer's books is important to ensure the accuracy of the treasurer's reports. An audit protects both the treasurer and the organization. The auditor may uncover sloppy bookkeeping practices or even recommend a better way of doing things.

The auditor's report is an endorsement of the financial report, and it relieves the treasurer of any responsibility for the period covered by the report, except for fraud. Treasurers should insist that the books be audited once a year, and anyone newly elected to the office should not accept unaudited books. In small organizations, an audit committee should be appointed. In larger organizations, the audit should be done by independent accountants.

BOARDS

Boards are considered deliberative assemblies. This means they have the authority to meet to determine courses of action to be taken in the name of the organization.

Robert's Rules Of Order, Newly Revised, defines them as

> An administrative, managerial, or quasi-judical body of elected or appointed persons which has the character of a deliberative assembly with the following variations:
> (a) boards have no minimun size and are frequently smaller than most other assemblies;
> (b) while a board may or may not function autonomously, its operation is determined by responsibilities and powers delegated to it or conferred on it by authority outside itself.

A board may come in any size. It may be a governmental body such as a village board that makes laws for the village, or it may be the governing body of a corporation. Within a club, it may be a body that has been given administrative powers for the organization.

All boards are set up by some enactment. In public bodies, they are brought into existence by state legislatures or by county and local governments. In incorporated organizations, they are usually brought into existence by the corporation charter. In small un-incorporated organizations, they are established in the bylaws.

A board may have various names: board of directors, board of trustees, executive board, or board of managers.

For an organization to have an executive board, there must be a provision in the bylaws. If it isn't in the bylaws, then no small group of members can act like an executive board.

Bylaws and Boards

Boards get their powers and duties from the bylaws and can only do what the bylaws allow them to do. Boards are primarily the administrative arm of an organization, and they transact the business of the organization between regular meetings.

Board membership is defined in the bylaws. The bylaws should state who comprises the executive board. It may be the officers and committee chairmen and a few elected directors. Or the board may be composed of members elected by the membership, who in turn elect their own officers from the members of the board. Usually the president and the secretary of an organization serve on the board in the same capacity as they do in the regular membership meetings.

Bylaws should set the quorum of the board, specify how vacancies are filled, define how vacancies are created, set the number of board members, explain their duties, and determine how often the board meets.

Boards cannot disobey the orders of the assembly or act outside of their prescribed duties. Any action of the board can be counteracted by the assembly, unless the bylaws specifically give a particular authority to the board.

Board Meetings

Board meetings are usually held in "executive session" (closed to the membership), unless the bylaws state that the meetings are open to the members. The minutes of the board meetings are not made public to the membership unless the board members vote to let the membership read the minutes or unless the membership votes by a two-thirds vote, or with previous notice a majority vote, to have the board minutes read.

This, however, does not mean that the board keeps its activities secret. It should give a periodic report of its activities to the members. When drafting bylaws, an organization should carefully consider how much power it assigns to the executive board.

For example, in homeowners' associations, the board members usually make all the decisions for the association. Often the only power the members of the association have is the ability to elect members to the board. This can lead to tyranny. Therefore, board members should be selected for their understanding of democratic principles, especially the concept of "consent of the governed."

Everything said at board meetings is confidential, and board members should respect this and not tell other members about what has transpired until the entire membership hears the report. *Individual board members cannot speak for the entire board.*

All board members are equal, but the chairman presides at the meetings. The chair does not have more power than any other board member unless it is given to him or her in the bylaws. (See "Board Meetings" in Chapter 11 for specific procedures.)

Those elected to the board, especially in governmental bodies such as school boards or village boards, should remember that compromise is a key element in serving on the board. Board members should work for the good of the entire organization, not for the agenda of one group or special interest. Too often people run on a platform, and when they have accomplished "their agenda," they lose interest in the rest of the board's proceedings.

Serving on a board is a privilege. Each board member should be thoroughly familiar with the governing documents of the organization, as well as parliamentary law and procedures.

Ex Officio Board Members

Many organizations have "ex officio" board members. Ex officio means "by virtue of office"; in other words, the member serves on the board because he or she holds a certain office either within the organization or in the community. For example, if the bylaws state that the president of the state organization shall be an ex officio board member, the president becomes a member of the board because he or she is the state president. When the member's term as state president ends, the term as ex officio board member also ends. The new state president becomes the ex officio member. Another way members become ex officio members is by virtue of some office they hold in the community. Sometimes a mayor is asked to serve as an ex officio member of a board even though he or she is not a member of the organization.

The most frequently asked question about ex officio members is, "Can ex officio members vote?" If an ex officio board member is a regular member of the organization, there is no distinction between the ex officio member and the other board members. The ex officio board member is counted in the quorum and has the right to make motions, debate motions, and vote on all questions.

If an ex officio member is not a member of the society, he or she is not counted in the quorum. However, the ex officio member still has the right to make motions, debate motions, and vote on all questions.

When the bylaws state that "the president is an ex officio member of all committees," the president is not counted in the quorum because it would be too difficult to attend all the committee meetings. But if the president attends the meeting, he or she has the right to make motions, discuss motions, and vote on all questions.

When a person is appointed an ex officio member by virtue of holding a public office (such as mayor), his or her membership on the board or committee ceases when the term in office expires.

PASSING THE TORCH

In each Olympics before the Olympic games begin, we have the dramatic lighting of the Olympic flame by a torch that was lit in Greece and that was carried by plane, boat, and on foot to the location of the present games.

At the beginning, the members of an organization may be fired up with this Olympic flame of enthusiasm, but as the torch passes from one administration to another this enthusiasm often wanes.

How can organizations keep their members and officers alight with enthusiasm? Here are some suggestions:

- Have officer training sessions for new officers.

- Listen to the members and meet their needs.

- Recognize and use the talents of all the members.

Training Sessions

Perhaps you are in an organization that elects officers and then says, "Here's last year's file, a list of your duties, and a copy of Robert's Rules. Good luck!" The newly elected officer or committee chairman scratches his or her head and says, "Now what do I do?"

How often have you met long-term members who expect everyone to know as much as they know and criticize the efforts of those who don't intuitively know what to do; yet these same long-term members don't offer any guidance or training to new officers or new members?

Successful organizations know that a productive, happy membership requires investments in the members. These organizations have training sessions for new officers, they appoint mentors to explain the ropes to new members, and they listen to the reasons why people have joined the organization and then try to meet those needs.

An officer training session might include the following:

- The outgoing officer meeting with the new officer, going over the files, explaining the duties, and sharing the things that worked or didn't work.

- A group training session in which the outgoing officers explain to all the new officers how the organization works. It might also include individual officer training.

- On-the-job training in conducting meetings, taking minutes, and writing and giving officer reports.

Each organization should come up with a plan for training new officers. Members are more likely to serve if they feel competent in performing the tasks at hand. By investing time and effort in training officers, the transition from one administration to the next will be less painful.

8

Nominations and Elections

In every organization, the process of nominating and electing officers and board members is very important, and the procedure should be clearly stated in the by-laws. This chapter explains the nominating and election process from start to finish. It discusses the various ways a candidate can be nominated and the ways a vote can be taken. The duties of the tellers' committee—those appointed to count the vote—are described, and the reader is taken step by step through the teller's sheet and report.

NOMINATIONS

Candidates can be nominated in several ways:

1. By a nominating committee
2. From the floor
3. By ballot
4. By mail
5. By petition

The most common nominating procedure is done by a nominating committee with the assembly given the opportunity to present nominations from the floor. The nominating process should not be confused with the election to office. *Robert's Rules of Order* states that a person does not have to be nominated to be elected to office. If the vote is taken by ballot, there is always the opportunity to write in a name. In this case, a person could win as a *write-in candidate* without ever being nominated.

Nominations by Committee

Many organizations have a nominating committee. The composition of this committee and how it is selected should be specified in the bylaws. This is the one committee a president should not be a member of or help to select. If at all possible, the nominating committee should be elected by either the board or the membership.

Duties of a Nominating Committee

The duty of a nominating committee is to find the best candidate for each office. The bylaws should not tie the hands of the committee to find more than one person to fill each slot. The committee should be instructed to find the best candidate for each office.

The committee should be given a copy of the membership list, the bylaws, a description of the duties of each office, and the eligibility requirements. They should meet and carefully review the membership list and select the people who they think will do the best job. Then a member of the committee should be designated to call each nominee to see if he or she would be willing to serve if elected. If not, then the committee needs to meet again and find another candidate.

If no candidate can be found, then the committee can leave that slot open for nominations from the floor. Or they can let it be known that they do not have a nominee for a certain office. This allows members to volunteer. No one should be nominated without his or her consent because, if elected, the person may decline to serve and the members will have to hold another election.

Report of the Nominating Committee

The nominating committee should have a designated time to report at a meeting. This usually appears on the agenda under "special orders."

When called on to give their report, the chairman of the nominating committee should state the nominations for each office.

Chairman of Nominating Committee:

> Madam President, the nominating committee submits the following nominations: for president, Judy Smith; for vice president, Dave Jones; for secretary, Ricky Shores; and for treasurer, Sarah Thomas. [*hands the nominations written on a sheet of paper to the president and sits down*]

Sometimes there is a split in the nominating committee over who to nominate. If a minority of the committee wishes to nominate someone else, the nomination is made during nominations from the floor.

As soon as the committee has reported, it is discharged from its duties. Sometimes the committee is revived to make nominations to fill vacancies. After the committee reports, the chair states:

President: The nominating committee has nominated Judy Smith for president, Dave Jones for vice president, Ricky Shores for secretary, and Sarah Thomas for treasurer. Nominations are now open from the floor. Are there any further nominations for president?

Nominations from the Floor

As soon as the president opens nominations from the floor, any member can bring forth a nomination. However, the rules for a member nominating a candidate are the same as for the nominating committee. A member should know if the person he or she wishes to nominate is eligible to serve and if the person is willing to serve.

When the nomination is from the floor:

1. A member does not have to get recognition, and often in small assemblies a member can call out a name while still seated.

2. A nomination does not need a second.

3. A member can be nominated for more than one office.

4. A member can't nominate more than one person for an office until everyone has had the opportunity to make nominations.

5. After each nomination, the president repeats the name to the assembly. For example, the president would say:

President: Denise Harmon, for president. Are there further nominations for president?

6. A motion to close nominations is usually not necessary unless it becomes apparent that members are nominating people just to honor them, and that the nominees have no intention of serving.

7. Usually the president closes nominations when no further nominations are coming forward from the assembly.

If at anytime during the nominating process a member realizes that he or she will be unable to serve if elected, the member should stand and request that his or her name be removed from nomination. It is better to remove your name during the nomination process than after you are elected.

Nominations by Ballot

Instead of nominations from the floor, the nominations can be by ballot. Each member is given a nominating ballot and writes the name(s) of a candidate(s) on it. Then the tellers' committee counts the ballots and writes a list of the nominees to give to the president to announce. Then a vote is taken for election. Care should be taken that the nominating ballot does not become the electing ballot.

Nominations by Mail

When members are widely scattered, it may be helpful to take nominations by mail. The secretary is responsible for mailing the nominating ballots to each member, with instructions on how to fill out. After the members mail back the nominations, the secretary composes the ballot from which the members then vote.

Nominations by Petition

Sometimes the bylaws provide for nominations by petition. In this case, a nominee must be nominated by a signed petition of members before the nomination is put on the ballot. The nominating petition may be enclosed with a newsletter or mailed to the members.

Other Nominating Procedures

If the bylaws do not state how nominations are to be conducted, any member can make a motion proposing a nominating process. This is an incidental main motion. It needs a second and is not debatable but is amendable. The best practice, however, is for the bylaws to state the procedure.

UNDEMOCRATIC PRACTICES IN THE NOMINATION AND ELECTION PROCESS

Members should be alert to some undemocratic political practices in organizations. For instance, if a person is elected and then resigns, the office is considered vacant and the president or board fills it by appointment instead of having another election. This may allow an unpopular or hand-picked candidate to get the office even though he or she was not elected.

In writing the nomination, election, and vacancy conditions in the bylaws, the organization should make sure that if a vacancy is created early in the term of office, the vacancy is filled by election instead of by appointment, whenever possible. In some national organizations that meet yearly or biennially (every 2 years), this would be difficult.

When nominations are being taken from the floor or when a nominating ballot is being used, a good practice is to provide the members with an eligibility list so that they are not nominating people who will not be able to serve. When the secretary mails the members a notice about the nomination and election meeting, the letter can include a request that members who do not wish to be considered for office notify the secretary in writing. When the secretary prepares the eligibility list for the meeting, only those members who are willing to serve are on the list.

ELECTIONS

After the nominating process is finished, the members must vote on the proposed candidates. If the bylaws do not state how the vote is to be taken, a member can make an incidental motion regarding how to take the vote. If the bylaws state that the vote must be taken by ballot, even if there is only one candidate for each office, the vote must nevertheless be taken by ballot. A ballot vote still allows the members to write in a candidate's name. If the bylaws require a ballot vote, the members must vote by ballot even if all candidates are running unopposed. It is out of order to ask one person (for example, the secretary) to cast the electing ballot for the entire assembly. Such a motion is wrong because it takes away members' rights to write in a candidate.

The vote for election can be taken by

1. Voice
2. Ballot
3. Roll call
4. Cumulative voting

Election by Voice Vote

When there is only one candidate for office, election by voice vote is a good method to use if the bylaws do not stipulate how the election should take place. However, anytime an election is by voice vote, members forfeit their right to write in a candidate.

When more than one person has been nominated and the election is by voice, the chair takes the vote on the candidates in the order in which they were nominated.

Members must remember to vote yes for the candidate they want and vote no for the other candidates as they are voted on. The first candidate to receive a majority vote wins.

The presiding officer takes the vote this way:

President: All those in favor of Member G for president, say "Aye." Those opposed say "No."

Then the president announces the vote:

President: The ayes have it, and Member G is elected president.

If Member G loses, the chair announces it this way:

President: The noes have it, and Member G is not elected. All those in favor of Member X for president say "Aye." Those opposed say "No."

Then the president announces the results of this vote. This procedure continues until someone receives a majority vote.

When more than one candidate is nominated, the problem with a voice vote is that those nominated first are more likely to get elected. If there is a motion to make an election by voice vote unanimous that vote must be by ballot. If there is one "no" vote, the election is not unanimous.

Election by Ballot Vote

There are two ways a ballot vote can be taken:

1. As a slate of all the officers on one ballot

2. As an individual ballot after nominations are closed for each office

Slated Ballots

In large organizations, such as conventions, it is usual to have a prepared, printed ballot listing all the names of the candidates, with room for further nominations or write-ins from the membership.

Members go to the polls once. When there is no election for a particular office or for several offices, members must continue to vote on those offices until someone is elected. With this kind of ballot, it is best to have the election early in the meeting. In the event that another vote is needed, it can be accomplished before the convention or meeting adjourns.

Individual Ballots

In the second way of taking a ballot vote, members are given a blank piece of paper by the tellers' committee after nominations have been closed for an office. The members write on the blank piece of paper the name of the person they wish to see elected for that office. The tellers then collect the ballots, count them, and the chair of the tellers' committee reads the reports. The president declares who is elected and proceeds to take nominations for the next office. After nominations are closed, the tellers again give members blank ballots to write the candidate of their choice. They collect the ballots, count them, and the chairman reads the report. This goes on until the members elect someone to each office.

This kind of balloting works well in small organizations where members can pause briefly to count the ballots without taking a recess or proceeding with other business.

When electing officers, if there is a tie vote or no one receives a majority vote, then the members keep voting until someone is elected. The members do not proceed to the next office until they have elected someone for the unelected office. For example, if no one receives a majority vote for the office of president, the members keep voting until they elect someone. They proceed to vote on the office of vice president only after they have elected a president. In cases where the members are voting on several directors at one time, those receiving a majority are elected to office. If any positions are not elected on the first ballot, the members keep voting on the rest of the candidates until the positions are filled. If more candidates receive a majority vote than there are positions available, those candidates receiving the highest votes are considered elected. For example, the Soccer Club has an executive board of five people. Seven people are nominated, and the members are instructed to vote for five candidates on the same ballot. There are twenty people present and voting. It takes eleven votes to elect. The following candidates received this number of votes:

Candidate Smith, 14 votes

Candidate Jones, 15 votes

Candidate Baker, 19 votes

Candidate Torry, 16 votes

Candidate Green, 13 votes

Candidate Frank, 12 votes

Candidate Bates, 11 votes

Although all candidates received a majority, only five can be elected to the board. In this case, the five candidates who received the most votes are the winners:

1. Baker with 19 votes ⎫
2. Torry with 16 votes ⎪
3. Jones with 15 votes ⎬ top 5 candidates
4. Smith with 14 votes ⎪
5. Green with 13 votes ⎭
6. Frank with 12 votes
7. Bates with 11 votes

If three candidates had received the same vote—for example, if Smith, Green and Frank had each received 13 votes—then the membership would have to hold another election. Even though Candidate Bates received the lowest vote, his name would remain on the ballot. No one is removed from the ballot unless the bylaws state that the member with the fewest votes should be removed—because that person may end up being the compromise candidate.

The actual counting and recording of the ballots is accomplished by the *tellers' committee,* members who are appointed to count the vote during a meeting. For information on this aspect of the voting process, see "Counting and Recording the Ballots by Tellers' Committee," later in this chapter.

Election by Roll Call Vote

If the members take the vote by roll call, the same methods used for a ballot vote can be followed: either voting for all candidates at once or voting for one at a time. The presiding officer should explain the procedure. As the secretary calls the roll, each member states for whom he or she is voting. The secretary records the vote and repeats it to make sure it is accurate.

Election by Cumulative Voting

When an organization has elections for positions in which more than one candidate is elected (for example, the Soccer Club), the bylaws may provide for cumulative voting. (Note that cumulative voting cannot take place unless it is stated in the bylaws.) *Cumulative voting* is the ability to cast all your votes for one candidate or to weight your vote in some way. In the earlier example of electing the five board members, the membership voted for five different candidates. In cumulative voting, a member could give two votes to Mr. Smith and three votes to Mrs. Baker. This allows a minority group to get together and elect one of their candidates. But this practice is not in accord with the parliamentary principles of one person, one vote.

Election by Other Types of Voting

If an organization's membership is spread over a large distance, the bylaws can provide for a vote by mail ballot. In this case, it is wise to allow candidates to be elected by a plurality vote because, if no one receives a majority vote, the vote is difficult to retake.

Plurality Vote

In a *plurality vote,* the winning candidate must receive the most votes but not necessarily a majority of those cast.

For example, let's say an organization has 500 members. There are three candidates running for president. Of the 500 ballots sent to the members, 375 ballots are returned in the mail:

It takes 188 to elect by majority vote.

Candidate A receives 180.

Candidate B receives 125.

Candidate C receives 70.

No one receives a majority vote, but Candidate A received a *plurality,* the most votes, and is therefore elected president.

COUNTING AND RECORDING THE BALLOTS BY TELLERS' COMMITTEE

A *tellers' committee* is a small group of members appointed to count the vote during a meeting when there is a ballot vote or a rising counted vote. Depending on the size of the group, the committee is usually two to three people. In many small organizations, the presiding officer will appoint several members to count ballots or to count a rising vote when the time comes.

If the organization does not have a tellers' committee, then a secretary who is well versed in counting the ballots can be very helpful. The secretary can assist those appointed to be tellers during the counting of the ballots. Tellers who are appointed at a meeting to count a ballot vote should be appointed because of their accuracy and dependability, not because they have something to gain from the outcome of a vote. They should have the confidence of the assembly. If the issue is a controversial one, the tellers should include members on each side of the issue and a neutral person to count the ballots.

If a tellers' committee is needed to count ballots for an election of officers, the committee should be appointed before the meeting and should be trained in the correct procedure for counting the ballots.

In larger organizations or at national conventions, a tellers' committee is appointed for the entire convention and is usually a large committee headed by a chairman. The chairman is in charge of the ballots and ballot boxes and is responsible for training the tellers on the proper way to count the ballots and on the various methods of counting a rising vote. The tellers' committee is present during the entire session to count any doubted voice vote, when requested to do so by the presiding officer or the membership.

Teller's Sheet and Report

For each ballot vote taken, the tellers should have a sheet of paper that helps them tally the ballots. A teller's sheet might look like this:

TELLER'S SHEET AND REPORT

Office_____

Number of votes cast_____

Number of votes to elect_____

Number of illegal votes_____

Candidates:

1._____

2._____

3._____

4._____

5._____

Signed Tellers' Committee:

1._____

2._____

3._____

4._____

Counting the Ballots

1. When three tellers have been appointed to count the ballots, Teller One should open each ballot and determine whether it is a legitimate ballot. All blank ballots are put aside because they are not counted in the total number of votes cast. *Illegal ballots,* those that have writing on them but are not readable or that contain the name of a person who is not eligible for election, are put in another pile.

2. Teller One counts the legal ballots and writes the total on the teller's sheet on the line "Number of votes cast." If there are illegal ballots, these are counted and the number is put on the line "Number of illegal votes cast." Then the number of illegal and legal ballots is totaled. This number is used to establish the number for the majority vote. The number is written on the line "Number of votes to elect."

3. Next, Teller One reads aloud the names on each ballot. The other two tellers record the name of the person as it is read and mark a tally by the name on the teller's sheet that they have been given.

4. When all the ballots are counted, the tellers' committee totals the votes for each candidate and writes the number of votes received by each name. The tellers' committee then writes the word "elected" by those receiving a majority vote. If no one receives a majority vote, the phrase "no election" is written on the teller's report or is written by any office for which no candidate has received a majority vote.

5. Each member of the tellers' committee signs the teller's report, and the chairman of the committee, or Teller One, reads the report to the assembly and gives it to the presiding officer.

In our election of candidates for the Soccer Club board, there were no blank ballots, so the tellers would write on their sheets "20" for the number of ballots cast. There were no illegal ballots, so they would write "0" on that line. On the line that gives the number to elect, they would write "11."

Filling Out the Teller's Report

TELLER'S SHEET AND REPORT

Office: Executive Board_____

Number of votes cast__20__
Number of votes to elect__11__
Number of illegal votes__0__

Then the tellers' committee would fill in each name as it was called by the member opening the ballots.

Teller One reads off the names on the first ballot:

Teller One: Smith, Jones, Baker, Torry, Green.

Tellers Two and Three now write those names in the blanks under "Candidates" and make a tally mark after each name.

Candidates:

1. Smith_____|_____
2. Jones_____|_____
3. Baker_____|_____
4. Torry_____|_____
5. Green_____|_____

The next ballot is opened. This ballot has two names that were not on the first ballot. On this ballot Teller One reads the following names:

Teller One: Frank, Bates, Smith, Baker, Torry.

Tellers Two and Three add the two new names, **Frank** and **Bates**, to the bottom of the list, and make a tally mark by each candidate. The teller's sheet now looks like this:

Candidates:

1. Smith_____ ||_____
2. Jones_____ |_____
3. Baker_____ ||_____
4. Torry_____ ||_____
5. Green_____ |_____
6. Frank_____ |_____
7. Bates_____ |_____

This process goes on until all the ballots are cast and recorded by the two other tellers. As soon as one candidate receives five votes, Teller Two calls out "tally." Teller Three then checks to see if his or her sheet matches Teller Two's. If it doesn't, the committee should immediately stop and recount the ballots to see where the mistake was made.

When the count is finished, the report should look like this, with the word "elected" written by those who received a majority vote.

TELLER'S SHEET AND REPORT

Office: Executive Board_____

Number of votes cast_____ 20_____

Number of votes to elect_____ 11_____

Number of illegal votes_____ 0_____

Candidates:

1. Smith ̶̶H̶H̶ ̶H̶H̶ IIII 14 elected
2. Jones ̶̶H̶H̶ ̶H̶H̶ ̶H̶H̶ 15 elected
3. Baker ̶̶H̶H̶ ̶H̶H̶ ̶H̶H̶ IIII 19 elected
4. Torry ̶̶H̶H̶ ̶H̶H̶ ̶H̶H̶ I 16 elected
5. Green ̶̶H̶H̶ ̶H̶H̶ III 13 elected
6. Frank ̶̶H̶H̶ ̶H̶H̶ II 12
7. Bates ̶̶H̶H̶ ̶H̶H̶ I 11

Signed:

1. Joyce Bell

2. Robert McGregor

3. Bill Walsh

Giving the Tellers' Committee Report

The chairman of the tellers' committee rises, addresses the chair, is recognized, and reads the teller's report. The chairman reads the entire report including the number of votes cast, number to elect, any illegal votes, and all names and the vote totals for each candidate, even for those who are not elected. It is the right of the members to know who received what number of votes. However, the teller reading the report does not read "elected" by those who are elected. The presiding officer announces who is elected. The report does not include the number of eligible voters. Only the officer responsible for the membership roll is able to give this if needed.

Chairman: The Tellers' Committee Report for Election of Board Members:

> Number of votes cast were 20.
>
> Number to elect is 11.
>
> Mr. Smith received 14 votes. (elected)
>
> Mrs. Jones received 15 votes. (elected)
>
> Mrs. Baker received 19 votes. (elected)
>
> Mr. Torry received 16 votes. (elected)
>
> Mr. Green received 13 votes. (elected)
>
> Mrs. Frank received 12 votes.
>
> Mr. Bates received 11 votes.
>
> Joyce Bell
>
> Chairman

She then gives the report to the presiding officer and sits down.

Note: The words in parentheses are written on the report, but not read aloud.

The presiding officer repeats the report and announces the election of each candidate:

President: The Tellers' Committee Report reads:

> Number of votes cast were 20.
>
> Number to elect is 11.
>
> Mr. Smith received 14 votes. (elected)
>
> Mrs. Jones received 15 votes. (elected)
>
> Mrs. Baker received 19 votes. (elected)

> Mr. Torry received 16 votes. (elected)
>
> Mr. Green received 13 votes. (elected)
>
> Mrs. Frank received 12 votes.
>
> Mr. Bates received 11 votes.

Note: The words in parentheses are written on the report, but not read aloud.

> The members have elected: Mr. Smith, Mrs. Jones, Mrs. Baker, Mr. Torry, and Mr. Green to the executive board. Do these members accept the position? [*All members nod yes; no one rises to reject election.*]

The presiding officer states when the election is effective, according to the bylaws:

> Thank you. You will take office at the close of our annual meeting. [*as stated in the Soccer Club's bylaws*]

Those elected take office immediately unless the bylaws state differently. In this organization the newly elected board members take their places at the close of the annual meeting.

If an organization usually has an installation of officers but fails to hold it, those elected still take office unless the bylaws provide that those elected take office when installed. An installation is only a ceremony and is not the activity that enables those elected to take office. Also, because an installation is considered a ceremony, a quorum is not needed to conduct the installation.

The complete teller's report is then entered into the minutes. If a recount is not a possibility, the ballots can be ordered destroyed or filed with the secretary for a certain number of days and then destroyed.

9

Committees

Committees are considered the workhorses of any organization. It is in committees that much business is discussed, investigated, and carried out. This chapter concentrates on the two types of committees found in organizations—standing committees and special committees. It explains the purpose of each and the important role of committee chairmen.

ROLE OF THE COMMITTEE

A committee can do only what the organization has asked it to do. It cannot act independently of the organization. However, if a committee originates an idea that it feels will benefit the group, it can bring the idea to the assembly in the form of a motion.

The bylaws should state who has the power to appoint the members of committees. With the power to appoint members of the committees comes the power to appoint the chairman and to fill vacancies.

It is the secretary's duty to let members know of their appointment to a committee, and to give committee chairman the proper documents so that the committee can accomplish its assigned work. If a motion is referred to a committee, the secretary needs to give the chairman a copy of the motion and the instructions that go with it.

The committee chairman should preserve all documents given to him or her and return them to the secretary in the same condition in which they were received. Each year the committee should keep a record of its activities and place them in a file. This file becomes a continuous record of the activities of the committee and is given to the new committee chairman each year.

STANDING COMMITTEES

Standing committees are listed in the bylaws and are considered a permanent part of the organization. In a standing committee, the committee members usually change when new officers are elected, but the purpose of the committee and its functions and duties do not change.

The standing committee has certain functions to perform that are essential to the harmonious operation of the organization. When the board or the membership receives business that is handled by one of these committees, the business is usually referred to the appropriate committee. That committee investigates and then reports back to the board or to the membership. Examples of standing committees may be finance, program, or membership.

SPECIAL COMMITTEES

The other type of committee is a *special committee,* also called a select committee or ad hoc committee. This committee is created to perform a specific task and is dissolved when the task is completed and the final report is given. The membership should not create a special committee to do something that is within the designated function of a standing committee.

Special committees have two functions. One function is to "investigate," and the other is "to carry out" what the assembly has adopted. The size of these committees and who is appointed to serve on them is determined by the purpose of the committee. If the special committee has been created to investigate a question, it is important that all the different views of the membership be reflected in the committee members. This practice allows many differences to be resolved in the committee instead of at the assembly meeting, where they take up a lot of time. Such a committee is thus usually a large one in order to represent all viewpoints.

If the special committee has been created to carry out something the membership has adopted, only those in favor of the membership's wishes should be on the committee. If members who are opposed to the action are on the committee, the action might not be carried out or could be delayed. This committee is usually a small one so that the members can easily meet and get the work done.

APPOINTMENT OF THE COMMITTEE CHAIRMAN

The committee chairman is the most important member on the committee. He or she is responsible for calling the committee meetings, overseeing all the work, and completing the work. Most committee chairman are appointed by either the president or an executive board. Sometimes the assembly elects a chairman and its committee members after they have voted to establish a special committee.

When selecting a committee chairman, those who do the appointing (either the president or the executive board) should select a chairman who is enthusiastic about the committee work, who has the time to devote to the committee, and who knows how to do the work. This person should also be able to work with others and inspire them to do the work. The other committee members should be appointed for what each can contribute to the work of the committee and for their ability to work with others on the committee. Committee work is teamwork, not a one-man band.

10

The Role of the Member

So far we have been talking about the roles of officers, boards, and committees, but what roles do the members play? After all, the members are the ones who run for office, serve on boards and committees, and come to meetings to present ideas. Without members taking an active role in the organization, it can't function or exist.

In organizations there are those who seek active roles and those who want to sit on the sidelines and "let the next person do it." It is important for the betterment and advancement of the organization to engage all the members in active participation in all the functions of the club. Unfortunately, in many organizations only a few are allowed to rise to the top. This causes cliques and small groups to develop. When only a few are considered leaders or are asked to serve on committees, resentment and ill will are created, and, worst of all, other members' talents are left untapped.

For an organization to grow, to be successful, and to be truly democratic, all the talents of the members need to be recognized, cultivated, and used. The cream should be allowed to rise to the top, but everyone can be trained and cultivated for leadership roles in organizations.

This chapter looks at ways to involve new members, the duties of a member, and situations requiring a member to assume special responsibility.

MEMBERSHIP INVOLVEMENT

Here are proven techniques for incorporating new members immediately into the organization and making them feel welcome and useful:

1. Make sure that each new member receives a copy of the bylaws and other documents that govern the club.

2. Listen to the member. Why did he or she join the organization? If the member's needs are not being met, he or she will probably not renew the membership.

3. Assign the new member a mentor, someone to explain how the organization operates and to advise where the member can best use his or her talents.

4. Give a training session on parliamentary procedure and explain that at meetings all members are encouraged to present ideas to the club in the form of motions.

5. Immediately appoint the new member to a committee where his or her talents are useful and where the member is interested in the work.

Toastmaster's International is an example of an organization that immediately includes all new members. At every meeting, each member is assigned a task or is able to participate in some way. This practice trains all members for leadership roles. If the same people always do the work, always are elected to office, or always get the limelight, the result will be a schism in the organization—which may ultimately destroy the organization.

The biggest mistake an organization can make is to have a probationary period for new members or to set up barriers to service. If you wait too long to include the new member, you may not have a new member at all.

DUTIES OF THE MEMBERS

Members, too, have duties and responsibilities. Here are a few:

1. Members should attend meetings, be on time, and know the rules of parliamentary procedure. It takes two to tango and to make a meeting go smoothly— both the presiding officer and the members need to know the parliamentary rules.

2. Members need to prepare themselves for leadership roles.

3. Members should accept committee assignments and perform the tasks given to them in a timely manner.

4. Members need to work harmoniously with other members even though they don't always agree with them.

5. In debate, each member has the right to sway the membership to his or her point of view. If a member votes with the losing side, the member must respect the fact that the majority rules and cheerfully carry out the membership's wishes.

6. Members must be impartial, fair, and courteous in meetings. This means respecting the rights of others, especially in debate. Members should call out a "point of order" only when a serious breach of

the rules has taken place. Members should listen attentively and courteously to the other members and wait in turn to speak. All members must ensure that "majority rule" does not become "mob rule" by protecting the rights of the minority and by not "gaveling through" or "railroading through" any business. It is important that each member diligently follow this principle, for today one might be with the majority, and tomorrow with the minority.

7. When the bylaws or other rules of the organization are not being followed or when members' rights are being taken away in a meeting, members have a responsibility to courteously call the violation to the attention of the membership.

A SPECIAL RESPONSIBILITY FOR MEMBERS

Every now and then there comes along a presiding officer that does not respect the rights of the members and will not entertain a legitimate, seconded motion because he or she does not agree with it. In such situations, a member can pursue the following actions:

1. Raise a point of order.

2. If the chair rules it out of order, the member can appeal the decision. (See Chapter 6, "Appeal from the Decision of the Chair.")

3. If the chair ignores the point of order, the member can make the motion again. If it is seconded and the chair still ignores it, the member can place the motion before the assembly, ask for debate, and take

the vote. This means that the member stands in his place and takes over during this part of the meeting until the main motion is disposed of—either permanently or temporarily. The member has a right to do this under *Robert's Rules of Order*. This is a good example of the principle that power is vested in the membership, not in the leadership.

PART IV

MEETINGS AND STRATEGIES

11

Meetings

A *meeting,* as defined by *Robert's Rules of Order,* is a single official gathering of the members in one room, with a quorum present to transact business. The members do not leave the meeting except for a short recess, or when the business has been completed or the chair declares the meeting adjourned. This chapter covers the many types of formal and informal meetings, including conventions and mass meetings, which are formal types, and board and committee meetings, which are informal. It also explains how to manage and evaluate meetings and how to form strategies—and counterstrategies—for meetings.

THE BASICS

Even though there are many types of meetings, each designed to accomplish a different purpose, all meetings have some things in common:

1. A quorum must be present.

2. Someone is in charge of conducting the meeting.

3. Someone is responsible for taking the minutes.

4. Business is conducted according to specific rules that state who can attend and participate in the discussion of the business and who can vote.

5. All members are notified of the meeting's date and time and the purpose for which the meeting is called. The parliamentary term for this procedure is the **call to the meeting**.

Most organizations have both formal and informal meetings. A *formal meeting* can be defined as one in which the entire membership meets to hear reports of officers, boards, and committees, and to propose business, discuss it, and vote on it. An *informal meeting* is one in which a small group of the organization meets, in either committee meetings or small boards, to help the organization carry out its goals. The primary difference between these two types of meetings is the chairman's role in participating in the meeting.

Meeting procedures vary according to the type of the meeting. In formal meetings, the members usually follow strict parliamentary procedures. This means that the person in the chair stands while presiding and while stating the motion and taking the vote. He does not participate in the debate unless he leaves the chair. Members must rise and be recognized in order to obtain the floor, to make motions, and debate. Debate is restricted to ten minutes each time a member speaks unless there is a rule to the contrary, and each member may speak twice to a motion.

In informal meetings, for example those of committees and small boards, the person presiding is usually seated and takes an active role in making, discussing, and voting on all issues. There are usually no limits on debate, and members can discuss an issue without a formal motion.

TYPES OF FORMAL MEETINGS

Types of formal meetings range from annual meetings and regular periodic meetings to conventions and mass meetings, plus less-common types such as adjourned (continued), executive, and special meetings and sessions. This section defines each type and explains its particular requirements.

Annual Meetings

The term *annual meeting* can mean two things:

1. The meeting of a society that has only one meeting a year.

2. A regular, periodic meeting of a society, designated by the bylaws as the annual meeting. The bylaws may prescribe this meeting as the one to hear the annual reports of officers, boards, and committees; elect officers; and perform other such once-a-year business.

In organizations with regular meetings, business not completed at the annual meeting can carry over to the next regularly scheduled meeting, if the time interval between meetings is quarterly or more often.

When organizations meet only once a year, business can carry over to the next annual meeting only by referring the business to a committee.

Regular Meetings

A *regular meeting* is the periodic meeting of an assembly, which is held weekly, monthly, quarterly, or at similar intervals. The day of the meeting should be stated in the bylaws (for example, "the first Monday of each month"), and the hour of the meeting should be stated in the standing rules (for example, "8:00 p.m."). If an organization has meetings quarterly or more frequently than quarterly, main motions can carry over to the next meeting through the following procedures:

1. Postponing to the next meeting

2. Referring to a committee

3. Laying on the table

4. Reconsidering the motion

If meetings quarterly or more often, a main motion can be carried over to the next meeting only by referring it to a committee, with instructions to report at the next meeting.

Adjourned Meetings

An *adjourned meeting* is a continuation of the meeting in a session. An adjourned meeting means that the meeting (as well as its time, place, and purpose) is a continuation of the meeting that established it. It is set up with a motion to "fix the time to which to adjourn" or by a main motion to "adjourn until a specified time." In an adjourned meeting, the minutes of the meeting being continued are read first, and then business is taken up where it left off from the continued meeting.

Executive Sessions

An *executive session* is a secret meeting of an assembly. In some organizations all meetings are secret. An example is the "lodge system." In an ordinary assembly, board and committee meetings are usually held in executive session. Other members can be invited to attend, but they do not have the right to attend unless the bylaws provide for it.

In many organizations, guests who attend the meeting are able to observe the business proceedings of the organization. However, at times members may not want the guests present to hear the discussion. In these situations, a motion may be made to **go into executive session**. This motion is a privileged motion and is adopted by a majority vote. If the motion is adopted, all nonmembers are requested to leave the meeting, until the members vote to end the executive session.

Business conducted in an executive session is confidential and known only to its members. Members are not supposed to divulge the proceedings of an executive session and can be punished under a disciplinary provision if they violate the secrecy. Anyone else who is not a member, but who is allowed to stay during the executive session, is honor bound not to tell what happened in the executive session. Minutes of an executive session are read and approved only in an executive session.

All disciplinary action against a member *must be* held in executive session.

Special Meetings

A *special meeting* (or a *called meeting*) is a separate meeting of a society held at a time different from the regular meeting. The bylaws must provide for the call of a special meeting, or the special meeting can't be held. The bylaws should specify the proper procedures for calling a special meeting, including who can call it, the conditions under which it can be called, and the number of days notice that the members must be given. Notice of the time, place, and purpose of the meeting must be sent to all members in advance of the meeting. At this meeting, the members can discuss only the business that was stated in the notification. (This is referred to as the call to the meeting.) If some emergency business is transacted for which no notice was given, that business must be ratified by the organization at a regular meeting or at another special meeting.

Sessions

A *session* is a series of connected meetings held by a group and devoted to a single order of business or program. If the session has more than one meeting, each meeting is scheduled to continue business from the point where it left off in the preceding meeting. This is very common in conventions.

Conventions

Conventions differ from regular meetings in that they are assemblies of delegates chosen from the units of the organization, which may be scattered over a large geographical area. The delegates are sent as representatives of these units. Usually a convention is held once every year or two, and lasts about a week, although it could last longer, if necessary, as in a constitutional convention. The voting members are those who hold proper credentials as delegates or those who in some other way hold membership and voting rights. Before delegates can participate, they must report to the credentials committee. This committee gives them the necessary documents to enter the convention floor and to participate in the convention business.

Other names sometimes used for conventions are: congress, conference, convocation, general assembly, house of delegates, and house of representatives.

Of the various types of conventions, the most common is the convention of an established state or national society. The delegates are chosen by, and from, the local chapters of the society. Sometimes a convention is called for the purpose of forming a new association of persons to address a common problem or concern. This type of convention is handled like a **mass meeting** (see the later section, "Mass Meetings.")

Conventions vary in terms of how often they are held and how long the sessions are. They range from one-day conventions held annually or biennially to weeklong (or longer) conventions held yearly. The variation is dependent on the size of the organization and the amount of business that needs to be done. Usually the rules relating to a society's conventions are stated in the bylaws.

In its bylaws regarding conventions, a state, regional, or national society should have provisions that do the following:

- Authorize a periodic convention.

- Define its powers and duties.

- Fix the quorum.

- Specify the voting members (who can vote and who can't).

- Define the qualifications of delegates and alternates, how they are elected, and how many there are.

- Explain how the convention should be organized and operated.

The procedures of a convention differ from those of a regular meeting. After opening ceremonies and any presentations such as inspirational speakers, the first business in order is the report of the credentials committee.

The Credentials Committee

The credentials committee is one of the most important committees in the convention. This committee is responsible for registering the delegates, giving each delegate the proper identification to enter the assembly, and providing a copy of the program and other information such as time and places of workshops or other meetings.

The credentials committee is the first to report at the convention, and no business can begin without the credentials committee report. This report states the number of those in attendance and establishes the membership of the meeting and quorum. Usually at a convention the quorum is the number of members present. The credentials committee report is adopted by the members present at the beginning of the meeting and also at the beginning of each session and often before a vote is taken, especially if new delegates have arrived and registered. Because delegates are continually arriving or leaving the convention, the credentials committee report is changing and must be voted on as it changes. *It takes a majority vote to adopt the credentials committee report.*

The credentials committee mans the registration table, and its members are present at stated times during the entire convention to register delegates as they arrive, or arrange for alternates to replace those delegates who must leave the convention.

Standing Rules for the Convention

The convention adopts standing rules, which are prepared by a committee on standing rules. These rules contain both parliamentary rules and standing rules for this particular convention. Parliamentary rules may be those that set a time limit on debate. For example, each speaker can speak for three minutes; members shall use voting cards instead of voice votes or rising votes. There may be standing rules particular to the convention, such as all speakers shall come to the microphones and must wear badges to come into the assembly. These rules are drafted by the committee and are presented immediately after the credentials report. They may be amended by the assembly and are adopted by a two-thirds vote.

Program

A convention usually adopts its own order of business. This order of business is called the *program* and specifies when certain issues are to be taken up and when certain events are to occur. The program, or agenda, is developed by the program committee and adopted after the standing rules of the convention by a majority vote. After the program is adopted, it takes a two-thirds vote to change it.

Some organizations have a resolutions committee or a reference committee whose basic purpose is to screen all main motions before they are presented to the assembly.

In some organizations, a standing committee will function as a reference committee to allow members to come to an open meeting sponsored by the committee for the sole purpose of getting the members' input before resolutions or proposed bylaw amendments go to the entire assembly. It is usually the bylaws committee that acts as a reference committee to help expedite the amending of bylaws. The bylaws committee can provide an informal setting where members can raise questions, state their objections, or give suggestions for improvement of proposed bylaw changes. The committee can then reevaluate the proposed amendments and make changes that are more acceptable to the membership. Because members have already raised questions and given suggestions to the committee, much time is saved during the regular session when the bylaw amendments are presented. In most cases, the controversial issues can be resolved because the bylaws committee can then propose a compromise amendment during the business meeting.

Adjournment Sine Die

When the convention has finished its business and program, it adjourns *sine die,* which means "adjournment without a day." In other words, this particular group of delegates will not meet again. The next convention is a "new" convention where the delegates will start all over by adopting standing rules and a program. A convention is a complete unit in and of itself, and that is why it always adjourns sine die.

Mass Meetings

A *mass meeting* is a meeting of an unorganized group. It provides a meeting place and an orderly way to bring people of the same interests and concerns together for the purpose of forming an organization or solving a community problem.

Because a mass meeting has no written rules to help in conducting the meeting, some basic parliamentary principles govern it:

1. Those sponsoring the meeting have the right to restrict the discussion and any proposals to the purpose they have announced.

2. Those attending have the right to determine the action by making motions and by debating and voting on the proposals.

3. The sponsors have the right to keep out of the meeting any who are opposed to the purpose or would try to subvert the purpose because the organizers have invested both time and expense in calling the meeting.

Calling a Mass Meeting

Those who want to have a mass meeting have a variety of ways they can notify those interested: telephone or mass mailer or through media announcements and posters—any means by which they can reach the intended audience. The call to the meeting should state the purpose of the meeting; the date, time, and place; and who is invited to attend. For example, it may be residents of a certain neighborhood, registered voters, or those interested in a certain issue.

Preparing for a Mass Meeting

Like other meetings, a mass meeting must have structure. Those who are calling the meeting need to prepare an agenda and decide who is going to call the meeting to order, who they want to nominate as a temporary chairman and secretary, who will explain the purpose of the meeting and what the sponsors want to accomplish, and, finally, by which rules they will abide.

Conducting a Mass Meeting

Although a mass meeting has no governing documents to provide structure, the basic parliamentary rules of conducting a meeting apply. However, in *Robert's Rules of Order, Newly Revised,* there are specific rules given for conducting a mass meeting. The following rules are for the "first" mass meeting that is called by a group. If there are a series of mass meetings, those meetings will follow the order of business as outlined in Chapter 2.

The first item of business in a mass meeting is electing a chairman and secretary. When the time arrives for the meeting to begin, the person selected to preside calls the meeting to order and requests nominations for a chairman. Those sponsoring the meeting should be ready to nominate a candidate for the office. It could be the person who called the meeting to order. Another way to accomplish this is for the person presiding to immediately nominate the candidate that the sponsors want to be chairman. After the sponsors nominate their candidate, the person presiding asks for nominations from the floor. Then he or she takes a voice vote.

After the person is elected chairman (that person should be the sponsors' candidate), the next business in order is to elect a secretary. The sponsors again nominate a candidate for this office. After the election of the secretary, the chairman asks the secretary to read the call to the meeting. Then the chairman recognizes the person who is designated to explain the purpose of the meeting.

After the purpose is explained, it is in order to propose a resolution or series of resolutions to accomplish the purpose. Those present are considered members of the assembly and have the right to propose amendments, or any other motions that would help expedite the purpose of the meeting. The only motions that are not allowed are those that are contrary to the purpose of the meeting, and the chairman has the responsibility to rule those motions out of order. For example, if the meeting is called to oppose the construction of a shopping mall in the neighborhood, it would be out of order to propose a motion in favor of the shopping mall.

Adjournment of a Mass Meeting

Here is a word of caution about adjournment. If the assembly needs to have another meeting, the date, time, and place of the meeting need to be established prior to adjournment. If the members adjourn without adopting a motion to set the time for another meeting, the assembly dissolves and has to start from the very beginning again if another meeting is called.

Using a Mass Meeting to Establish an Organization

A mass meeting can be used to bring an organization into being. The procedures are the same as those for the first type of mass meeting except for the following:

1. The chairman and secretary elected are considered chairman pro tem and secretary pro tem, and serve until permanent officers are elected. Pro tem means for the time being.

2. A motion is presented to establish the organization.

3. A bylaws committee is appointed to draft bylaws for the new organization.

4. A time and a place are set for the next meeting, the purpose of which is to consider the proposed bylaws.

5. After the bylaws are adopted at the next meeting, the members recess in order to enroll the members.

6. After the membership is established, the permanent officers are elected.

INFORMAL MEETINGS

Informal meetings are distinguished from formal meetings by the size of the group and how the meetings are conducted. In meetings having an attendance of fewer than twelve, the rules can be less formal: The person presiding is usually seated and can make motions, discuss motions, and vote on motions. The members do not have to rise to address the chair, and often ideas can be discussed before a motion is made. However, even though the informal meeting has a more relaxed approach, it is still important for the members to follow an agenda and limit discussion to the subject of the meeting. If these techniques are not practiced, time is wasted and things do not get accomplished. The two most common types of informal meetings are board and committee meetings.

Board Meetings

Board meetings are like other deliberative assembly meetings in the way business is conducted. Boards must transact business in a properly called meeting, one in which the members have been notified and there is a quorum present. The minutes of the board meeting are kept by the secretary and are accessible only to members of the board (unless the board votes to release them to the general membership). However, the general membership can vote to have the board's minutes released and read to the membership. At board meetings, the executive committee (if there is one) should report to the board what it has been doing since the last board meeting.

The formality of the rules in board meetings is determined by the size of the board. *Robert's Rules of Order* sets the dividing line between large and small boards as twelve members. Large boards operate under the same rules as other deliberative assemblies. Small boards can use more relaxed procedures, and these differ from the procedures of large boards in the following respects:

- Members do not have to stand up and obtain the floor before speaking. They can speak while seated.

- Motions do not need to be seconded.

- Members can speak any number of times, and there is usually no motion to close debate.

- Members can discuss a subject while no motion is pending.

- When all the members know what they are voting on, it is not necessary to have a formal motion before voting. However, for the sake of having a clear record in the minutes of the issue being voted on, it is always best to put the discussion in the form of a formal motion before taking a vote. Then there is no question about what everyone is voting on. Unless they agree by unanimous consent, members must vote on proposed board actions just like other assemblies. Also, a vote can be taken by a show of hands, which is often more convenient than other ways of voting.

- The chairman doesn't have to stand up to put a question to a vote.

- The chairman can enter into the discussion and usually remains seated while conducting the meetings. He or she usually makes motions and votes (unless board custom dictates otherwise).

If a board meeting ever disintegrates into chaos, or a lack of order prevents business from being accomplished, a wise presiding officer will return to the formal rules of conducting a meeting and advise the members that parliamentary rules are in place—rising and addressing the chair before speaking, making a main motion before beginning to speak, observing the formal rules of debate, and stating the question before taking the vote.

Committee Meetings

The chairman (or the first named member, who usually acts as the chair in the case of a new committee) is responsible for calling together the committee—that means he sets the time, date, and place of the meeting and notifies all the committee members. The chairman can be appointed by the presiding officer of the assembly or can be elected by the committee.

If for any reason the chairman won't call a committee meeting, then two members can call the committee meeting. A quorum is a majority of the committee's members.

The rules in a committee meeting are the same as those specified for small boards. The chairman usually acts as the secretary of a small committee. In a large committee, someone is usually chosen to act as the secretary.

Committees operate under the same bylaws, parliamentary authority, standing rules, and special rules as those that govern the organization creating the committee. Committees do not make their own rules (except when authorized by a higher authority).

The chairman of a committee plays a very active role in the committee. He or she can make motions and can also debate and vote in the committee. Because debate is not limited in a committee, it can continue as long as necessary to reach an acceptable conclusion.

A committee doesn't really decide anything (unless it has been given power by the assembly to make certain specified decisions). Usually a committee just makes recommendations, which are then discussed and voted on by the parent assembly. (The committee is basically a "child" of the organization that created it.)

Should the committee wish to take action beyond the scope of its powers, it can report to the assembly that it wishes to be empowered to do so. Then, if the assembly assents, it can empower the committee to take the action requested.

When committees are about to decide on an important issue, they should invite members of the society to appear and offer their views on the subject being discussed. They can also invite nonmembers who have expertise in the subject. This is called a *hearing*. After everyone who has an interest in the proceedings has been heard, the committee deliberates privately. During actual committee deliberations, only committee members have the right to be present. Any vote taken to decide the will of the committee including what is to be included in committee reports is by a majority vote.

- In a committee, the motion **to reconsider the vote in committee** is handled differently than in regular meetings of assemblies. The differences are:

  - The motion to reconsider can be made and taken up any number of times in a committee. Also, there is no limit on the amount of time elapsed since the original motion was considered and voted on.

  - The motion to reconsider in committee can be made by any member who did not vote with the losing side. This means that the person could have been absent or abstained when the vote was taken.

  - A two-thirds vote is required to adopt the motion to reconsider in committee (unless all the members who voted on the prevailing side are present or have been notified, in which case a majority will suffice).

Committee of the Whole

The membership of a large assembly can designate that the members present act as a committee. This is called a **committee of the whole,** and is a variation of the motion to **refer to a committee.** An assembly must vote to go into a committee of the whole. The motion needs a second, is debatable, and takes a majority to adopt. The advantage of functioning as a committee of the whole is that members may speak an unlimited number of times to an issue. Any actions by a committee of the whole are not decisions of the assembly but are recommendations of the committee of the whole to the assembly. The chair of the committee of the whole is appointed by the presiding officer of the assembly, who then steps down while the committee of the whole is in session. Also, in the case of a committee of the whole, a vote cannot be reconsidered because it really is not a binding vote but is only a recommendation that will be voted on later by the assembly.

Quasi-Committee of the Whole

Another form of the motion to act as a committee of the whole is the **quasi-committee of the whole,** which is designed for medium-size assemblies. In this form of the motion, the presiding officer of the assembly remains in the chair and presides. Decisions are reported to the regular assembly for consideration.

Informal Consideration

A technique suited to small assemblies, *informal consideration* removes the limit on the number of times members can speak in debate. The regular presiding officer remains in the chair and presides. The results of votes taken while in informal consideration *are* decisions of the assembly and are not voted on again in the assembly.

To go into a **committee of the whole**, a **quasi-committee of the whole**, or **informal consideration**, a member makes a motion to do so. If the motion is adopted by a majority vote, the assembly begins carrying it out. In the case of a committee of the whole, one member is appointed chairman and another secretary of the committee. The secretary keeps minutes of the committee's proceedings. Eventually the committee of the whole reports to the assembly, which then may consider, discuss, and vote on the recommendations from the committee, if any.

In the quasi-committee of the whole, the presiding officer of the assembly presides and the secretary of the assembly keeps the minutes of the committee's votes and recommendations. Eventually they report the committee's actions are reported to the assembly. To end a committee of the whole or a quasi-committee of the whole, the chairman rises and reports.

In the case of informal consideration, no separate committee is created and the actions and votes of the assembly are recorded in the minutes.

MEETING MANAGEMENT

Anyone who works with a group who wants to get things done finds that one of two things happens. Either one person wants to do all the work so it will get done, or a meeting is called about it, and then more meetings. At work and in our organizations, many of us are being "meetinged" to death, and the meetings aren't accomplishing all that they should. Is there a way to solve the meeting dilemma but still preserve democracy and not waste everyone's time? Yes, it's called meeting management. Many of the techniques previously explained in this book, such as preparing and following an agenda, rotating debate and keeping debate within its limits, and insisting that members keep to the topic, certainly are elements in meeting management.

The following suggestions apply mainly to informal meeting settings, such as board and committee meetings, where the most time is wasted because people don't know how to stay on the subject. Often what is supposed to be a committee meeting to get something done turns into a social event, or the members get sidetracked by discussing something or deciding something that is not within the scope of the meeting or the duties of the committee or board.

Here are some helpful techniques for managing a meeting so that you can accomplish what you set out to do in an efficient, timely manner.

First, don't have a meeting if you can accomplish the objective some other way. Perhaps phone calls, e-mail, faxes, or even letters will suffice.

Second, if you need to meet, minimize attendees and time spent. Only call those who really need to be there. Give attendees as much notice as possible. Include time, place, start and end times, subject, and agenda in the call of the meeting. If visual aids are needed (charts, videos, overheads, etc.), have them set up well in advance and tested to ensure they function properly.

Third, start the meeting on time. Don't allow latecomers to waste the time of those who arrive in time. Allot a reasonable amount of time to accomplish the meeting's objectives and stick to the schedule. Follow the agenda to cover each item as quickly as possible. Don't allow discussion to get off the subject of the agenda. Have someone take the minutes or notes on what the committee or group decides to do. The chairman should keep a list of assignments and target dates for action. In recurring meetings, discuss issues from previous meetings and give progress reports. Before ending the meeting, have the recorder summarize plans that were agreed upon and target dates. End the meeting on time.

Know what your responsibility and authority is in the meeting. This should be stated in the bylaws. Be sure you have the authority to make decisions about the issues being discussed at the meeting. Foresee what is likely to happen in the meeting, and prepare for it. Use committees. This means delegating responsibility and the work to smaller groups. If you are the chair of a committee, break up the work among the members. A wise meeting manager will use committees to get a lot of work accomplished for the organization.

When giving directions or assigning tasks to others, make sure that they understand the directions or what they are expected to do and when it is to be done.

Make sure the leader of the meeting does what a leader is supposed to do: He or she should know the agenda items and what decisions and action plans are going to be proposed. The leader should be impartial but have the facts surrounding any proposed action plans. The leader should allow debate on the agenda items but make sure discussion sticks to the agenda and doesn't wander and waste time on irrelevant issues. The leader should follow the agenda and keep the meeting moving along.

One final technique for expediting business without compromising anyone's rights or the democratic process is to use general consent instead of a vote on noncontroversial issues such as:

- Paying bills
- Approving the minutes of the previous meeting
- Answering correspondence
- Closing nominations
- Considering reports and recommendations
- Adjourning

The chairman would say:

> If there is no objection, we will do . . .

If no one objects, the action can be done in the name of the organization. The chairman says:

> Hearing no objection, we will do . . .

Managing Meetings at the Office

Can these same techniques be used at the office? Can a knowledge of democratic principles and formal rules and procedures help in conducting meetings in the business world? Most definitely yes! Incorporating meeting management techniques and the basic principles of parliamentary procedure in business meetings will save time, encourage input from all the participants, and give structure to the meeting.

The basic principle of taking up one thing at a time is applicable in any meeting. The person planning the meeting or facilitating the meeting should have an agenda or a list of things to accomplish at the meeting. These should be arranged in the order of priority. Everyone attending the meeting should be given a copy of the agenda.

The principle of impartiality is also applicable. The key question the meeting planner should ask is: Do I really want the ideas of others or do I just want to tell them what to do? How this question is answered will determine how the meeting proceeds.

If the person conducting the meeting really wants the input of employees or colleagues, he or she will be impartial—refraining from passing judgment on what is said and allowing all to speak. In this kind of meeting, it will be important to alternate the discussion in order to bring out the best ideas. The meeting leader will not allow one person or a small group of people to dominate the discussion and will solicit opinions from those who are not participating in the discussion to see what they have to say.

Here are some other important points to remember in conducting a meeting:

1. When calling the meeting, explain the purpose and what you hope to accomplish at the meeting. An example might be "how to cut down the time between when an order is received and when it is shipped."

2. Include in the meeting all the people involved in solving the problem.

3. Set a meeting time and place that is convenient for all attendees.

4. If several departments in a large organization are involved, have the meeting in a neutral place and choose a facilitator who is impartial.

5. Prepare for the meeting. Gather information in advance and send it to those who will attend. Ask them to consider the information and to come with solutions.

6. Start the meeting on time. If there is more work to be done, set another meeting and encourage the members to continue thinking about solutions.

The most effective meetings in the business world are those in which employees know their ideas are taken seriously and implemented. When employers call meetings just to meet or talk "at" their employees, no one takes these meetings seriously, and everyone will make excuses not to attend.

The Meeting Environment

Another part of meeting management is the meeting room itself. Some obvious factors should be checked in advance. Is the room large enough to seat the group comfortably? It should not be too large or too small. Is it temperature-controlled so that it doesn't get too hot or too cold? Is it quiet enough for the audience to hear the speakers and the leaders? Does it have facilities for audio, video, overhead projectors, computers, or whatever else may be needed by the speakers to present their information?

Does it have a properly functioning public address system (if needed)? Are there enough exits into and out of the room for safety's sake but not so many that admission can't be controlled? Are there enough tables and chairs? All of these matters should be checked in advance and properly prepared.

The seating arrangement can facilitate the meeting. For smaller meetings of fewer than thirty people, some experts suggest that circular or semicircular seating helps focus the members' attention on the leader and on each other. This arrangement is good for promoting inter-action. The circular seating pattern fosters a sense of equality (like the Knights of the Round Table). It is good for intense face-to-face interaction but may not be so good for problem solving. The semicircle or U-shaped seating pattern focuses attention on the leader who is seated at the top of the U. The door to the room should be at the bottom of the U so that meeting participants are not distracted by persons coming and going. The diameter of the semicircle should be about 15 feet for a 15-person meeting. If there are more than 15 people, a second row of chairs should be set up. This way everyone can see each other easily, see the leader, and also see any visual aids at the front of the room.

Try to get people to sit close together. This promotes a feeling of group cohesiveness. If you know that someone has left the meeting and will not return, take away the empty chair and have the group move together to fill the empty space. Empty spaces are to be avoided because they suggest something missing or a vacuum— psychologically negative suggestions for a group which is trying to accomplish something together.

Evaluating Your Meetings

After the meeting is completed, it is a good idea to evaluate the meeting so that you can plan better meetings in the future. The following checklist will help you identify mistakes and avoid future ones:

- Was a detailed meeting agenda provided so that everyone knew what was supposed to happen?

- Did everyone receive sufficient notice of the meeting so they could plan to attend?

- Did the presiding officer follow the agenda?

- Did the chairman announce the results of the votes and the effect the votes would have?

- Did the chairman keep the discussion on track? Or did members raise and discuss unrelated issues?

- Was there adequate time to conduct the business on the agenda?

- Did the members listen to the discussion and wait their turn to speak? Or was cross-talk allowed to disrupt and distract the business at hand?

- Did the members and the chairman follow the rules of parliamentary procedure? Or did they make up the rules as they went along?

- Did the chair allow the speakers to make their statements? The chair should interrupt only to call the meeting to order, to call time, or to redirect the discussion to the business at hand.

- Did everyone speak and participate? Or was discussion dominated by one, two, or a few members?

- Did the chairman enter the discussion without stepping down from the chair? Did the chairman try to "railroad" an issue or stifle discussion on an issue?

- Were any decisions made in haste and without sufficient consideration?

- When a decision was made, were there clear instructions regarding what was to be done, who was to do it, when they were to have it completed, and when they were to report back to the organization?

- Were there any hidden agendas at work in the discussion?

- Was there discord in the meeting? Was it resolved? If so, how was it resolved?

- Did the members see alternative courses of action? Were any presented?

- Did all members participate in the discussion? If some didn't, did the chairman try to bring them into the discussion? If they still didn't participate, did anyone try to find out why?

- Regarding committee reports, did committees report on what they had done rather than what they were going to do?

- Was the room comfortable for the meeting? Or was it too hot, too cold, too large, too small, too noisy, too bereft of chairs or tables, or deficient in any other way?

- Was the seating arrangement appropriate for the meeting?

- Did the audio and video equipment (if any) operate properly?

- Were there any other problems that could be identified and corrected in future meetings?

MEETING STRATEGIES

This section is designed to give readers plans of action for either adopting a motion or defeating a motion while preserving the highest ideal of democratic proceedings in meetings. Although the word "strategy" has a favorable definition—a careful plan or method to achieve a goal—it also connotes a plan of action to defeat an enemy by trickery.

The intent of this discussion is not subterfuge but information. This section will describe the procedure or procedures that give the counteraction of any motion presented in a meeting. There are always two sides (sometimes many sides) to each issue, and if one group prevails by subverting the democratic process and preventing the other side(s) from being heard, the action is doomed to failure. Often such action means the breaking up of the organization. However, it is the right of each side to use parliamentary procedures in a fair, just, and honest way to obtain its goal.

Here is a word of advice from Henry Robert:

> Where there is radical difference of opinion in an organization, one side must yield. The great lesson for democracies to learn is for the majority to give to the minority a full, free opportunity to present their side of the case, and then for the minority, having failed to win a majority to their views, gracefully to submit and to recognize the action as that of the entire organization, and cheerfully to assist in carrying it out, until they can secure its repeal.

It is important that all members know fully the rules of procedure, their rights as members in an organization, and how to protect their rights. Remember that if an opposition "sleeps on its rights," it may be too late to correct the action. Therefore, members must pay attention to what is happening in the meeting and point out to the chair and the assembly any mistakes *when they are happening*—not after the meeting has adjourned and everyone has gone home.

This discussion will present strategies first for members and then for the presiding officer.

Types of Strategies

When organizations have to consider a controversial issue, both sides commonly come to the meeting with a plan to achieve their goals. If the organization is divided on the issue, and the presentation of the debate has been equal, it is usually the side having the best understanding of parliamentary procedure that wins. Therefore, all members should understand the types of strategies and how to counter each one.

There are several types of meeting strategies: those necessary to adopt an action, to delay an action, to defeat an action, to bring a compromise, and to change an action.

One of the most important strategies is to come prepared for the meeting. Have the person who will make the motion already assigned and rehearsed, have the motion carefully worded, and be prepared for the debate. Let someone play devil's advocate so that members can counter the opposition's objections. Plan what you will do when motions are made to defeat the proposed action; if possible, work with a parliamentarian. The same advice goes for those opposing the action.

If you are the person who has to preside during a controversy, think about all the situations and motions that could arise, and prepare for them. Be ready to keep order and handle points of order and appeals from the decision of the chair. Seek advice from a parliamentarian before the meeting, and, if possible, hire a parliamentarian to help you during the meeting.

Strategy to Adopt an Action

Often a proposed action comes from a committee or the board of an organization. If this is the case, the great advantage is that the proposal is coming from an official organ of the organization. Usually in the eyes of the membership, such a proposal carries more authority than if an individual member makes the motion. There is also more than one person who is supporting the idea. The other advantage is that in presenting the idea to the members, the committee or board gives a report explaining the whys and wherefores of the motion. Many objections can be met in the report by providing enough information. The other advantage a board or committee has is being able to give to the assembly written information attached to the agenda or sent out with the **call to the meeting**.

An individual presenting a motion wouldn't be able to give a report or attach printed materials to the agenda without the permission of the assembly. Nor would an individual have a small group of people who are already in favor of the action. However, one way to get more information to the group about the motion is to present it in the form of a resolution. In this form, the reason for the proposed action can be stated in a preamble. (See Chapter 6, "Motions.")

A defensive strategy in adopting a motion is to watch for those who would try to shut off debate prematurely, or those who would try to kill a motion by **laying it on the table** instead of making the motion to **postpone indefinitely.** During the meeting if you feel you are losing ground or you need to consult with others, make a motion to **recess.** If the members seem to need more time to think about the motion or more facts need to be gathered, use a delaying strategy.

Strategy to Delay an Action

Delaying an action can sometimes be the wisest move to make. There are two ways to delay an action: first by referring the motion to a committee, and second by postponing it to a later time. (Sometimes the motion to **reconsider the vote** delays the action if this motion is not taken up at the meeting but is called up at the next meeting.)

A delaying strategy is helpful if a member makes a motion that no one is prepared to discuss or has even thought about. In this instance, the motion to **postpone to the next meeting** enables the members to gather information, formulate their reasons pro or con, and get the absent members to attend the next meeting. In cases where the members are uncertain because they don't have enough information, or when they want to know how the details are going to be worked out, it is best not to push for a decision at that meeting but to make a motion to **refer to a committee**.

Strategy to Defeat a Motion

Members don't always agree, and those who oppose an action have just as much right to try to defeat it as those who are trying to get it adopted.

The most obvious ways to defeat an action are to:

1. Debate against it.

2. Postpone it indefinitely.

3. Postpone it to another meeting, hoping more support can be gathered to vote against it.

However, if something detrimental to the organization or a member is proposed, the wisest action is to **object to consideration of the question** immediately after it is stated by the chair. This motion should seldom be used, and then only when something would truly harm the organization even to discuss it. (For information on making this motion, see "Using Incidental Motions" in Chapter 6.)

Compromise as a Strategy

An alternative to defeating a motion is to compromise. Very rarely is an issue either a "yes" or a "no." Most issues are negotiable and can be resolved through discussion, carefully listening to others, and then using the amending process. Let's say the membership is divided about the time of the meetings. Group A wants the meetings changed to an earlier time, but Group B wants to keep the current time. After much discussion and proposing of amendments, the members vote on a time that neither one really wants but that is in-between the current meeting time and what Group A has presented. It is a compromise that everyone can accept.

Other Strategies

Besides the strategies already discussed, there are others that can be used effectively to change an action, correct a mistake, cool down tempers, keep a motion alive, or deal with various situations arising in a meeting.

A Point of Order

A point of order can correct a multitude of errors. If the chair does not correct a serious mistake in a meeting, a member can **raise a point of order**. This motion should be used only when a serious mistake has been made in the meeting, for example, when members' rights are being taken away. The chair always rules on the point of order *before proceeding with any further discussion or motions*. If a member does not agree with the chair's ruling, he or she should **appeal the decision** of the chair.

Parliamentary Inquiry

If a member realizes that the assembly doesn't understand what is going on, he or she can rise to **parliamentary inquiry**, which can be done at any time. This is not considered debate, so it can be made while a nondebatable question is pending. This action might be of help, for example, when someone has moved the previous question to try to cut off a member's right to debate. A member could rise and ask the chair what will happen if the members vote for the previous question.

Point of Information

A **point of information** can be raised anytime during debate to ask for factual information. It is not considered debate, so a member could lead the discussion without debating by asking all the right questions.

Motion to Recess

A **motion to recess** can help cool things off in debate or can provide time to plan strategies with those who are of like mind. Or, it can buy time to call in additional support from members not present. If someone moves the previous question early in debate, a motion to recess can rally votes to stop this motion. If things aren't going your way, move to take a recess.

Move the Previous Question

When nothing new is being said in debate and it is going on and on, make the motion to stop debate by saying:

I move the previous question.

If adopted, this closes debate and brings the motion to a vote.

Lay the Pending Motion on the Table

If there is a motion being debated on the floor, and a member needs to leave the meeting early but wants to make a motion before leaving, he or she can move to

lay the pending motion on the table. If adopted, the pending motion will be temporarily laid aside, and the member can now make the new motion. Once this issue is decided, someone can move to take the original motion from the table. If the motion is adopted, the assembly proceeds with the meeting where it left off.

Postpone to Later in the Meeting

If a motion is being discussed and a member who has important information about the subject has not arrived, a member can move to **postpone the motion to later in the meeting**.

Or, if a member is not at the meeting but another member knows that with a simple telephone call the member would come to the meeting, he or she could make a motion to **recess**. During the recess, this person can call the member and find out when the member would be able to arrive at the meeting; then he or she can make the motion to **postpone to later in the meeting** to give the member time to arrive. If the member can't make the meeting, a motion to **postpone it to the next meeting** can be made.

Reconsider and Enter on the Minutes

When a temporary majority results from an unrepresented attendance at the meeting pushes through a motion that many absent members would have opposed, the best strategy is to vote on the prevailing side and then move to **reconsider and enter on the minutes**. (See "Other Helpful Motions" in Chapter 12.) This motion needs a second. It stops all action on the motion, and can be brought up only at the next meeting. In the call letter for the next meeting, there must be a notice about this motion.

Fix the Time to Which to Adjourn

If members want to go home but important business still needs to be discussed and might die if the meeting adjourned because of a time element, then set the time for an *adjourned meeting*. To do this, make the motion to **fix the time to which to adjourn**. Set the hour, date, and place for the meeting. Then make the motion to **adjourn**. At an adjourned meeting, business is taken up where the members stopped at adjournment.

Consider the Intent of a Motion

When a motion is not worded in proper parliamentary terms, the intent of the motion should be considered. For example, a member may move to "table something to the next meeting." This is really the motion to "postpone the next meeting." If the chair places it before the assembly as the motion to lay on the table, a member should raise a point of order because it is taking away the members' right to debate by a majority vote. Another example might be if a member makes a motion that would in effect rescind something previously adopted where no previous notice was given. Alert members will point out that the vote needed to adopt this motion is a two-thirds vote or a majority of the entire membership. By understanding intent, the membership will know the proper rules governing any situation.

Voting Strategies

If a voice vote is taken and a member feels the vote is not decisive, he or she should call for a **division**. The chair must retake the vote by asking the members to rise. If a question is controversial, and a member thinks having a secret vote would deliver the most honest and representative vote, he or she should move to **take the vote by ballot**. This motion needs a second, is undebatable, and requires a majority vote.

The Best Strategy in a Meeting

When you don't understand what is going on in a meeting or you've gotten lost in the procedures, the best strategy is to ask the chair by rising to a **parliamentary inquiry.** If more members would use this tool, much misunderstanding could be prevented in meetings.

Another way to use a parliamentary inquiry is to ask the chair if it is in order to do something. The chair's duty is to assist the members in presenting business.

Still another way of asking for help in a meeting is **a point of information.** If you want more facts about the subject being discussed or don't understand what someone has just said, ask! A member might say,

> Mr. Chairman, I rise to a point of information.
> Did I understand the previous speaker to
> say . . . ?

Be assured that if you didn't understand something or are lost in the procedures of a meeting, others are probably having the same problem.

Paying Attention Can Pay Off

Members can often stop illegal actions before they occur in a main motion by remembering these points:

1. A main motion can't conflict with national, state, or local laws. It can't conflict with the bylaws (constitution) or rules of the assembly. If such a motion is adopted, even by a unanimous vote, it is null and void.

   If such a motion is made, the presiding officer should rule it out of order. If the presiding officer does not rule it out of order, a member should call a point of order, stating that it conflicts with the existing laws, bylaws, or rules.

2. A motion can't be made that presents substantially the same question as a motion that has been previously rejected during the same meeting. A motion can be removed if there is a change in wording or a difference in time or conditions.

   However, if a member votes on the prevailing side, he or she can move to reconsider the vote on the motion that was defeated. If the motion to reconsider is adopted, the motion is again before the assembly as if it never had been voted on, and the members can amend it or substitute something more to the liking of the membership.

   Here's an example. The assembly has voted against having a booth at the County Fair because no one had the time to man the booth. After some progress in the meeting, a member who voted against the motion comes up with a creative solution, so the member moves to "reconsider the vote." The vote is reconsidered, and the motion is now before the assembly again. It is then amended to everyone's satisfaction and adopted.

3. A motion can't conflict with a motion previously adopted and still in force.

   However, a member can move to rescind the action or to amend the action. (This is called amend something previously adopted.) If an action is rescinded, it is no longer in force.

4. A main motion can't conflict with, or present substantially the same question as, a motion that has been temporarily set aside. For example, if a motion has been postponed, laid on the table, or referred to

a committee (or if a reconsideration has been moved and has not been taken up), someone can't make a motion that conflicts with the motion that has been temporarily put aside.

If such a motion is made, the chair should rule it out of order and state the proper procedure. If the chair does not rule the motion out of order, a member can raise a point of order.

The correct procedures for handling motions that conflict with, or present substantially the same question as, a motion that has been temporarily set aside are:

- If a motion is laid on the table, make the motion to take it from the table.

- If a motion has been postponed, move to suspend the rules and take up the motion.

- If a motion has been made to reconsider the vote and has not yet been called up, call up the motion to reconsider.

- If a motion has been referred to a committee and the committee has not yet reported, move to discharge the committee.

5. A main motion that proposes action outside the organization's purpose (as defined in the object of the bylaws or corporate charter) can be considered only by a two-thirds vote.

Strategies for Presiding Officers

The presiding officer's duty is to ensure that all meetings proceed in a democratic fashion and that all procedures and proposed actions are in accord with the governing documents of the organization and parliamentary rules.

Therefore, a presiding officer should be thoroughly familiar with the following:

1. The bylaws and other governing documents of the organization

2. The organization's adopted parliamentary authority

3. The agenda and any controversial issues that might be coming before the assembly

4. Procedures for presiding, the ranking of motions, and the rules of debate

Strategies for Presiding Officers When Conducting Business Meetings

Should a presiding officer have a meeting strategy? Yes, in the sense that he or she is well prepared to conduct the meeting. An effective presiding officer will be thoroughly familiar with the agenda and will preside from a meeting script. (See Appendix C for a sample meeting script.) The officer will have reviewed different procedures from the organization's parliamentary authority and will have consulted beforehand with the parliamentarian about any tricky items that might come up.

The presiding officer's goal should be to expedite business in a timely fashion while still allowing it to be presented in a fair manner. He or she should not try to push things through solely to get things done in record time.

Most presiding officers are familiar with the members and know which are the hot-button issues. When a presiding officer knows that an agenda item is one of those issues, the officer should be thoroughly prepared to keep control of the meeting so that it doesn't get out of hand.

Techniques for keeping order in a meeting are:

1. Read up on how to handle debate and any motions that members might use to block the democratic process, such as **previous question, lay on the table, points of order,** and **appeals from the decision of the chair.**

2. Before debate begins, remind the members of the rules of debate:

   - The member making the motion has the first right to speak to the motion.

   - Everyone gets a turn to speak, and debate will be alternated between the pros and cons.

   - Members must rise, address the chair, and be recognized before speaking.

     When members know that the chair is impartial and in control of the situation, they will be more likely to behave.

3. If things start to get out of control, declare a recess. If a brawl begins, adjourn the meeting to protect the membership. (You can't adjourn the meeting because you think it is going on too long or because you don't like the members questioning your decisions.)

4. Know when and how to use general consent in taking a vote, and when to assume a motion and take the vote. Instead of waiting for someone to move to pay the bills, say:

   > All those in favor of paying the bills say "Aye." Those opposed say "No." [*Announce the vote.*]

   To vote by general consent, say:

   > Is there any objection to paying the bills? Hearing none, the treasurer will pay the bills.

5. Keep the meeting going forward! If members are not rising to debate an issue, take a vote. Don't wait for someone to **move the previous question**. When debate is going on, alternate between those who are in favor and those opposed. Ask:

> Does anyone want to speak for the motion?

Then,

> Does anyone want to speak against the motion?

If members are making substantially the same points, ask:

> Is there anything new to add to the discussion?

If no one rises to speak, take the vote! Or ask if there is any objection to closing debate and taking a vote.

   If one person objects, you must first take a vote on closing debate (a rising vote and two-thirds); then if debate is closed, take a vote on the motion. The chair should be good at reading the assembly and knowing when they are ready to vote. The chair can use this procedure of closing debate when the members aren't readily rising to debate. By asking the question, if the members **"are you ready for the question?"** or **"is there any objection to closing debate and taking a vote?"** the chair is telling the members that if they don't rise to discuss the issue further the chair is going to take the vote now.

6. When handling debate, remember that the member who made the motion has the first right to speak to the motion. *Robert's Rules of Order, Newly Revised*, says, "The chair should turn toward the maker of the motion to see if he wishes to be assigned the floor first in debate . . . ." Be watchful in this

situation. Many times members who are opposed will move the previous question. If this happens, you do not have to recognize the member or entertain the motion since there has been no debate. If it is a controversial question, you have an obligation to see that debate is not stopped before the minority has been able to present its side.

7. Remember to remain impartial and courteous at all times and conduct the meeting in a democratic way. If you feel strongly about an issue, step down and let another officer preside until the vote is taken. (However, this officer must not yet have debated the issue.)

    One way to handle this situation is to find someone in the membership who feels the same as you do and have that member speak to the motion. If you know that something is coming up at the meeting, you can give facts and information to that member to present to the membership. By remaining impartial and unbiased, you retain the respect of the members.

8. If in doubt about why a member has risen and addressed the chair, especially when a nondebatable question is pending, say:

    For what purpose does the member rise?

9. You don't have to wait for someone to make the motion to adjourn. If no further business is coming forward, take a vote on adjourning the meeting by saying:

    Is there further business? [*pause*] All those in favor of adjourning the meeting, say "Aye." Those opposed say "No." The ayes have it, and the meeting is adjourned.

Or you can say:

> Is there any objection to adjourning the
> meeting? [*pause*] Hearing no objection, the
> meeting will adjourn. [*pause*] The meeting is
> adjourned.

10. When you anticipate a complicated procedure (such
    as adopting bylaws) or a series of motions, the most
    efficient way to conduct the meeting is to instruct
    the members in the correct procedures for that part
    of the meeting.

12

Strategies for Individual Motions Illustrated

This chapter provides strategies that you can use with various classes of motions. It explains the purpose of each strategic motion and how that motion can be used in a meeting to help adopt—or defeat—another motion. Its countermotion is also explained. The motions are given in the same order as found in *Robert's Rules of Order, Newly Revised,* according to each motion's rank. (For additional information on any of these motions, see Chapter 6, "Motions.")

MAIN MOTIONS

Before a topic can be discussed at a meeting, it must be stated as a *main motion.* Then the motion needs a second before the topic can be discussed. If it does not get a second, it is not before the assembly. However, if members begin debating a motion that does not have a second, the fact that it was never seconded is a moot point. (After discussion begins, no one can stop the discussion because the motion was not seconded.) A second does not mean someone is in favor of the motion, only that another wants to hear it discussed. The maker of the motion has the first right to discuss the motion. After the chair states the motion, it belongs to the assembly, not to the maker of the motion, and members can now alter the motion as they see fit.

Besides applying subsidiary motions to the main motion to change or defeat it, members can take two immediate counteractions: **object to its consideration** and **motion to substitute**, both of which are explained next.

Object to Its Consideration

If a member believes that the main motion would be detrimental to the organization or a member even to discuss, he can immediately object to its consideration. It requires a two-thirds vote in the negative (that is, against consideration) to sustain the objection and not consider the main motion. In taking the vote the president asks,

Shall the motion be considered?

(See Chapter 6, "Incidental Motions.")

Motion to Substitute

To obtain a different version of the main motion, a member can make the **motion to substitute** his or her motion for the original main motion. This is a form of amending, and can be done only after the maker of the motion has spoken to the main motion. (Also see "Motion to Substitute," later in this chapter under "Subsidiary Motions.")

SUBSIDIARY MOTIONS

The following subsidiary and privileged motions can help either adopt or defeat the main motion. Countermotions are given for each motion.

Postpone Indefinitely

The motion to **postpone indefinitely** has three purposes: to kill the main motion, to test the strength of opposition on the motion, and to enable a member to speak two more times to the main motion. It needs a second and is debatable. In debate, members can discuss the main motion. If the motion to postpone indefinitely is adopted, it kills the main motion without taking a vote on the main motion; the main motion is killed for the duration of the meeting. The main motion can be brought before the assembly at another meeting, but it can be brought up at the same meeting only by a motion to **reconsider the vote** (only an affirmative vote can be reconsidered).

Strategies for countering a motion to postpone indefinitely are:

1. **Amend**—If members are against killing the main motion, they can move to amend it to make it more agreeable to the opposition. If the motion to amend is made, it takes precedence over **postpone indefinitely**.

2. **Refer to a committee**—If the main motion is referred to a committee to investigate, then **postpone indefinitely** does not go to the committee. However, the committee could recommend that it be killed.

3. **Postpone to a certain time**—If members want to gather support for or against the motion, it can be postponed to the next meeting. Or the members could **fix the time to which to adjourn** (set a time for an adjourned meeting) and then **postpone the motion to the adjourned meeting**.

Motion to Amend

The purpose of the **motion to amend** is to change the main motion to make it more agreeable or to defeat it. In the latter case, the motion may be a *hostile amendment*. For example, if someone moved "to give the secretary a raise, someone else could propose an amendment "to give the secretary a decrease in salary."

Another way an amendment can be used to defeat a motion is to **substitute another motion for the main motion.**

Strategies for countering a motion to amend are:

1. If a motion is poorly worded and fixing it with amendments would take too long, someone should suggest that the motion be withdrawn. If the assembly agrees, then start again.

2. If you are unhappy about how your main motion is being amended, move to refer it to a committee to investigate and come up with a solution.

You can always speak and vote against any proposed amendment with one exception: The maker of a motion can *vote against but not speak against* his own motion.

Motion to Substitute

If a member does not like a motion, he or she can *strike out* the entire motion and *insert* another motion. This is called the **motion to substitute.** This method can be used to strike out an entire paragraph, section, or article—even an entire motion or resolution. In the case of a main motion, it is replacing one motion with another motion. This motion can also be used to make more than one change at a time.

There are specific procedures for using the motion to substitute. Let's say a member makes the following motion:

Member 1: I move to buy a new word processing typewriter.

Another member could amend the motion by substitution:

Member 2: I move to amend the motion by striking out the entire motion and substituting "to buy a computer and a laser printer."

The motion to substitute needs a second and is debatable. It is considered a primary amendment and must be moved before another primary amendment is made. Debate can be on the merits of the original main motion and the substitute. In debating, the membership is deciding which motion will be the main motion.

The chair states the motion this way:

Chairman: It is moved and seconded to amend the motion by striking out the main motion and substituting "to buy a computer and a laser printer." Is there any discussion?

Member 2: I believe that buying a computer and a laser printer would be a better investment for us than a word processing typewriter because it does more than word processing. The treasurer could keep all the financial records on the computer. Others could use it too and have their own files. A word processing typewriter will soon be obsolete.

Member 1: I speak against the substitute motion and for the typewriter. Right now this is all the organization needs, and we need to think of our budget.

Debate goes on until the members are ready to vote.

The chair takes the vote this way:

Chairman: The question is on the motion to substitute. Shall the motion to buy a computer replace the motion to buy a typewriter as the main motion of the assembly? As many as are in favor say "Aye." Those opposed say "No." The ayes have it, and motion to substitute is adopted. The pending question (to be considered now) is to buy a computer and a laser printer. Is there any discussion?

If the noes have it, the chair would say:

Chairman: The noes have it, and the motion to substitute is lost. The question is on buying a word processing typewriter. Is there any discussion?

It must be remembered that the members are voting to determine which motion is to be the main motion. The vote taken does not adopt either the main motion or the substitute motion but decides which will be considered as the main motion. After it is decided by a vote, the motion is considered by the membership just like any other main motion. However, there is one exception, which is explained next.

The Perfecting Process

During the substitution process, both the main motion and the substitute motion can be amended. This is called the *perfecting process*. It allows members, if they wish, to make the pending main motion more attractive to the group. Those in favor of the substitution may want to **amend to compromise**, so that the **motion to substitute** will be adopted.

If members want to amend either the pending main motion or the substitute motion, the chair must first take amendments on the pending main motion—the motion that was made first. When the members have finished amending the pending main motion, then the chair takes amendments on the substitute motion. When this is finished, the chair takes a vote to determine which of these motions will be considered as the main motion.

In the perfecting process, the members must remember this rule: If the substitute motion is adopted as the main motion, it can't be amended further except for adding nonmodifying matter. For example, if the substitute motion has been amended to "buy a computer and a laser printer not to exceed $2,000," then no one may strike out and insert anything further in the motion—to strike out "laser" and insert "ink jet" would be out of order. But a member could add at the end "by July 1." It is important that all changes to the substitute motion be made in the perfecting process. If the motion to buy a typewriter is voted to be the main motion, it can be further amended because it was the original main motion.

Fill in the Blank

Another helpful form of amending that can be used as a strategy to get more input from the members is the incidental motion **fill in the blank**. This motion is a way to consider more than a primary and a secondary amendment at the same time. When members have many different ideas about a dollar amount, date, time, place, color, names of nominees, etc., this is a helpful procedure.

Fill in the blank allows members to strike out a date, place, time, or number in the motion and to create a blank. The blank lets members consider many alternatives without having to go through a long amending process. This motion must be seconded, is not debatable, and must be voted on immediately.

For example, a member makes a motion to "buy a computer and a laser printer not to exceed the cost of $2,000." A second member moves to strike out "$2,000" and insert "$3,000."

What if several members had other ideas about the cost? Someone could move to create a blank.

Member 1: Madam President

President: [*assigns the member the floor*]

Member 1: I move to strike out "3,000" and create a blank.

Member 2: Second.

President: It is moved and seconded to strike out "$3,000" and create a blank. As many as are in favor say "Aye." Those opposed say "No." [*None are opposed.*] The ayes have it, and a blank is created. The chair will now take suggestions on filling the blank.

Any member can rise and without recognition insert an amount to fill the blank. These proposals do not need a second. Each member can give only one suggestion to fill the blank and cannot give a second suggestion unless he or she has unanimous consent to do so. The suggestion that was struck out to create the blank also becomes one of the suggestions to fill the blank.

When the members have finished giving their suggestions, debate is open on all pending suggestions. After debate is finished, the chair takes a voice vote or, in small assemblies, takes a vote by a show of hands, on all the suggestions until one suggestion receives a majority vote. It is important for members to vote for or against all suggestions because the first suggestion to get a majority vote is adopted and fills the blank. If members do not vote on earlier suggestions, one of those suggestions may be adopted and the blank filled. The chair should begin the voting with the least likely suggestion to be adopted, or with the least popular choice, in the case of filling the blank with an amount. Here is an example of filling the blank:

President: The motion to fill the blank has been created. Are there any suggestions?

Member 2: One thousand five hundred dollars.

President: One thousand five hundred dollars. [*writes it down*]

Member 3: Two thousand five hundred dollars.

President: Two thousand five hundred dollars. [*writes it down*]

Member 4: Four thousand dollars.

President: Four thousand dollars. [*writes it down*] Are there any more suggestions? [*looks around and sees no one rising*] Is there any discussion on the proposed suggestions?

Member 2: Madam President

President: [*assigns the floor*]

Member 2: I believe we can get the computer and printer that we need for $1,500, and anything over that would be unnecessary for our needs.

Member 3: Madam President

President: [*assigns the floor*]

Member 3:   I am for the amount of $2,500. Most laser
printers cost between $500 and $600, and to
get a computer that has all the programming
we need will cost over $1,500.

Member 1:   Madam President

President: [*assigns the floor*]

Member 1:   I am for $3,000. If we buy one that costs less,
we will have to install it ourselves. I know of a
good computer system that we can buy from
a company who will install it and teach us
how to use it.

President: Is there any further discussion? [*pause*] If not,
the question is on filling the blank.

Before the vote is taken, the president should explain
the voting procedure and then repeat all the suggestions
for filling the blank.

President: The suggestions proposed, beginning with
the largest amount, are $4,000, $3,000,
$2,500, $2,000, and $1,500. The chair will
take the vote beginning with $4,000 and
work to the smallest sum until an amount
receives a majority vote. Each member needs
to vote yes or no when each amount is
presented. Voting will go on until one of
these amounts receives a majority vote. As
many as are in favor of "$4,000 say "Aye."
[*One person says aye.*] Those opposed say
"No." [*The rest say no.*] The noes have it,
$4,000 is defeated, and the question is on
"$3,000." As many as are in favor say "Aye."
[*A majority says aye.*] Those opposed say
"No." [*Two say no.*] The ayes have it, and
the blank is filled with "$3,000."

When the blank is filled, voting on the proposals to fill the blank stops. The president then takes a vote on the amendment.

President: The question is on the amendment "not to exceed $3,000." As many as are in favor say "Aye." Those opposed say "No." The ayes have it, and the amendment is adopted. The question is on the motion as amended, "to buy a computer and a laser printer not to exceed $3,000."

The president continues the discussion of the motion as amended or takes a vote.

Presiding Officer's Prerogative to Propose Creating a Blank

If a member does not call for creating a blank, and the presiding officer thinks that one is needed, the president can say:

President: The chair suggests creating a blank by striking out "$2,000." If there is no objection to creating a blank [*pause and look to see if there is an objection*], the blank is created. [*pause*]

The presiding officer should pause and wait to see if there is an objection. If there is an objection, he or she can take a vote on creating a blank. The incidental motion to create a blank can be made when either a primary or a secondary amendment is pending.

Special Note About Filling the Blank

When filling the blank with amounts of money, apply one of the first two rules:

1. When buying something or spending money, arrange the proposed amounts from the highest to the lowest.

2. When selling—or accepting a sum of money in settlement of something—start with the lowest amount and proceed to the highest.

3. In filling the blanks with names or colors, arrange the suggestions in the order they were given.

Refer to a Committee

One of the purposes of the motion to **refer to a committee** is to appoint a small group to investigate the motion and bring back their findings. In meetings where people are undecided about a motion or where there is a lot of amending going on, the motion to refer to a committee is helpful. It lets a small group work out the details and then present it to the assembly. This could ultimately save time.

Another use of this motion is to make sure a motion will be put on the agenda in organizations that have meetings annually or semiannually.

However, if a member does not want the motion to be referred to a committee because he or she wants it decided now, the member can move that the assembly act as the committee. This takes away the limits on debate and allows for flexibility in the discussion.

If one member moves to refer a motion to a committee but another member wants to consider it now, the second member can either debate against referral or amend it by striking out "the committee" and inserting that "the assembly act as the committee." If this amendment is adopted and the motion that the assembly act as the committee is adopted, then a solution may be reached at the meeting.

When members have many conflicting viewpoints about a matter, another helpful use of the motion to **refer to a committee** is to establish break-out groups of ten to twelve people who meet during a recess. Each group has an appointed moderator, and the groups meet in informal discussion to come up with solutions. After the meeting is reconvened, the moderators of each group give their reports. The reporting is a form of debate. The motion must then be returned to the assembly for a final decision.

Strategies for countering the motion to refer to committee are:

1. Strike out one committee and insert another committee. Or strikeout the name of the committee and insert "that the assembly go into a committee of the whole (or quasi-committee of the whole for informal consideration)."

2. Stipulate the date when the committee is to report back.

3. Stipulate what the committee is to do.

If the organization meets quarterly and a member wants a motion decided before then, he or she can make the motion to **fix the time to which to adjourn** (in other words, set the time for an adjourned meeting and then have the committee report back at that meeting). Alternatively, a member can make the motion to **recess** and then have break-out groups meet to see if issues can be resolved without having to refer it to a committee that reports back at another meeting.

When referring a motion to a committee, the assembly needs to be alert to those who would use this as a tactic to let something "die" in committee. Not only should members be watchful about when the committee is to report back to the assembly, but also about who is appointed to serve on the committee. If, for instance, in an organization, a member moved that a committee be appointed to do a feasibility study of selling the building and building a new one. Many of those appointed to the committee did not want to sell the building. The committee did not do what it was instructed to do. As a result of inattentive selection of committee members for this committee, the whole issue "died in committee." The proper procedure for correcting such a problem is to **discharge the committee** and appoint a new one.

Postpone to a Certain Time

The motion to **postpone to a certain time** is very useful when a member believes that too few members are present to make a representative decision. Let's say there are just enough members present to conduct the meeting and a controversial motion is made. A member could move to postpone it to the next meeting, arguing in debate that this motion would best be discussed when more members were present.

Postpone to a certain time can also be used to delay a motion until later in the meeting, especially when members who may be informed about the subject are known to be arriving late.

This motion can be used to postpone a pending motion until later in the meeting so that the members can take up other business. Another use is to postpone to the next meeting so that members have more time to think about an issue.

If a motion is controversial and members are getting angry in the debate, it could be postponed to give members more time to think about the issue and to let everyone cool off.

If a member is concerned about a motion being postponed either to later in the meeting or to the next meeting and it not being taken up, then he or she can amend the motion to make it a **special order** for a definite time. The special order will ensure that the motion is taken up by the assembly at that specific time.

Strategies for countering motions to postpone to a certain time are:

1. If someone moves to postpone a motion to the next meeting but the motion includes a time that occurs before the next meeting, then **to postpone** is out of order. For example, if a motion is to sign a lease by August 16, and the next meeting is September 1, then the motion to postpone to the next meeting is out of order. If the chair does not rule it out of order, a member can raise a point of order.

2. To prevent someone from trying to delay the decision, the time element of the motion can be amended. If a member moves to postpone the motion to the next meeting, another member can amend it by striking out "the next meeting" and inserting "later in this meeting." Or it can be amended by making it a special order and adding the phrase "at 8 p.m. and make it a special order." The amendment ensures that it will come up again at that exact time. (See "Postpone to a Certain Time" in Chapter 6 for more details.)

3. If members want more discussion time for the motion than the current meeting allows, someone can move to **fix the time to which to adjourn**. If the motion is adopted, then someone can move to **postpone the motion to the adjourned meeting**.

4. If a member does not want the motion postponed, he or she can debate against it, amend it to an earlier time than the time proposed in the motion and make it a special order, or vote against it. For example, if a member moves to postpone the motion to the next meeting, another member could amend the motion by adding at the end, "and make it a special order for 7 p.m." This will ensure that the motion is taken up promptly at 7 p.m. and interrupt pending business at that hour.

To Limit or Extend the Limits of Debate

The motion to **limit debate** is useful when a lot has to be accomplished at a meeting and the members are long-winded. Before any business is proposed, a member can make an incidental main motion that limits debate to, say, five minutes per person, or that limits the debate for each subject discussed to fifteen minutes. During debate, a motion could be made to "limit debate to ten more minutes and take a vote."

After members have adopted a motion to limit debate, they may change their minds later in the meeting and want to extend the debate. They can either **reconsider the vote** on the motion to limit debate or **suspend the rules** and **extend the debate**.

When you need to keep brevity in a debate, the most useful form of this motion is to limit the amount of time each member can speak. Most people can get their points across in five minutes. However, it is possible to counter the motion.

Strategies for countering this motion are:

1. **Amend**: After the motion to limit debate is made, another member can always propose an amendment to the amount of time.

2. If a member wants to stop debate now, he or she can **move the previous question**.

3. If a member does not want debate limited, he or she can **move to recess** and talk to other members to vote this motion down.

4. Since this motion is nondebatable, a member can raise a **parliamentary inquiry**, asking the chair what the implications of this motion are and what effect it will have on the discussion. This action will allow the members to think about how they will vote.

Previous Question

The purpose of the motion **previous question** is to stop debate immediately and take the vote. It is one of the most misunderstood and misused motions in a meeting, and members need to know how to defend themselves from its abuses.

The first abuse occurs when members call out "**question**" and the chair immediately stops debate and takes a vote on the motion. If this happens, a member can call out "**point of order**" and remind the chair that someone needs to make a formal motion to close debate, the motion needs a second, and the vote must be two-thirds in the affirmative to close the debate.

Another abuse in meetings occurs when a member makes a main motion and then someone immediately **moves the previous question**. If the chair allows this tactic, a member again should raise a **point of order**, stating that members have the right to debate. Since no debate has been allowed, this motion is out of order.

Another often-used tactic occurs when the maker of the motion speaks for the motion and then another member immediately moves to close debate. Again the chair should rule this motion out of order. If the chair does not, a member should raise a **point of order**. Debate means just that—all sides must be heard. If someone is allowed to debate for the motion, the opposition should have the right to debate against it.

One motion that is most helpful in counteracting previous question is to **recess**. It is a higher-ranking motion and takes precedence over previous question. If recess is adopted, members have the opportunity to persuade the other members to vote against closing the debate.

Strategies for countering the previous question are:

1. Make the motion to **recess**.

2. Raise a **parliamentary inquiry** to let members know the implications of closing debate.

3. Make sure the correct procedures are followed with this motion and that the vote is taken as a rising vote (where everyone stands up to be counted).

4. Vote in the negative.

Lay on the Table

This is the other most misused motion in meetings. Because people have seen it misused so often, its misuse becomes acceptable.

The most frequent form is "let's table this to the next meeting." Technically, there is no such motion in *Robert's Rules of Order*. To "table to the next meeting" is the motion to **postpone to the next meeting**. If the chair does not restate this as the motion to **postpone to the next meeting** and call for debate, then a member should raise a **point of order**.

To **lay on the table** is correctly used to take up a more urgent item of business or to hear a speaker who can't stay for the completion of the pending business. It is incorrect to use it to kill a motion or delay it to a later time. Its only purpose is to temporarily put business aside so that the members can take up a more urgent matter.

Strategies for countering this motion are:

1. Raise a **point of order** when it is misused.

2. Make a motion to **recess** when members want to get support to defeat it.

3. Raise a **parliamentary inquiry** when a member wants the other members to understand the implications of adopting this motion.

4. If the motion to **lay on the table** is adopted, remember to make the motion to **take from the table** after the more important business has been decided. That way the members can again discuss and vote on the motion that was laid on the table.

PRIVILEGED MOTIONS

Privileged motions do not relate to the main motion or to subsidiary motions but to special matters of immediate importance that come up in a meeting.

Raise a Question of Privilege

The motion to **raise a question of privilege** is most useful when a member can't hear what is being said or when the room is too hot or too cold, and you need to take care of these environmental problems now. This is a good motion for members to have in their parliamentary vocabulary.

Member: Mr. President (or Madam President), I rise to a question of privilege of the assembly.

This is one of the higher-ranking motions and usually can be made at any time during a meeting and can be made even when another has been assigned the floor. However, it can't interrupt voting or verification of a vote.

Another form of raising a question of privilege is to **go into executive session** when the members need to have a confidential discussion or when members have sensitive information to give to the assembly concerning the subject under discussion. This is especially helpful in city government meetings, such as school board meetings, when sensitive issues like hiring and firing must be discussed. (Government meetings operating under "open meeting laws," however, need to abide by the state laws for going into executive session.) If members want the nonmembers to leave the room, a member can move to "go into executive session."

Strategies for countering these two motions are:

1. Use the higher-ranking motions such as to **recess**, **adjourn**, and **fix the time to which to adjourn**.

2. To counter **go into executive session**, debate against it and vote against it.

Recess

Recess can be used in a multitude of ways. It can be used: to cool off a heated argument in debate, to caucus with other members before a vote is taken, to give time to count ballots, or to let members get up and stretch. It can be used to counteract the motions **limit debate**, **close debate**, and **lay on the table**.

Strategies for countering motions to recess are:

1. **Amend**—Change the amount of time for the recess.

2. **Adjourn**—Let's not take a recess but instead end the meeting.

3. **Point of order**—If someone proposes to take a recess of a day or several days, a member should point out that a recess means a short duration of time, not a day or several days. The correct motion in this case is **fix the time to which to adjourn**.

4. **Raise a parliamentary inquiry**—Ask the chair to explain the implications of a recess. Since a parliamentary inquiry is not a debatable motion, it allows the members to decide whether they want to take a recess.

5. To prevent an amendment to recess, someone can **move the previous question**. (There are two times when previous question can be applied to a higher-ranking motion than itself: recess and fix the time to which to adjourn.)

Adjourn

When the assembly has no set time to adjourn, members have the right to make the motion to **adjourn**. If this motion is made and defeated, it can be made again after there has been progress in the debate or business.

If a business meeting is getting out of hand, **adjourn** is a good way to put an end to it.

This motion is out of order when the assembly is engaged in voting or in verifying a vote, or before the result of the vote is announced by the chair. However, there is one exception to the rule that you can't adjourn while the assembly is engaged in voting. That exception occurs when a ballot vote has been taken and all the ballots have been collected but the result has not yet been announced.

Strategies for countering the motion to adjourn are:

1. **Fix the time to which to adjourn**—If a member thinks the members are going to vote to adjourn the meeting and important business has not yet been taken care of, the member can move to set the time for an adjourned meeting. This motion can be made after the chair has announced that the motion to adjourn has passed and before the chair declares that the meeting is adjourned. (See Chapter 6, "Adjourn.")

2. **Raise a parliamentary inquiry**—Ask what will happen to the important business if the meeting adjourns.

3. **Raise a point of order**—Anytime a member believes that this motion is out of order or would dissolve the assembly then he or she can **raise a point of order**.

4. Vote against adjourning.

Fix the Time to Which to Adjourn

The motion to **fix the time to which to adjourn** is used to set the time and place for the continuation of this meeting (an adjourned meeting). It is helpful if the bylaws do not allow for calling of special meetings. Let's say an organization is revising or amending bylaws and needs a series of meetings for this. The organization's bylaws either do not allow for special meetings or state that bylaws can be amended only at the annual meeting. At their meeting, the members can move **to fix the**

time to which to adjourn in order to set another meeting for continuing their work with the bylaws. This process can go on at each meeting until all the bylaws have been proposed and voted on.

Strategies for countering motions to fix the time to which to adjourn are:

1. **Amend**—The time, date, place, or any other variable can be amended.

2. **Previous question**—If previous question is adopted, then no amendments can be made. However, this strategy may not serve any good purpose.

3. **Parliamentary inquiry**—Ask the chair what effect this motion will have if adopted. This is a way to get the information to the assembly. By having the chair explain the purpose of the motion, members can decide whether they want to have an adjourned meeting.

INCIDENTAL MOTIONS

The preceding discussions of counteractions have mentioned several incidental motions: **point of order**, **parliamentary inquiry**, and **point of information**. One motion that has not been mentioned as a strategy is to **appeal from the decision of the chair**.

Members need to realize that anytime the chair makes a ruling, a member can appeal the ruling. The purpose of an appeal is to let the assembly decide. Presiding officers do make mistakes, and the assembly has the right and obligation to correct them. Correcting a mistake in the meeting procedures may even determine how the assembly decides an issue.

Another helpful incidental motion is the motion to **withdraw**. This action should be used only when it becomes apparent that the motion being discussed is poorly worded or that something has changed so that the motion is not relevant anymore.

A situation that assemblies need to be aware of, however, is one occurring when a member gets mad because "his" or "her" motion is being amended and the member is unhappy and wants to withdraw it. Because members are not informed, they allow the motion to be withdrawn. If you want the motion to continue to be discussed and voted on, then object to its withdrawal. This way the presiding officer will have to take the vote on the motion to withdraw.

MOTIONS THAT BRING A QUESTION AGAIN BEFORE THE ASSEMBLY

Rarely is it ever too late to revisit an issue or for the assembly to change its mind after it takes a vote. This section discusses the motions that enable the assembly to do so.

Reconsider the Vote

Reconsider the vote is an important motion to use in situations where the assembly has already adopted a motion but during the meeting new information comes to light. By **reconsidering the vote** on a motion, the members can change their minds about what they have adopted, or at least consider it again by taking into account the new information. To prevent a misuse of the motion, only a member who voted on the prevailing side can move to reconsider.

If a member did not vote on the prevailing side but wants the motion reconsidered, he or she can rise when no business is pending and briefly state reasons for reconsidering the motion. If a member who voted on the prevailing side agrees with the reasons, perhaps he or she will then make the motion. While business is pending, a member can request permission to state his or her reasons for reconsideration. Another tactic a member can use is to make the motion to **recess**. During the recess the member can approach members who voted on the prevailing side and try to convince one of them to make the motion to reconsider.

In one organization, a bylaw amendment was defeated. A member who did not vote on the prevailing side wanted it reconsidered. A recess was taken, and the member was able to convince another member who had voted "no" (the prevailing side) to make the motion to reconsider. The members voted to reconsider the vote. The member gave persuasive reasons why the amendment should be adopted, and it was.

An important point to remember is that the motion **to reconsider** must be made on the same day that the motion it is reconsidering was adopted, unless the organization has adopted rules to the contrary. City and county government officials frequently misuse this motion, believing they can reconsider a vote on a motion a month later. In such cases, if the action is adopted, it must be rescinded. If the motion was defeated, the motion can be renewed; that is, presented again. However, city and county governments may have statutes or laws concerning the presentation of business, for example approval of building permits, zoning, and other public issues. Government bodies need to check with their attorneys about such laws and proceed carefully concerning these parliamentary rules. Some government organizations have adopted rules of order that allow the vote on a motion to be reconsidered at the next meeting.

Rescind

Should a member want **to rescind** an action, the key strategy is to give previous notice. By giving previous notice, either in the call to the meeting or at the previous meeting, only a majority vote is needed to rescind an action. If a member does not give previous notice, a two-thirds vote is needed to rescind or a majority of the entire membership. Members need to be alert to situations where members move to rescind an action without giving previous notice and then the vote is taken only by a majority. This action violates the principle of protecting the rights of the absent members. Members must also be aware of the rules regarding rescinding the motion. (See "Rescind and Amend Something Previously Adopted" in Chapter 6.)

OTHER HELPFUL MOTIONS

Many members believe that after they have adopted a motion or after a motion has been defeated no one can do anything about it.

A common misconception is that once a motion is defeated at a meeting it can't be brought up again. People leave the meeting upset because they think they are helpless. The rule is that a motion can't be brought up again at the same meeting unless the vote on the motion is reconsidered. However, a motion that is defeated can be brought up again at the next meeting, later in the meeting if changed by time or circumstances, or at later meetings. It has been known to happen that a persistent person keeps bringing up a motion at every meeting and ultimately gets it adopted.

If a motion is adopted and the members change their minds afterward, they can rescind or amend the action; or during a meeting they can reconsider the vote.

If an unrepresentative temporary majority at a meeting ramrods something through, two members can stop the action by moving to **reconsider and enter on the minutes.**

Reconsider and Enter on the Minutes

Reconsider and enter on the minutes is an unusual form of the motion to reconsider. By making this motion and seconding it, two members can stop action on an adopted motion.

The same rules apply to this motion that apply to the motion to reconsider. The maker of the motion must have voted on the prevailing side. The only purpose of this motion is to prevent an unrepresentative temporary majority in attendance at a meeting from taking advantage of its position and adopting a motion that a majority of the membership would normally oppose.

Let's say that a small group has been trying at each meeting to get the organization to buy a new stove for the clubhouse. The motion has been defeated at every meeting at which it has been presented. However, at this particular monthly meeting, many of the members can't attend, but there is a quorum present. The majority of those present are those who want to buy a new stove. They see this as the only opportunity to adopt this motion, and they do it.

To stop the action, a member who is opposed to buying the stove needs to vote on the prevailing side—those who voted yes. (This may seem like an unusual thing to do, but only a member who has voted on the prevailing side may make the motion to reconsider.) Immediately after the vote is announced, this member should make the motion to **reconsider and enter on the minutes**. It needs a second. What this does is suspend all action on the motion until the next meeting. The absent members must be notified of the proposed action. To reconsider and enter on the minutes can't be brought up on the same day, but on the next day or another day as long as the time between meetings is within a quarterly time interval.

This motion can be subject to abuse. It is possible that two members could hold up a legitimate action.

The strategy for countering this motion is:

Fix the time to which to adjourn—Set the time for an adjourned meeting. That way the motion can be taken up before the next regular meeting.

There are two conditions under which **reconsider and enter on the minutes** is not in order:

1. If delaying it would defeat the object of the motion.

2. If there is more than a quarterly time interval between meetings.

In such cases, a member should raise a **point of order** if the chair does not rule the motion out of order.

13

Most Frequently Asked Questions

We have found that members of organizations generally ask the same questions about parliamentary procedure and meetings. Most questions concern voting, a quorum, the motion to lay on the table, the agenda, minutes, bylaws, and what to do about a tyrannical presiding officer. If you have a question or a problem, the best advice is to look in your organization's bylaws and governing documents and then consult your parliamentary authority. The bylaws and other governing documents always take precedence over the parliamentary authority.

This chapter provides answers for commonly asked questions about parliamentary procedure and issues in meetings. The questions are grouped by topic: voting, the secretary and the minutes, the president, other officers, ex officio officers and members, quorums, meetings, and motions.

VOTING

Q: I am trying to find some sound guidelines to establish our method of proxy voting. Are there minimum requirements in order for proxy voting to be valid?

A: *The first thing you should do is consult the statutes regarding proxy voting in the state in which your organization is incorporated. If the state statutes allow proxy voting for your kind of organization, they may require certain procedures for conducting and counting the proxies.*

If you are not incorporated, then check the statutes for the state in which you reside to see what they say about this proxy voting.

Second, check to make sure that proxy voting is provided for in your bylaws. Unless it is stated in the bylaws, proxy voting is not permitted. The exception to this is if the state statutes say that it must be allowed. State statutes may provide that an organization can use proxies only if it is in the bylaws.

Note that Robert's Rules of Order *is against proxy voting for nonprofit organizations. Proxy voting is, however, an advisable method when a financial interest is inherent, for example business corporations, homeowner's associations, neighborhood associations, and owners.*

Here are questions to consider as you write your bylaws concerning proxy voting:

1. *Are proxies counted in the quorum and how?*

2. *Will the proxy be a general proxy or a limited proxy? A general proxy gives the person holding the proxy the right to vote as the holder sees fit on all issues and motions. A limited proxy is a signed proxy in which the signer stipulates the way that the holder is to vote on specific issues. The proxy holder must cast the member's vote the way the signer has designated on the proxy. The difference between a general proxy and a limited proxy is that a general proxy gives the proxy holder the discretion to cast a vote based on information discussed in the meeting.*

3. *Who is in charge of validating the proxy?*

4. *What is the procedure for counting the proxies with voting members present?*

5. *What is the form of the proxy?*

6. *Does your organization really need proxy voting? Will it complicate your meetings, or allow members to stay away so that they don't participate in the discussion? Could this method of voting ultimately put control of the organization in the hands of a few people?*

7. *Is the proxy valid for one meeting or does it expire after a short period of time?*

8. *Is it revocable?*

As you consider the preceding questions, remember why we have meetings: so that members can meet face to face, discuss and debate the issues, and arrive at a reasonable agreement through a vote. Members often come to meetings with their minds already made up, but after hearing the discussion they change their minds and vote differently. Proxies cut out that process.

Q: If a quorum is not present at a meeting, can the proxies be used to make up the quorum in order for a vote to be taken using the proxies?

A: *If an association's bylaws authorize voting by proxy, then the quorum should be based on attendance at meetings in person or by proxy.*

Q: Yesterday at our church these questions arose. Can the chair of a committee vote? Can ex officio members of a committee vote?

A: *The answer to your first question is yes. The chairman of a committee is a member of the committee and has all the rights that the other members have. Usually the chairman is the most active participant in the committee and has been selected because of his or her knowledge or interest in the committee work.*

The answer to the second question is also yes. Ex officio members of a committee can vote. According to Robert's Rules of Order, Newly Revised, *" . . . If the ex officio member of the board is under the authority of the society (that is, if he is a member, officer, or employee of the society), there is no distinction between him and the other board (or committee) members." If the ex officio person is not a member, he or she has all the rights and privileges and none of the obligations, and the ex officio person should not be counted in the quorum of the committee or board.*

Conferring ex officio status on members is a way to have people serve on committees or boards without having to appoint or elect them. The bylaws of an organization may state that the president is an ex officio member of a committee or that the pastor is an ex officio member of committees. Instead of someone being appointed to a committee by a board or elected to the committee by the membership, the person is appointed by virtue of his or her position or office in the organization or the community. Therefore, the ex officio person is a member of that committee with all the rights of membership unless your bylaws state differently.

Q: At a zoning board meeting, five votes were necessary to obtain a variance. By what authority was it specified that five votes were necessary to obtain a variance? I assumed that if there were no bylaws the abstaining votes go to the majority vote.

A: *If there are no bylaws, and if the board's parliamentary authority is* Robert's Rules of Order, *then the abstentions count as zero. However, if there is a state, city, or municipal law that says five votes are necessary for a variance, you follow that law. If not, then a simple majority should be enough to get the variance adopted. Consulting a lawyer about the legal status of the vote might be in order.*

If your organization has a rule that says it takes five to obtain any variance, then it takes five votes in the affirmative. If only six attend the meeting and the vote was four in favor and one opposed, an abstention is not a vote and is not counted either way. This is important to remember. However, since you did not get five affirmative votes, the one present who refused to vote did affect the vote. They in essence cast a "no" vote.

Q: **What is the proper way to break a tie during an election of officers? Should the president cast the tie-breaking vote? We recently had our yearly election, and there was a tie for one office. The president cast the tie-breaking vote after the ballots were counted. Should he have waited until the meeting came back to order, or was he right in casting the tie-breaking vote before the meeting resumed?**

A: *According to* Robert's Rules of Order *the president always votes in a ballot vote. Therefore he cannot break a tie vote because he cannot vote twice. He should have announced that the vote was a tie vote and that the members would keep voting until someone received a majority vote. If it is desired for the president to cast the tie-breaking ballot, he must hold his ballot until the result of the vote is announced. Then the president announces the result vote with his ballot.*

Q: When a roll call is taken on a motion, what is the order of the roll call vote? In other words, who votes first, second, etc.? Does this order change from motion to motion?

A: *The secretary takes the roll call in alphabetical order, but the president's name is read last. When a member's name is called, he or she can vote "yes," "no," "abstain," or "present" (which also means to abstain). If the member is not ready to vote, the answer is "pass." After the secretary reads the roll once, the secretary calls again the names of those members who answered "pass," giving them one more opportunity to vote.*

As the secretary calls each member's name, the secretary repeats how each member votes and marks it by the member's name. At the conclusion of the roll call, the president can ask if everyone has voted who wants to vote. At this time, members can also change their votes before the secretary tallies the votes and the result is announced by the president.

The secretary gives to the president the final number of those voting on each side and the number of those abstaining. The president announces the result and declares the motion adopted or defeated.

Q: I am the president of a volunteer fire company. We have recently had many discussions about the value of abstaining during the vote. We feel that the abstaining vote is actually a vote against the motion. Could you please provide the rules for how to handle this and tell us what alternatives we have?

A: *You need to find out the rules of your fire department regarding what constitutes a majority vote. If the rules state that all motions are adopted by a majority vote, then that means a majority of those voting. An abstention means, I am not voting. In that situation, an abstention does not affect the vote at all.*

If your rules say a "majority vote of those present," or a "majority vote of the entire membership," then an abstention could affect the vote.

Let's say you have ten at your meeting. Your rules say a "majority vote of those present." In this case, it would take six votes in the affirmative to adopt. So, if five voted for, two voted against, and three abstained, the motion is lost.

However, if the rules stated "a majority vote," then, taking the above vote, the motion carried because the majority was determined by those who voted, not by those present. The majority in that case is four.

In taking the vote, the presiding officer takes only the "aye" and "no" votes. He or she does not ask for abstentions. If the meeting is a big one, how can you tell who abstained? The only way is to take a counted vote, roll call, or ballot vote.

It is highly recommended that you have your rules or bylaws state "majority vote" because that means of those voting. However, if your group is a small board of fewer than ten members, having a rule that requires a majority vote of the entire board membership prevents a small group from getting together and pushing through business. Let's say there is a board of nine members, and five members is the quorum. If you have a rule that says just a majority vote, then at a meeting of five members, it could be possible for one or two to adopt motions if others abstain. Having all action adopted by a majority of the entire membership guarantees that at least five members are always in agreement, and this fact could solve problems that arise during controversial issues.

Q: When a main motion is before the assembly, may an assembly require more than a majority vote in order for the motion to be approved? More than a majority vote is not required by either parliamentary law or the rules of order of the assembly.

A: *If an assembly wants to change the vote required for the adoption of a main motion, some one has to make a motion to suspend the rules. This needs a second. It requires a two-thirds vote since it is taking away rights from the members.*

The member can state:

> I move to suspend the rules and have the vote taken on this main motion by a two-thirds vote.

Member 2: Second.

President: It is moved and second to suspend the rules and have the vote taken on this main motion by a two-thirds vote. All those in favor please rise. Be seated. Those oppose please rise. Be seated. The affirmative has it and the vote on this main motion will require a two-thirds vote.

If the negative won, the president says:

> There are less than two-thirds in the affirmative and the motion is lost. We will not be suspending the rules and requiring a two-thirds vote on this main motion. The motion will be adopted by a majority vote.

Q: Is it correct that for most elections abstentions are not counted as votes in determining the winner of an election requiring a majority? Are there any conditions where an absolute majority of eligible voters is necessary to declare a winner? In that case, can abstentions actually prevent a winner from being declared? Is the situation the same with invalid ballots, for example, someone voting for Mickey Mouse?

A: *Blanks are ignored because members may use them as a way of abstaining but yet appearing to vote. So, you are correct that abstentions are not counted.*

The only time when an absolute majority of eligible voters is required is when you have rules to that effect. For example, such a rule might say "a majority of the entire membership." In that case an abstention might prevent someone from getting elected. Let's take this example:

Your membership is 50.

A majority of the membership is 26.

Member X receives 25 votes.

Member Y receives 23 votes.

Two members abstain.

No one is elected because no one has a majority of the entire membership. It takes 26 votes for election.

Now about an invalid ballot? Robert's Rules of Order considers them illegal votes. A vote is illegal when:

1. *It has the name of someone who is not eligible to serve in the office, for example, Mickey Mouse. Or it could be a member who does not meet the requirements for office. A ballot that the tellers can't read is also considered an illegal ballot.*

2. *Two ballots are folded together, and each ballot has a name written on it. In this case, it is counted as one illegal ballot. If two ballots are folded together and one is blank, then the blank is ignored.*

An illegal ballot could affect the outcome of an election because it is counted in the total number of votes cast. Let's take this example:

30 votes are cast.

16 is the majority.

Member A receives 15 votes.

Member B receives 14 votes.

There is 1 illegal ballot.

The members will have to vote again because no candidate has received a majority vote. In this case, the illegal ballot did make a difference; it might have been cast for member A.

Q: I am aware that the president may vote to break a tie vote on a motion. Does the president have voting privileges on any other occasion or for any other reason?

A: *The president can vote to make or break a tie vote, can cast a ballot vote, and can vote in a roll call vote. The reason the president does not vote at other times is because his vote can influence the other members and how they vote. The president is to remain impartial. Since a ballot vote is secret, the president's vote can't influence others and that is why the president can vote at the same time as the members. In a roll call vote, the assembly is demanding that each member vote and that each state how he or she is voting for the record. The president has no choice but to vote in this vote and his name is called last.*

Q: What happens when the president's vote will cause a tie to occur on a motion? If the president's vote causes a tie vote to occur, then how is the matter resolved at that point?

A: *The motion is defeated.* Robert's Rules of Order *allows a president to vote to make a tie vote or break a tie vote. The president can also vote whenever his or her vote will affect the result. For example, the president can vote to cause a two-thirds vote or to prevent the attainment of a two-thirds vote.*

However, the president can't be forced to vote if he or she wants to remain impartial. In that case, if the motion is a tie, and the president does not want to vote, the motion is defeated. A tie vote is not a majority.

A tie vote means the motion is lost. Now what can you do? Another rule in parliamentary procedure is that members can't be asked to decide the same question twice at the same meeting unless they reconsider the vote. To reconsider the vote, a member must have voted on the prevailing side (in this case the negative vote could move to reconsider). However, the motion can be brought before the assembly again at the next meeting by anyone. It is handled as if it is a new main motion.

SECRETARY AND MINUTES

Q: **What is the main job of the secretary? If the secretary isn't cooperating with the board, does the board have any controls over him or her? Can the board dismiss the present officer and elect a new one? If so, how would you carry it out?**

A: *The role of a secretary is very important in any organization. The duties of the secretary should be listed in the bylaws, but* Robert's Rules of Order *also lists the secretary's duties. In general, the secretary is responsible for:*

1. *Keeping all the records of the organization, including committee reports, on file and the list of all the members.*

2. *Notifying members of their election to office, appointment to committees, and furnishing them with the proper documents.*

3. *Notifying members of election or appointment to be a delegate at a convention and furnishing them with credentials.*

4. *Signing all the minutes and other certified acts of the organization, unless the bylaws specify differently.*

5. *Maintaining the official documents of the organization including the bylaws, rules of order, standing rules and minutes. Keeping the bylaws and other governing documents up-to-date with any changes made through the amendment process and bringing these documents to the meeting.*

6. *Mailing to each member notice of each meeting.*

7. *Taking minutes at all business and board meetings, handling the correspondence, and preparing the agenda for the meetings unless the president prefers to do this. The secretary must know how to call a meeting to order if the president and vice president are absent and know how to preside until a temporary chairman is elected by the assembly.*

The secretary should cooperate with all members and be of service to the entire organization. The procedure to remove a secretary who is not cooperative (or any officer not performing his or her duties) should be found in your bylaws. If there is no provision for removing this officer, and if your bylaws do not state "or until the successor is elected," then you will have to hold a trial for removal.

If the bylaws provide for removal, follow that procedure. If your bylaws state "or until the successor is elected," you can rescind the election. This takes previous notice and a majority vote, or without previous notice a two-thirds vote or majority of the entire membership. The vacancy thus created can be filled by an election at the same meeting.

Q: With the advent of new technology, what is the appropriate method to use in binding minutes?

A: *You can purchase secretary's books of blank pages that can be printed on a computer and, when the book is finished, bound at a printer's. The books cost approximately $75. What you're buying is the original hardcover book with paper, and that is why it is expensive. It is refillable, however, so after the initial purchase you will just have to buy paper. After you've typed the minutes into the computer, remove the necessary number of blank pages in the book and use your printer to print the minutes on them. Replace the printed paper into the book. When the paper is used up, take all 150 pages to the printer's and have them bound and labeled with a date. Then order more paper and put it in the book. Any office supply store should be able to show you what is available.*

Q: Do you have any information on the proper forms of minutes? What should they include? What can be left out? Is there a difference between a formal meeting and an informal one as far as minutes are concerned? I am the secretary responsible for the minutes of four different types of meetings: a private company's board of directors' meetings, a private company's stockholders' meetings, the Kiwanis club's general meetings, and the Kiwanis club's board meetings. Where can I find out the proper and legal requirements of the minutes I am responsible for?

A: *For the most part, the form of the minutes is the same. Minutes record what was done at the meeting, not what is said. However, if any of these organizations publish the minutes, then you need a tape recorder because everything goes into the minutes word for word. Check with the Secretary of State's office in the state in which your company* *is incorporated to see if there are any specific guidelines for legal requirements of minutes. If so, you need to follow them. The important thing to remember about minutes is that they are the legal document of the meeting. Ask yourself: If we went to court, what would be most helpful to the judge or the jury in deciding an issue? Sometimes it is important to put background information into the minutes to explain why an action was taken by the assembly. Recording of a counted, roll call, or ballot vote may be proof of a quorum present.*

THE PRESIDENT

Q: Does a president of the board of directors have the authority to refuse to let a issue come before the board?

A: *No, a president does not have the authority to refuse to let an issue come before the board unless your organization has a written rule that says the president can. He or she can rule a motion out of order if it conflicts with your bylaws, corporate charter, national, state, and local law. He can also "object to consideration of the question," but that does not prevent the motion from coming before the board. This motion must be voted on by the rest of the board.*

Q: Does the president of the board of directors have the right to deny a guest permission to speak at a board meeting? The guest is a club member.

A: *Board meetings are usually conducted in executive session, which means that only members of the board can attend. So a guest would not be allowed to come to the meeting unless your board meetings are open meetings. The guest could attend if he or she was invited by the board to give input on an issue because the guest had special* *knowledge about the subject. In that case, after the guest had spoken and answered any questions, the guest would leave. He or she would not be allowed to participate in the debate.*

Q: Our committee has seven members, and an extra person has just shown up. Can I refuse to let that person speak or take part in the discussion?

A: *Committee meetings are conducted in executive session, and only members of the committee can attend. Unless a member is an ex officio member of the committee, he or she has no right to just "show up" and ask to participate in the committee meeting. Politely escort the member to the door and explain that only committee members are allowed to attend. (This is true unless your organization has rules to the contrary.)*

Q: One of our members is constantly causing problems because he and his wife don't like the club president. What can be done to stop it? This problem is wasting all our time and energy.

A: *Your president was voted in by a majority of the members and deserves everyone's support. It sounds to me as if you have a "democracy problem" in your organization—members not understanding the concepts of democracy, which require all members to abide by the majority rule even if they did not vote with the majority. The most diplomatic tactic would be for you to take them out to lunch and try to persuade them to be cooperative and encourage them to work with the president. These members need to see how detrimental their actions are to the entire organization.*

Q: How can a member of an organization bring items to the floor if the president refuses to put them on the agenda? The agenda does not include "old or new

business" or "unfinished business." It is also not customary for the association to approve the agenda at the beginning of the meeting. Can I ask for the approval of the agenda? Or can I make a motion at any time to include an item or items on the agenda?

A: *Yes, a member can bring items to the floor if the president does not put them on the agenda. The agenda is designed to serve the entire organization by bringing order to the meeting and helping members keep on track. It is not the "president's agenda" or his idea of what should go on at the meeting. The president has not been elected to enforce "his" or "her" will on the assembly. He or she has been elected to lead the organization and to be impartial and fair in conducting the meetings. The agenda should follow a standard order of business as found in* Robert's Rules of Order. *It should include unfinished business if there is any. Unfinished business is business left pending at the last meeting or postponed to the current meeting. It is found in the minutes of the previous meeting. The minutes should be read at the beginning of the meeting so that members know whether there is any unfinished business. If the president does not bring it up (the president and the secretary are responsible for putting it on the agenda), then a member can bring it up by rising to a parliamentary inquiry:*

Member: Mr. President (or Madam President), I rise to a parliamentary inquiry.

President: Please state your inquiry.

Member: The minutes state that X motion was postponed to this meeting. I noticed that the agenda doesn't list any unfinished business. Will the president kindly inform this member when it will be presented to the assembly?

The president is now responsible for telling you when motion X will be brought up. By using this technique, you are alerting the members that something has been left off the agenda, and you are doing it in a nice way.

Is your president a dictator or just uninformed? If the president is uninformed, then perhaps you can privately show him or her the order of the business meeting in your parliamentary authority. If the president is a tyrant who wants to do things his or her way, then you have a bigger problem.

After the minutes are read and before any other business is transacted, rise to a parliamentary inquiry and ask why no unfinished business or new business is on the agenda. Then ask that the following items be added to the agenda. If the president does not do this, then make a motion to adopt the agenda with unfinished business and new business added to the agenda. It will need a second and it takes a majority vote to adopt.

If the president still ignores you, then raise a point of order. If he ignores the point of order, then make the motion again. If it is seconded, and the president still ignores the motion, then you have the right to place the motion before the board, ask for discussion and take the vote.

You can use this technique anytime the president ignores a legitimate motion that has been seconded. However, all the steps that were just given have to be followed exactly.

Q: **What can be done when the president has overstepped his or her role as facilitator, and how do you correct the mistake? Also, is the president solely responsible for appointing members of committees from the board?**

A: *To correct the president during a meeting, the procedure is to stand and say:*

Member: Madam President (or Mr. President), I rise to a point of order.

Or just stand and say

> Point of order.

The president should respond,

President: Please state your point.

You now state the correct procedure. The chair then rules on your point. Either the chair agrees with your point and corrects what he or she is doing wrong, or the chair does not agree with your point and proceeds with what he or she is doing.

President: Your point is well taken.

or

> Your point is not well taken.

If you don't agree with the chair's ruling, you can appeal from the decision of the chair. This needs a second. However, if the chair really doesn't know the proper procedure, you should speak with him or her outside the meeting and share helpful information.

The answer to your second question is found in your organization's bylaws or standing rules. For the president to have the power to appoint committees, the bylaws must give him or her that authority. If the bylaws do not say who appoints committees, then the assembly will have to appoint them.

Q: Can business be conducted after a meeting has been officially adjourned? In this case, the meeting was adjourned, the office manager went to the door to ascertain that a certain leader had left, and then the manager reconvened the meeting to do business.

A: *What was done was unethical, undemocratic, and unkind. If any business was transacted after the meeting* *adjourned, it is null and void. When a meeting adjourns, it is over; it is finished.* Robert's Rules of Order *states the chair can call a meeting back to order in only one situation: when a member was trying to obtain the floor, before the chair declared the adjournment, for the purpose of*

> *Giving an important announcement.*

> *Making the motion to reconsider.*

> *Making the motion to reconsider and enter into the minutes.*

> *Giving previous notice about a motion to be made at the next meeting.*

> *Setting the time for an adjourned meeting.*

When the manager tried to reconvene the meeting, someone should have stopped him or her immediately. How is this group going to function harmoniously if members realize they are purposely being left out of business and discussion?

Q: Can a president make a motion or second a motion?

A: *It depends. In a board meeting of fewer than twelve members (unless you have rules to the contrary), a president can make motions, second motions, discuss motions, and vote on motions. If it is a general membership meeting, the president is to remain impartial. He or she should not make a motion or second it. However, there is an exception. Let's say the treasurer presents a bill to be paid. The president can assume a motion, and say:*

President: The treasurer has presented a bill for X
dollars. Is there any discussion? All those in
favor say "Aye." Those opposed say "No."

Then the president announces the vote. This is a great way to expedite business.

The other situation in which a president can make a motion is when he or she steps down from the chair and lets the vice president preside until the motion is dispensed with. However, the best practice is for the president to find another member who is willing to present the motion.

When someone is elected to the office of president, that person must remember that he or she serves all the members. The effective president in any organization is the one that remains impartial in conducting the meetings.

Q: At a recent city council meeting, the mayor said, "As chairman, I always have the last word in any discussion." He also said that he had looked this up in *Robert's Rules of Order* . . . . I have been a member of a board of education for the past 17 years and have used *Robert's Rules*; I do not remember ever seeing that the chair always has the last word. Maybe I don't have a complete copy. Maybe he is not accurate. Would you please let me know if there is such a reference?

A: *Oh, if we could all have the last word! There is one time when the chair has the last word, and that is on a debatable appeal to the chair's ruling. According to parliamentary rules, in a debatable appeal the presiding officer has the first right to speak to the appeal and the last right to speak to the appeal. The other time the presiding officer has the last word is when saying, "The meeting is adjourned" (and then only if the other members agree about adjourning!).*

NOMINATIONS AND ELECTIONS

Q: Do you need a second on a nomination? For example, I nominate John Smith as chairman. Do I need a second before his name can be put on the ballot for this position?

A: *No second is required. Any member who is eligible to serve can be written on a ballot.* Robert's Rules of Order *clearly states that a person does not have to be nominated to be elected. Thus, on a written ballot someone could be elected through a write-in campaign.*

Q: Are there any rules, in *Robert's Rules of Order* or elsewhere, that forbid a person from running for two offices at the same time, such as president and vice president, or president and senator. This has come up during nominations for officers and directors at our conservation club, and we need a clarification.

A: *There is no general parliamentary prohibition against a person being nominated for more than one office unless the bylaws of an organization prohibit it. However, it is usually understood that members hold only one office at a time. If a member is elected to two offices and he or she is present when the election takes place, the member should choose in which office he or she wants to serve. If the member is not present, then the other members can decide in which office they want him or her to serve.*

If you can await the logical sequence of events, the situation may resolve itself. Perhaps the member will be elected to only one office. If not, the preceding information will help you decide what to do next.

Q: Once the floor has been closed for nominations, can the president reopen the floor for nominations? And if so, in which cases or circumstances?

A: Robert's Rules of Order *says that nominations can be reopened for any reason by a majority vote. A member needs* *to make the motion to reopen the nominations, or the chair could assume a motion by stating:*

Chairman: Is there any objection to reopening the nominations? Hearing none, nominations are now reopened.

If there is an objection, the chair takes a vote.

Chairman: All those in favor say "Aye." Those opposed say "No."[*Then announce the vote.*]

One case for reopening nominations might be when someone has been elected to office and then has immediately declined the position. Another case might be when the assembly has voted many times but no one has received enough votes to be elected, and the members want to consider adding someone else's name to the list.

Q: Does the nominating committee have the only right to nominate an officer or can a member also nominate someone? And if a member can do it, what is the procedure for getting the floor and nominating someone?

A: *Check your organization's bylaws for specifics on the nominating and electing process. Those are the rules that the members must obey. But to answer your question in general parliamentary terms, the nominating committee should try to find the best candidate for the office and should not let personal feelings get in the way of nominating someone. And the person they want to nominate should be contacted to see if he or she is willing to serve. However, if the committee disagrees about the nomination, those on the committee who are in the minority may propose other nominees for some or all of the offices when the presiding officer asks for nominations from the floor (from the members).*

In Robert's Rules of Order, *this is the general procedure for nominations:*

1. *The nominating committee gives its report by stating the nominees for each office.*

2. *The presiding officer repeats the nominations of the committee for each office and asks,*

Are there further nominations?

At this time, any member can rise and nominate someone (a nomination does not need a second), unless your bylaws state differently.

3. *The presiding officer repeats the nomination and asks if there are any further nominations. This continues until no one responds, and the presiding officer closes the nominations for that office and goes on to the next office.* Robert's Rules of Order *says that the procedure an organization follows should be clearly written in the bylaws or standing rules.*

If your organization is not following this procedure of taking nominations from the floor, check the bylaws or standing rules to see whether they prohibit it. If there is no prohibition, and the presiding officer does not ask for nominations from the floor, you can raise a point of order. (However, it would be better to talk to the presiding officer before the meeting and show him or her the pages in Robert's Rules of Order *that explain the procedure.*

If your organization takes the vote by ballot, you can wage a write-in campaign. According to Robert's Rules of Order, *a member does not have to be nominated to be elected, but the member does have to be eligible to serve. So, in the case of a ballot vote, it is possible to write in the name of someone who has not been nominated.*

Q: Our church bylaws require the nominating committee to present "a slate of candidates" for the board of trustees (among other bodies). In terms of parliamentary procedure, does "a slate" mean only the number of candidates equal to the number of vacancies, or may it mean at least a number of candidates equal to the number of vacancies? (Webster's defines "slate" as "a list of candidates.")

A: *A slate means a nominee for each office. So if you have three offices to elect—president, secretary, and treasurer—the slate is a nominee for each office. A single slate is a nominee for each office. A multiple slate is more than one nominee for each office. From a parliamentary law point of view, it is best for the nominating committee to choose only one nominee for each office—the best nominee. If the committee members are required to come up with more than one candidate, they may have to choose someone who isn't as qualified. If they choose two who are equally qualified, one is sure to lose, and the loser may decline to be nominated again. Electing officers in organizations is different than our national elections where we always have two candidates from which to choose. In organizations, it is best not to make members compete against each other. Organizations need to promote cooperation. However, if the members feel that the nominating committee is playing politics and is not nominating the best candidate, then by all means the members should nominate someone else.*

OTHER OFFICERS

Q: We are a small neighborhood association (20 members) with a president, vice president, recording secretary, corresponding secretary, treasurer, and a chairman of the board. The chairman of the board's duties are not spelled out in the bylaws. Just *what* does a board chairman do?

A: *If your bylaws don't give the chairman any duties, then his or her primary duty is conducting the board meetings; the association president conducts the membership meetings.*

Q: Does the parliamentarian have a vote on motions, and can he or she speak to motions?

A: *If the parliamentarian is not a member of the organization, he or she would not be entitled to vote or debate motions.*

If the parliamentarian is a member and sits in front by the president, he or she is not entitled to make motions, discuss motions, or vote. People look to the parliamentarian as an authority, and therefore impartial, and it would be improper for him or her to sway the vote. However, the parliamentarian, if a member, can vote in a ballot vote just as the president can.

If a member is considered the parliamentarian and sits with the assembly during the meetings and does not advise the chair during the meetings, then perhaps the parliamentarian would have the right to make motions, discuss them, and vote.

Q: Could you please give me some insight as to how the parliamentarian should act during a meeting? I'd like to know how much input this person is allowed during discussion on a particular matter.

A: *How the parliamentarian should act during a meeting is dependent on several things. If the parliamentarian is a member of the organization, he or she has all the rights of the members: to make motions, debate, and vote except when he or she is seated in the front next to the president. When the parliamentarian is seated by the president, he or she gives up* the right to make motions, debate, and vote (except in a ballot vote). The parliamentarian is there only as an advisor. Any comments made to the president should be inconspicuous. He or she only gives advice; the president still makes the rulings.

If the parliamentarian is a member of an organization that wants him or her to function as a parliamentarian, the parliamentarian can choose not to sit by the president. In this way, he or she doesn't give up the right to speak and vote. Note that this decision does not prevent the parliamentarian from meeting beforehand with the president to go over the agenda. In many cases, the parliamentarian can write a meeting script for the president to follow if the officer is not familiar with conducting meetings. Before the meeting, the parliamentarian can discuss with the president any controversial issues or any procedures with which the officer is unfamiliar. The parliamentarian and the president then can discuss ways to handle any problems that may arise during the meeting. In the meeting if the members get lost, the president can ask the parliamentarian what the correct procedure is. The parliamentarian can speak from where he or she is seated and tell the assembly what the correct procedure is. Then it is the president's duty to decide what to do. (The president always makes the rulings.)

A parliamentarian is an advisor; the position is not one of power. Unfortunately, in many organizations this office is very misused.

EX OFFICIO OFFICERS AND MEMBERS

Q: I am the recording secretary for the Parking Advisory Board. We are trying to set up some bylaws.

We are looking for a definition of ex officio member, and need to know whether such a member has voting rights.

A: *You need to first adopt a parliamentary authority.* Robert's Rules of Order *is an example of a parliamentary authority. When you adopt an authority, it will help you define ex officio member. A person usually becomes an ex officio member of an organization by virtue of his or her office. Many times the president of an organization is an ex officio member of a board or committee. Perhaps you would like someone in the community who works in a related field to be an ex officio member of your board. If that person leaves his or her position, he or she is no longer a member of your board, but whoever follows that person would then become a member ex officio.*

An ex officio member has all the rights of membership: the right to make motions, debate, and vote. Members who are ex officio and who are also members of the organization are counted in the quorum. Those who are not members of the organization are not counted in the quorum, but they still have the other rights of membership.

Q: My church's bylaws provide for ex officio members on the various governing boards and committees. The bylaws are silent, however, regarding the voting rights of these ex officio members. Do the ex officio members count toward a quorum?

A: *If the ex officio members are members of the church, they count in the quorum and have the right to make motions, debate, and vote. If the ex officio members are not members of the church, they have the right to make motions, debate, and vote; but they are not counted in the quorum.*

QUORUM

Q: I am interested in the rules about quorums as set forth in *Robert's Rules of Order*. What is the least number needed to open the board of directors' meeting? Is it just one more than fifty percent?

A: *The quorum is, or should be, specified in your bylaws. If it is not,* Robert's Rules of Order *states that it is a majority (more than half) of all the members.*

In boards or committees, if the quorum is not established in the bylaws or by rule of a parent organization or even state statutes, it is a majority of the members of the board or committee. A board or a committee does not have the power to establish its own quorum unless the bylaws give them that power. So, look at your bylaws carefully to make this determination.

Q: I am looking for information on how many members must vote to form a quorum with committee sizes of 5, 7, and 9?

A: *The members do not vote to form a quorum. The quorum of your committees should be stated somewhere in your governing documents, preferably your bylaws. However, if no quorum is stated, then* Robert's Rules of Order *says it is a majority of the members of the committee:*

The quorum of a 5-member committee is 3.

The quorum of a 7-member committee is 4.

The quorum of a 9-member committee is 5.

MEETINGS

Q: What is the procedure for ensuring that items are not added to the agenda during the actual board meeting? Or how do you prevent this from occurring?

A: *If the agenda is not adopted at the beginning of the meeting, items can be added by any member just by making a motion to add an agenda item at the time when "new business" is called for by the chair. If the agenda is adopted at the beginning by a majority vote, then it takes a two-thirds vote to amend the agenda by adding something to it.*

The purpose of an agenda is to keep order, keep the meeting on track, and expedite business. The agenda should be flexible, enabling members to bring business before the assembly, not preventing them from bringing business. Only items requiring notice cannot be added.

One reason for adopting an agenda may be that the meeting time is short; adopting the agenda thus expedites the business so that it can all be completed. An agenda should not be adopted for the purpose of excluding ideas. The president should not impose his or her own agenda on the members. The president is to preside and see that the members' wishes are carried out and that all members have the right to bring business before the board. The chairman protects everyone's rights by preventing dilatory motions. The members should decide what is to come before the board.

Q: We are between sessions of a meeting that was adjourned to meet tomorrow. A controversial motion is on the floor, and we need to know who has a right to vote at the meeting on Friday. Our bylaws state only members who are current in dues and who have attended at least three meetings in the previous twelve months. The question is: Does the sign-in sheet for the first session on Wednesday serve as the sign-in for the second session? Or, if more qualified members attend, are they allowed to vote?

A: *An adjourned meeting is a legal continuation of a meeting. The meeting that happens tomorrow is therefore a legal continuation of the meeting held on Wednesday evening. It is not a second meeting. So the people who signed in at the Wednesday meeting are still considered present unless you mark them off the sheet as having "left" the meeting early. And anyone coming to this meeting who wasn't at the meeting on Wednesday would be signing in as someone who came in "late to the meeting." It might be wise to have a sign-in sheet entitled "Adjourned meeting" with Friday's date and then staple it to the sign-in sheet of the Wednesday meeting.*

The rule for voting privileges at the adjourned meeting is the same as the rule at the regular meeting on Wednesday evening. The Friday meeting is not considered a separate meeting.

Based on the information given in your question, if someone did not come to the meeting on Wednesday evening but attends tomorrow and is current in dues and has attended at least three meetings in the previous twelve months, that member would be allowed to vote. It is as if the person were coming in late. Would you allow latecomers to vote if this meeting were held all in one day? If you would, then they can vote at this adjourned meeting.

Q: We have received information that at an upcoming not-for-profit board meeting some people plan to attend who are not duly elected but who are concerned. It would seem logical that nonmembers cannot attend, because otherwise you would have a free-for-all at meetings. The organization's constitution is silent on the matter. Is there a source that answers this question?

A: Robert's Rules of Order *states that board meetings are customarily held in "executive session," which means only the elected board members can attend. Do these members of the organization have a specific issue that they want to bring to the board?*

1. *If they do, then why not give them a hearing. After they've had their say, politely ask them to leave; or escort them graciously to the door, assuring them that the board will conscientiously consider their request and will make the board's decision known.*

2. *Another course of action would be for the board to ask the members to put their concerns in writing. Then the board could take up their concerns at a meeting.*

3. *If these are curiosity seekers just wanting to see what the board is "up to," then explain that the meeting is "closed" and is for board members only and that the full body will receive the board's report at the next regular membership meeting.*

Usually the board is authorized to handle business between membership meetings, with the members having the right to override board decisions unless duties are specifically given to the board in the bylaws.

Q: Can the chair of a committee make a motion during the committee meeting?

A: *Yes, the chair can make motions, debate motions, and vote on motions. In committees, the chairman is usually the most active participant in the committee work. This is true for committees smaller than twelve. If it is a public body, then the rules may be different. If the committee is larger than twelve, then the chairman is more of a presiding officer at meetings, and the rules of formal meetings apply to committee work. That means he or she can't make motions, debate motions, and can vote only to make or break a tie vote, or to vote in a ballot vote.*

Q: If a member of a board has a profound conflict of interest, should he or she leave the meeting during the time the area of conflict is under discussion? Is there a specific citation for a ruling?

A: *Let's first define what a conflict of interest is. It means a question of direct personal or monetary interest that is not common to other members of the organization. However, if the member is being considered with other members in a motion or is being elected to office, he or she is allowed to vote. The general principle in parliamentary law is that when a member has a "conflict of interest," he or she does not enter into the discussion or vote on the matter. However, there is no rule that says the member has to leave the room when others are discussing the issue. The other principle of parliamentary law is that if the member is not allowed to vote, he or she is also not counted in the quorum. So be forewarned: If a member is not able to vote on an issue, and his or her participation is needed for a quorum, then no vote can be taken on the issue.*

Q: What is the procedure in a meeting where members are on trial for misconduct?

A: *Since a trial is a serious event for any organization and should rarely be used, there are specific procedures to follow to protect the rights of the accused.*

1. *A trial is held in executive session.*

2. *The accused has a right to due process—to be notified of the charges, given time to prepare a defense, and the right to appear and defend himself or herself.*

However, there are several steps that must happen before a trial can take place. The first step when members hear of misconduct by another member is to choose a committee to investigate the validity of the reports and to see if charges should be made. The members of this committee should be chosen for their integrity and good judgment. To establish such a committee requires that a resolution be made, seconded, discussed, and voted on. This resolution should avoid as much detail as possible to protect the parties, who may be innocent.

In the second step, the committee should quietly conduct its investigation and make a sincere effort to get the facts. Any information collected is confidential. The committee should also talk with the accused to hear his or her side of the story. If the committee members find that the reports of misconduct are untrue, then they should prepare a report and resolution for clearing the accused. If they find substantial evidence that the report of misconduct is true, the next step is to report the findings and prefer charges.

Next, the investigating committee prepares several resolutions. The first resolution includes setting a date and time for a meeting for the trial. It states that member X is to appear to show why he or she should not be expelled from the organization and states the specific charges. A second resolution establishes the trial committee and its members. It should have different members than those of the investigating committee.

If the members adopt the resolutions to have a trial, then the secretary immediately sends by registered mail a letter notifying the accused of the time, date, place of the trial, and the charges against him or her. (The letter should include a copy of the exact charges.) At the trial the secretary should have on-hand a copy of the letter that was sent to the accused and a "signed return receipt" to prove that he or she received the letter.

The trial is a hearing. The managers present the evidence against the accused. The accused has a right to be represented by counsel and to speak and present witnesses in his or her own defense. The defense counsel may be an attorney but must be a member of the organization, unless the organization agrees by a vote to allow a nonmember to represent the accused.

At the beginning of the trial, the charges are read and the accused is asked how he or she pleads. If the accused answers guilty, there is no reason to proceed with the trial. If he or she pleads not guilty, the members proceed with opening statements by the managers and then by the accused. Next are witnesses by the managers and then by the accused. Rebuttal of witnesses by the managers, then by the accused, is followed by closing arguments on both sides.

After closing arguments, the accused leaves the room and the assembly discusses and takes a vote. Each charge is read and debated and voted on. If the accused is found guilty, the next business in order is determining the penalty. Usually the managers propose the penalty. It is a debatable and amendable motion. One member can demand that the vote be taken by ballot. If the member is to be removed from membership, a two-thirds vote is needed. After the penalty is decided, the accused is brought back into the assembly and told the results.

A trial is an extreme measure. The best policy is to talk to the member and see what can be resolved before the situation ever reaches this proceeding.

MOTIONS

Q: Does a resolution need to have a second?

A: *A resolution is a formal way of phrasing a main motion. If it is proposed by a single member, it needs a second. If a committee of more than one has voted to present a resolution to the membership, it does not need a second.*

Q: If a motion has been rejected, can the same motion be brought before the membership to be voted on again?

A: *A main motion that is defeated usually cannot be brought up again at the same meeting (unless someone who voted on the prevailing side moves to reconsider the vote or changed by time or circumstance). However, it can be brought up again at another meeting. This is called renewing the motion.*

Q: I have read many guides that tell you what to do but not exactly how to do it. For example, when someone makes a motion to do something, what are the exact words to say and what are the responses from the chair?

A: *When a person makes a motion, he or she should phrase it in the positive and say "I move to . . . " or "I move that . . . " and state what it is he or she wants to do.*

The chair says:

Chairman: It is moved and seconded that . . . . [*repeats the motion*] Is there any discussion?

If the motion does not get a second, the chair can ask for a second:

Chairman: Is there a second?

If no second is forthcoming, the motion is not before the assembly and the chair says:

Chairman: Since there is no second, the motion is not before the assembly. Is there further business?

Q: **When a motion is made to table something and a second is made, does the full board then need to vote on the motion and the second? It has been my interpretation that a vote is not needed when a motion is made and seconded to table something.**

A: *A vote is taken on all motions made and seconded. The motion you asked about is the motion to lay on the table. The correct procedure is to take a vote immediately on the motion to lay on the table; it is not debated. Now, about this motion. It should be used only to set business aside temporarily for more urgent business. If you want to "table it to the next meeting" or "to later in the meeting," the correct motion is to postpone it. This motion needs a second and is debatable. To lay a motion on the table is taking away the members' rights to debate without taking a two-thirds vote. It is really a very undemocratic motion unless it is used correctly. The member who makes the motion should give the reason for wanting to temporarily set aside the pending business. If the president does not agree that the business is urgent, the president can rule the motion out of order or restate the motion as the motion to postpone to a later time.*

Another important point about the motion to lay on the table is that it is recorded in the minutes but is not put on the agenda if it carries over to the next meeting because it has been "temporarily put aside." It is normally taken from the table during the same meeting. Since the members moved to put it on the table, the members are responsible for making the motion to take it from the table. The assembly must be careful that this motion is not used as the motion to "kill." If the intent is to kill the motion, the chair should rule it out of order. The proper motion to kill is to postpone indefinitely.

PART V

APPENDICES

Appendices

APPENDIX A

How to Make Your Meetings Go More Smoothly

How many times have you attended a meeting that promised to be brief, and then went on and on for hours? There is a solution. Know the rules of order in a meeting and use them! The following tips are substantial meeting timesavers, and everyone in attendance—from the president to committee chairmen and general members—should be familiar with these tips and utilize them to create more effective meetings.

1. Presidents who know *Robert's Rules of Order* well, will know how to keep discussion moving and when to take a vote without someone having to **call for the question**. They know that no one can discuss an issue unless a motion is made and then seconded. This saves time! If a motion isn't seconded, it isn't discussed. (A second does not mean the person is in favor of the idea, just that he or she thinks it should be discussed.) How many times have you seen someone ramble on about a topic that no one else is interested in, and, because no one knows or follows the rules, valuable time is lost by allowing this person to keep talking without a motion being on the floor.

2. Another time waster is poorly worded or incomplete motions. Providing members with paper and pencil to compose a clearly worded motion can save time because it doesn't have to be amended many times

to make it clear, nor does it have to be withdrawn and the whole process started over again. A well-thought-out motion includes what the group is to do, how and when it is to be done, and how much time and money is to be spent.

3. In debate, a great deal of time can be saved by giving people the information they need before the meeting so they can have their ideas well formulated before they discuss them.

4. Avoid calling on committee chairmen to give reports when they don't have one to give or when they aren't there. The president should call every committee chairman before the meeting to make sure that he or she will be at the meeting and has a report to give. Only those chairmen who have a report ready should be called on.

5. To expedite the giving of reports, chairmen should sit in the front so that they don't waste time getting to the front to give their reports. If a committee is researching a project and is supposed to give a recommendation to the members in its report, the recommendation should be phrased as a motion, not a recommendation. The motion should come at the end of the report, and the reporting member of the committee (usually the chairman) states:

Committee Chairman:

> By direction of the committee,
> I move that . . .

A motion coming from a committee does not need a second because at least one other committee member has agreed that it should be discussed. Eliminating the second cuts out a step. If a committee makes a recommendation, someone still has to make a motion to accept the committee's recommendation. A motion from a committee of one requires a second.

6. The president needs to know when to call for the vote. Let's say someone has made a motion, and the chair has repeated it.

Chairman: It is moved and seconded to . . . Is there any discussion?

If the chair looks around and no one is standing to discuss it, the chair can say:

Chairman: As many as are in favor say "Aye." [*Wait for the response from the group.*]

Chairman: Those opposed say "No." [*Wait for the response; then announce the vote.*]

Chairman: The ayes have it, and the motion is carried. We will do . . . and [*give the member's name*] will carry it out.

or

Chairman: The noes have it, and the motion is lost. [*Then go on to the next business in order.*]

7. Many people forget that a member can speak only twice to a motion and can take a second turn only after everyone who wants to speak for the first time has done so. This keeps debate going and stops any member who is always popping up to talk after each member speaks.

8. Presidents can assume a motion. For example, a president does not have to wait for someone to move that the minutes be approved as read or corrected. He or she can state:

President: If no objection, the minutes are approved as read (or corrected).

Remember that the treasurer's report is not approved by the assembly; it is filed! However, the auditor's report is approved.

After the auditor's report is given, the chair should assume the motion and say:

Chairman: As many as are in favor of adopting the auditor's report say "Aye"; those opposed say "No." [*Then announce the vote.*]

If the treasurer presents bills to the assembly for payment, the president can ask whether there is any discussion or questions, and then assume the motion by saying:

Chairman: As many as are in favor of paying the bills say "Aye"; those opposed say "No." [*Then announce the vote.*]

Another motion that the chair can assume is the unqualified motion to adjourn. However, this is done only after all business has been brought forth, and no one is standing to present more. The chair can ask:

Chairman: Is there any further business? [*Pause, wait for someone to rise, and if no one does, then say:*]

Chairman: Is there any objection to adjourning the meeting? [*Pause to see if anyone objects.*] Since there is no objection, this meeting is adjourned.

Even though the chair has the authority to assume the unqualified motion to adjourn, the chair cannot close the meeting simply because he or she wants to go home or wants to prevent controversial business or any other business from coming forward. If the chair says the meeting is adjourned and one member objects, the chair must take a vote and say:

Chairman: As many as are in favor of adjourning the meeting say "Aye;" those opposed say "No."

9. A common time waster is asking for unfinished business when there is none. Before the meeting, the chair checks to see whether the agenda has any unfinished business on it. Part of the secretary's duty is to put all unfinished business on the agenda. This information is found in the minutes of the previous meeting. For example, a motion to postpone some business to the next meeting, or a motion left pending at the previous meeting when it was adjourned, is considered unfinished business. If there is no unfinished business, the chair goes right on to new business. Think of how many times you've been at a meeting when the chair asks for unfinished business and then looks around the room for someone to stand. Meanwhile, everyone else is looking around the room too, waiting for someone to stand. And no one does.

10. An effective president, a leader, provides the membership with information so that they too know how to keep meetings moving.

11. Every member should know the following:

- How to obtain the floor to make a motion or to speak to a motion.

- How to phrase a motion.

- The ranking of motions (presidents and secretaries need to know this too).

- Member's rights in debate.

- When the president has overstepped his or her role as facilitator and how to correct it.

The purpose of these timesavers is to keep a meeting going, not to take away the rights of the members!

APPENDIX B

Correct Parliamentary Terminology

This section gives the correct way to state a motion and the correct way for the presiding officer to repeat the motion to the assembly. Every motion listed in this book from a main motion to motions that bring a question again before the assembly is illustrated below. Examples for the member come first, then those for the presiding officer, and then those for how to take the vote and announce the vote. The motions are listed in order of rank, beginning with the main motion.

MAIN MOTIONS

* *To obtain the floor say:*

> [*rise*] Madam Chairman or Mr. Chairman; Madam President or Mr. President.

* *To make a motion say:*

> I move that . . .

or

> I move to . . . .

* *The chair states:*

> It is moved and seconded that . . . . Is there any discussion?

Voting

* *In taking the vote, the chair states:*

> All those in favor say "Aye." Those opposed say "No."

* *In announcing the voice vote, the chair states:*

> The ayes have it, and the motion is carried. We will be . . . , and [*give member's name*] will do it.

or

> The noes have it, and the motion is lost. We will not be doing . . . .

* *In taking a rising vote, the chair states:*

> All those in favor please rise. Be seated. Those opposed please rise. Be seated.

* *In announcing a rising vote, the voice states:*

> The affirmative has it, and the motion is carried. We will . . . , and [*give member's name*] will do it.

or

> The negative has it, and the motion is lost. We will not do . . . .

* *When a member doubts the result of a voice vote, the member calls out:*

> Division.

or

> I call for a division.

* *The chair states:*

> A division has been called for. All those in favor please rise. Be seated. Those opposed please rise. Be seated. [*Announce the vote.*]

Postpone Indefinitely (Kill a Motion)

* *To make the motion to postpone indefinitely:*

> I move that the motion be postponed indefinitely.

* *The chair states:*

> It is moved and seconded to postpone the motion indefinitely. Is there any discussion?

* *The chair takes the vote:*

> All those in favor of postponing indefinitely say "aye." Those opposed say "no."

* *Announcing the affirmative vote:*

> The ayes have it and the motion is carried. The motion is postponed indefinitely. That means it is killed for the duration of this meeting unless someone who voted in the affirmative moves to reconsider the vote. Is there further business?

* *Announcing the negative vote:*

> The noes have it and the motion is lost. Is there further discussion on [*the main motion; chair states what it is*]

Amend

* *To make a motion to amend, a member says:*

> I move to amend the motion by adding at the end . . . .

or

> I move to amend the motion by inserting . . . after . . . .

or

> I move to amend the motion by striking out . . . and inserting . . . .

or

> I move to amend the motion by striking out . . . .

* *How the chair states the motion to amend:*

> It is moved and seconded to amend the motion by adding at the end . . . .
> If amended, the motion would read . . . .
> Is there any discussion on the proposed amendment?

or

> It is moved and seconded to amend the motion by striking out . . . and inserting . . . . If amended, the motion would read . . . . Is there any discussion on the proposed amendment?

or

> It is moved and seconded to amend the motion by striking out . . . . If amended, the motion would read . . . . Is there any discussion on the proposed amendment?

* *How the chair takes a vote on amendments:*

> The question is on the adoption of the proposed amendment to add at the end . . . . All those in favor say "Aye." Those opposed say "No."

* *To announce the affirmative vote, the chair states:*

> The ayes have it, and the motion is amended. . . . will be added to the end. The question is on the adoption of the motion as amended. [*State the motion as amended.*] Is there any discussion?

* *To announce the negative vote, the chair states:*

> The noes have it, and the amendment is lost. The question is on the adoption of the motion . . . . Is there further discussion?

Refer to a Committee (Commit)

* *To make the motion to commit:*

> I move to refer the motion to the . . . committee, to do . . . and report back at the next meeting.

* *The chair states:*

> It is moved and seconded to refer the motion to the . . . committee, to do . . . and report back at the next meeting. Is there any discussion on referring to a committee?

* *The chair takes a vote:*

> All those in favor of referring the motion to the . . . committee say "Aye." Those opposed say "No."

* *In announcing the affirmative vote, the chair says:*

> The ayes have it, and the motion is referred to the . . . committee, to do . . . and report back at the next meeting. Is there further business? [*Or announce what the business is.*]

* *In announcing the negative vote, the chair says:*

> The noes have it, and the motion is not referred to the . . . committee. Is there further discussion?

Postpone to a Certain Time

* *To make the motion to postpone:*

> I move to postpone the motion to . . . [*State time or date or both, and if it is to be made a special order.*]

* *The chair states the motion:*

> It is moved and seconded to postpone the motion to . . . . Is there any discussion on postponing the motion?

* *The chair takes a vote:*

> [*If the motion is to be a general order, it is a voice vote.*] All those in favor of postponing the motion, say "Aye." Those opposed say "No."

* *In announcing the affirmative vote, the chair states:*

> The ayes have it, and the motion is postponed to . . . . Is there further business? [*Or announce it.*]

* *In announcing the negative vote, the chair states:*

> The noes have it, and the motion to postpone is lost. Is there further discussion on . . . .?

* *In taking the vote when the motion to postpone includes making the main motion a special order, the chair states:*

> All those in favor of postponing the motion to . . . and be made a special order for . . . please rise. Be seated. Those opposed please rise, be seated. [*takes a two-thirds vote to adopt*]

* *In announcing the affirmative vote, the chair states:*

> The affirmative has it, and the motion will be postponed to . . . and made a special order for . . . . Is there further business? [*Or announce what the business is.*]

* *In announcing the negative vote, the chair states:*

> The negative has it, and the motion to postpone is lost. Is there further discussion?

Limit or Extend Debate

* *To make the motion to limit or extend debate, a member says:*

> I move to limit debate to . . . .

or

> I move to extend debate to . . . .

* *The chair states the motion and immediately takes a vote:*

> It is moved and seconded to limit debate to . . . . All those in favor please rise. Those opposed please rise. [*takes a two-thirds vote to adopt*]

* *In announcing the vote, the chair states:*

> The affirmative has it, and debate will be limited (or extended) to . . . . Is there further discussion?

or

> The negative has it, and debate will not be limited (or extended) to . . . . Is there further discussion?

Close Debate (Previous Question)

* *To make the motion to close debate (previous question), a member says:*

> I move the previous question.

or

> I move to close debate.

Note: The Previous Question can be moved on the immediately pending question, on all pending questions, or on consecutive pending questions.

* *The chair states:*

> It is moved and seconded to close debate. If adopted, debate will cease on the pending question. All those in favor please rise. Be seated. Those opposed please rise. Be seated. [*requires a two-thirds vote*]

* *Or the chair could say:*

> The question is on the adoption of the previous question. If adopted, debate will stop on the pending motion. All those in favor please rise. Be seated. Those opposed please rise. Be seated. [*requires a two-thirds vote*]

* *In announcing an affirmative vote on the previous question, the chair states:*

> There is a two-thirds vote in the affirmative. Debate is closed. All those in favor of the pending motion say "Aye." Those opposed say "No."

* *In announcing a negative vote on the previous question, the chair states:*

> There are less than two-thirds in the affirmative. The previous question is lost. Debate will continue. Is there further discussion?

Lay on the Table

* *To make the motion to lay on the table, a member says:*

> [*Remember the member must state the reason why.*] I move to lay the motion on the table because . . . .

* *The chair states the motion:*

> It is moved and seconded to lay the motion on the table. All those in favor say "Aye." Those opposed say "No."

* *In announcing an affirmative vote, the chair states:*

> The ayes have it, and the motion is laid on the table. [*The person who moved to lay on the table should be given the first opportunity to be recognized to introduce new business.*]

* *In announcing a negative vote, the chair states:*

> The noes have it, and the motion is lost. Is there further discussion? [*if it is in order at that time*]

PRIVILEGED MOTIONS

Call for the Orders of the Day

* *To call for the orders of the day, a member rises:*

> Madam President [or Mr. President], I call for the orders of the day.

* *The chair states:*

> The orders of the day are called for. The orders of the day are . . . .

* *To set aside the orders of the day by the initiative of the chair:*

> The orders of the day are called for. The orders of the day are. [*State what they are.*] The question is: Will the assembly proceed to the orders of the day? All those in favor of proceeding to the orders of the day please rise. Be seated. Those opposed please rise. Be seated. [*A two-thirds vote in the negative is needed to set aside the orders of the day, so the vote must be a rising vote.*]

* *In announcing the affirmative vote, the chair states:*

> The affirmative has it, and we will proceed to the orders of the day.

* *In announcing the negative vote, the chair states:*

> There is a two-thirds vote in the negative, and the orders of the day are set aside. We will continue discussing . . . .

Raise a Question of Privilege

* *To raise a question of privilege, a member rises:*

> Madam President [or Mr. President], I rise to
> a question of privilege concerning the assembly.

* *The chair responds:*

> Please state the question. [*The question may
> be about conditions in the room, such as too
> hot, too cold, too noisy, too dark, etc.*]

* *The chair rules on the question of privilege.*

Recess

* *Three ways to make the motion to recess:*

> I move that the meeting recess until ———
> time.

   or

> I move to recess for 10 minutes.

   or

> I move to recess until called to order by the
> chair.

* *The chair responds:*

> It is moved to recess for 10 minutes. All those
> in favor say "Aye." Those opposed say "No."

* *In announcing the vote, the chair states:*

> The ayes have it, and the meeting stands in recess for 10 minutes. [*one rap of the gavel*]

or

> The noes have it, and we won't recess. Is there further discussion?

* *Calling the meeting back to order, the chair states:*

> The meeting will come to order. [*one rap of the gavel*]

or

> The meeting will be in order.

Adjourn

* *In making the motion to adjourn, a member says:*

> I move to adjourn.

or

> I move that the meeting adjourn.

* *The chair responds:*

> It is moved and seconded to adjourn the meeting. All those in favor say "Aye." Those opposed say "No." [*Announce the vote.*]

* *Announcing the affirmative vote:*

> The ayes have it and the meeting will adjourn. [*Pause; look around to see if anyone is rising to do any one of the five things that are still appropriate at this time. See Chapter 6, "Adjourn."*] The meeting is adjourned. [*one rap of the gavel*]

* *Announcing the negative vote:*

> The noes have it and the motion is lost. The meeting will not adjourn. Is there further business? [*or it could be discussion, depending on what was gong on when the motion to adjourn was made*]

Fix the Time to Which to Adjourn

* *To make the motion to fix the time to which to adjourn, a member says:*

> I move that when the meeting adjourns, it adjourn to meet at 8 p.m. tomorrow.

or

> I move that when this meeting adjourns, it stand adjourned to meet at 3 p.m. on Tuesday, May 1, at town hall.

or

> I move that on adjournment, the meeting adjourn to meet at the call of the chair.

* *The chair responds:*

> It is moved and seconded that when the meeting adjourns, it adjourn to meet at 8 p.m. tomorrow. All those in favor say "Aye." Those opposed say "No." [*Announce the vote.*]

* *Announcing the affirmative vote:*

> The ayes have it and the motion is carried. When this meeting adjourns, it will meet again tomorrow at 8 p.m. Is there further business? [*Or discussion, depending on what was happening when the motion was made.*

> *Or if the motion to adjourn was pending when someone made the motion to fix the time to which to adjourn, then the chair would take the vote on the motion to adjourn.]*

* *Announcing the negative vote:*

> The noes have it and the motion is lost.
> [*The chair then returns to the business that was pending.*]

INCIDENTAL MOTIONS

* *To make a point of order:*

> Mr. President [or Madam President], I rise to a point of order.

* *The chair responds:*

> Please state your point.

* *To make a parliamentary inquiry:*

> Mr. President [or Madam President], I rise to a parliamentary inquiry.

* *The chair responds:*

> Please state your inquiry.

* *To make a point of information:*

> Mr. President [or Madam President], I rise to a point of information.

* *The chair responds:*

> Please state your point.

* *To appeal the chair's ruling:*

> I appeal from the decision of the chair.
> [*needs a second*]

* *If the appeal is debatable, the chair states:*

> The ruling of the chair is appealed. The chair ruled that . . . [*State the ruling and the reason for the ruling.*] The question is, shall the decision of the chair be sustained? Is there any discussion?

* *In taking the vote on the appeal, the chair states:*

> All those in favor of sustaining the chair's decision say "Aye." Those opposed say "No." [*Announce the vote.*] The ayes have it and the chair's decision is sustained. [*Announce the decision.*]

or

> The noes have it and the chair's decision shall not stand.

* *To object to considering the question, a member says:*

> Mr. President [or Madam President], I object to the consideration of the question. [*does not require a second*]

* *The chair responds:*

> The consideration of the question is objected to. Shall the question be considered? Those in favor of considering the question rise. Be seated. Those opposed to considering the question rise. Be seated. [*A two-thirds vote against consideration is needed to sustain the objection.*]

* *In announcing the vote (those in favor of considering the question), the chair states:*

> There are less than two-thirds opposed, and the objection is not sustained. The question is on the motion . . . .

* *In announcing the vote (those opposed to considering the question), the chair states:*

> There are two-thirds opposed, and the question will not be considered. Is there further business?

* *To suspend the rules, a member says:*

> I move to suspend the rules and take up . . . . [*needs a second*]

* *The chair responds:*

> It is moved and seconded to suspend the rules and take up . . . . All those in favor rise. Be seated. Those opposed rise. Be seated.

* *In announcing an affirmative vote, the chair states:*

> There are two-thirds in the affirmative and the rules are suspended and we will take up . . . .

* *In announcing a negative vote, the chair states:*

> There are less than two-thirds in the affirmative and the rules are not suspended. We will . . . .

MOTIONS THAT BRING A QUESTION AGAIN BEFORE THE ASSEMBLY

Reconsider

* *To reconsider the vote, a member says:*

> I move to reconsider the vote on the motion . . . . I voted on the prevailing side. [*requires a second*]

* *The chair responds:*

> [*if no other motion is pending*] It is moved and seconded to reconsider the vote on the motion . . . . Is there any discussion? [*assuming the motion is debatable*]

* *If business is pending, the chair states:*

> Will the secretary make a note that the motion to reconsider was made and seconded?

* *To call up the motion to reconsider, a member says:*

> I call up the motion to reconsider the vote on the motion to . . . .

* *The chair responds:*

> It is moved and seconded to reconsider the vote on the motion to . . . . Is there any discussion?

* *In taking the vote on reconsider, the chair states:*

> All those in favor of reconsidering the vote on the motion . . . say "Aye." Those opposed say "No." [*Announce the vote.*]

* *Announcing the affirmative vote:*

> The ayes have it and the motion is carried.
> We will reconsider the vote on the motion
> to . . . . Is there any discussion? [*Members
> again debate the motion and take another
> vote. See Chapter 6, "Reconsider," for more
> details.*]

* *Announcing the negative vote:*

> The noes have it and the motion is lost. We
> will not reconsider the vote on . . . . It will be
> carried out.

Take from the Table

* *To take a motion from the table, a member says:*

> I move to take from the table the motion . . . .
> [*needs a second*]

* *The chair responds:*

> It is moved and seconded to take from the
> table the motion . . . . All those in favor say
> "Aye." Those opposed say "No."

* *In announcing the affirmative vote, the chair states:*

> The ayes have it, and the motion is taken
> from the table. Is there any discussion?

* *In announcing the negative vote, the chair states:*

> The noes have it, and the motion is not
> taken from the table. Is there further
> business?

Rescind

* *To make the motion to rescind, a member says:*

> I move to rescind the motion that was adopted to . . . .

* *The chair responds:*

> It is moved and seconded to rescind the motion that was adopted to . . . . Is there any discussion?

* *Taking the vote:*

> [*if no previous notice has been given the chair states*] Since no previous notice has been given, this takes a two-thirds vote to adopt. All those in favor please rise. Be seated. Those opposed please rise. Be seated.

> [*if previous notice was given, the chair states*] Since previous notice was given, it takes a majority vote to adopt. All those in favor say, "Aye." Those opposed say, "No."

* *Announcing the affirmative vote:*

> [*if a two thirds vote is required*] There are two-thirds in the affirmative and the motion to rescind is adopted and the previous action . . . is rescinded.

> [*if the vote was a voice vote*] The ayes have it and the motion is carried. The previous action . . . is rescinded.

* *Announcing the negative vote:*

> [*if taken as a rising vote, it is announced this way*] There are less than two-thirds in the affirmative and the motion is lost. The previous action stands as adopted.

> [*voice vote announced this way*] The noes have it and the motion is lost. The previous action stands as adopted.

Amend Something Previously Adopted

* *To amend something previously adopted, a member says:*

> I move to amend the motion that was adopted at the last meeting to . . . by striking out . . . and inserting . . . .

* *The chair responds:*

> It is moved and seconded to amend the motion that was adopted at the last meeting to . . . by striking out . . . and inserting . . . . If amended the action would be . . . Is there any discussion on the proposed amendment?

The vote is taken and announced the same way as the motion to rescind. If no previous notice is given, it needs a two-thirds vote to adopt. See Chapter 6.

ADDITIONAL POINTERS FOR THE CHAIR

1. When a nondebatable motion is pending and a member rises to address the chair, the chair should say:

> For what purpose does the member rise?

2. When more than one motion is pending, the chair should state it this way when taking the vote on each motion:

> The question is on the adoption of the motion to . . . .

3. There are several correct phrases to use when taking the vote:

> As many as are in favor say "Aye." Those opposed say "No."

or

> All those in favor say "Aye." Those opposed say "No."

or

> The question is on the adoption of the motion to . . .

APPENDIX C

Meeting Script

Preparing the agenda is the very first step in getting ready to conduct the meeting. After the agenda is written down and the presiding officer knows what is going to come up, the next step is writing a meeting script. The benefit of presiding from a meeting script is that all the presiding officer has to do is read it and follow any directions written on the script. Presiding officers don't get lost, the meeting goes smoothly, and less time is wasted.

In writing a script, write in complete sentences and put all directions of things to do in italics. It's like writing a script for a play. After the agenda is set, then write it out like a play. Here is an example. This is a general script that takes you through a complete order of business. It is easy to adapt this script to many kinds of meetings.

The outline of the agenda given to the members and secretary might look like this:

Agenda for March Meeting

Pledge to the flag

Reading and approval of the minutes

Treasurer's report

Board report

Social Committee report

Elections and nominations

Unfinished business: donation to Children's Museum

New business

Announcements

Adjournment

Now from this outline the presiding officer writes the script.

Meeting Script for March Meeting

1. The meeting will come to order. [*one rap of the gavel*]

2. The members will rise and say the pledge to the flag. [*Lead members in the pledge.*]

3. The first business in order is the reading of the minutes. The secretary will read the minutes of the previous meeting. [*Sit down while the secretary reads the minutes.*]

   [*After the secretary sits down, rise and ask*] Are there any corrections? [*If no corrections, say*] The minutes are approved as read.

   [*If corrections, then say*] Is there any objection to making the correction? Are there further corrections? [*If none, say*] The minutes are approved as corrected.

4. The next business in order is the reports of the officers, the board, and committees. [*Reports of officers are given in the same order as they are listed in the bylaws.*]

The first report will be that of the treasurer. May we have the treasurer's report? [*Sit down while the treasurer gives the report.*]

[*After the report, stand and ask*] Are there any questions? [*If questions, ask the treasurer to answer.*]

[*When the report is finished, state*] The treasurer's report is filed.

The next report will be that of the executive board. Mrs. Smith . . . . [*Sit down while report is given. After report, stand and say*] Are there any questions? [*If questions, ask chairman to answer; then state*] The report is filed.

The next report is the report of the Social Committee. Mr. Jones . . . . [*Sit down while chairman gives report. Repeat the motion from the Social Committee to the assembly.*]

The question is on the adoption of the motion to have the Spring Banquet at Chez Paul on Friday, April 28, at 7:30 p.m. at the cost of $15.00 per person. Is there any discussion? [*After discussion and any amendments, repeat the motion and take the vote.*]

All those in favor say "Aye." Those opposed say "No." [*Announce the vote and tell what the members have decided.*]

5. The next business in order is nomination and election of officers. First we will hear the report of the nominating committee. Then the chair will take nominations for each office from the floor. After nominations, we will vote on the officers by ballot. Will the chairman of the nominating committee give the report? Member A . . . . [*Sit down while the nominating committee reports; then repeat the nominations from the committee and ask for nominations from the floor for each office. Take the vote.*]

    The nominating committee has nominated the following:

    Member B for President

    Member C for Vice President

    Member D for Secretary

    Member E for Treasurer

    Are there any further nominations for President? [*If there are nominations from the floor, repeat them.*] Hearing none, nominations are closed for President.

Are there further nominations for Vice President? Hearing none, nominations are closed for Vice President.

Are there further nominations for Secretary? [*If there are nominations from the floor, repeat them.*] Hearing none, nominations are closed for Secretary.

Are there further nominations for Treasurer? [*If there are nominations from the floor, repeat them.*] Hearing none, nominations are closed for Treasurer.

The tellers will hand out the ballots. Members are to put an "X" by the name of the candidate they want for a particular office. If you are writing in any of the candidates nominated from the floor, write the name under the office for which the person was nominated, and be sure to put an "X" in front of the name written in. Are there any questions concerning how to mark your ballot? [*Give members a few minutes to mark their ballots.*]

Will the tellers collect the ballots? [*Before the tellers leave the room, ask*] Has everyone voted who wishes to vote? [*Look around to see if anyone is calling for a teller.*]

The polls are closed, and the tellers will count the ballots. We will take a short recess while the ballots are being counted. This meeting stands in recess. [*one rap of the gavel*]

[*When the tellers come in, call the meeting to order and announce the result of the vote. If any officers do not get a majority vote, you will have to re-ballot for that office or offices.*]

The meeting will come to order. [*one rap of the gavel*] May we have the report of the tellers' committee? [*Sit down while the tellers' committee gives the report. Then read it and announce the vote. Declare the winners; if no winners, take another vote.*]

6. The next business in order is unfinished business. The motion that was postponed to this meeting to give a $100 donation to the Children's Museum is now pending. Is there any discussion?

   [*Be ready to handle any amendments or other subsidiary motions. Take a vote on each, and then a vote on the final motion.*]

7. The next business in order is new business. Is there any new business? [*When there is no further business, ask for announcements and then adjourn the meeting.*]

8. Our next meeting will be next month on Tuesday, instead of Thursday, at 7 p.m. Remember to get your money to the Social Committee before next Thursday for the Annual Banquet. Are there further announcements? Is there further business?

9. Adjourn the meeting.[*one rap of the gavel*]
   If there is no objection, we will now adjourn
   the meeting. [*Pause; look around the room.
   If no one objects, say*] Hearing no objection,
   this meeting is now adjourned. [*one rap of
   the gavel*]

Special note about preparation: Before the meeting, it is important that you call all those giving reports to see if they will be making a motion at the end of their reports. If so, have the committee chairman or officer give the motion to you before you write the script.

If an officer makes a motion after his or her report, it will need a second. A committee of more than one does not need a second because the committee has already voted on presenting the motion. In that case, the presiding officer places it before the assembly this way:

Chairman: The question is on the adoption of . . . . Is there any discussion?

After the script is prepared, stand up and read it aloud! You may find some awkward phrasing that you want to rewrite. Practicing aloud also familiarizes you with everything on the agenda and gives you confidence in presiding.

This written script, however, cannot prepare you for any unexpected things that might come up in the meeting. Leave blank spaces in the script where the members can bring up business or amend proposed motions. In the blank spaces, you can write down the motions that are being made. If you don't leave blank spaces, then put a blank sheet of paper on the lectern so that you can write down motions that the assembly makes. Spend time reviewing the motions, the ranking of motions, and how to take the vote on several pending questions. Time spent in preparation will make you a better presiding officer and make your meetings more efficient.

This script can also be given to the secretary to help him or her follow along, or the secretary can be given an agenda with everything in an outline form.

Finally, if you write this using a computer, you can use the basic script outline for every meeting, and you can make changes easily.

APPENDIX D

Sample Minutes

The following examples are minutes from two meetings—
a regular meeting and an adjourned meeting.

MINUTES OF A REGULAR MEETING

Secretary: The regular meeting of Student Government
was called to order April 10, at 3 p.m. by
the President. The Secretary was present.
The minutes of the April 3 meeting were
approved as read.

Since the Treasurer had not arrived, the
President proceeded to unfinished business.
The motion to buy a computer and a laser
printer not to exceed the cost of $1,000,
which was postponed from the previous
meeting, was taken up. Keith called for
the orders of the day. The motion was lost.
Members continued discussing the motion
to buy a computer. After amendments, the
motion to buy a computer and a laser printer
not to exceed $2,000 was adopted as
amended.

The treasurer gave his report.

Balance on hand as of April 3, $9,800.

Receipts from T-shirt sales were $200.

Expenditures for the bike-a-thon, $100.

Balance on hand as of April 10, $9,900.

The treasurer's report was filed.

The secretary presented a bill for $50 for photocopying. The members approved the payment of the bill.

Mark moved to take from the table the motion to send five delegates to the state convention. The motion was adopted. Olivia moved to amend the motion by striking out "five" and inserting "two." Doc moved to refer the motion and its pending amendment to the finance committee to see what other funds are available. The previous question was ordered on all pending questions. The members voted to refer the motion and its amendment to the finance committee and report back at the next meeting.

Leslie, who voted on the prevailing side, moved to reconsider the vote on buying the computer and laser printer. The members voted to take a 15-minute recess. The meeting recessed at 3:45 p.m. and then reconvened at 4 p.m. The motion to reconsider the vote on buying the computer and laser printer was adopted. The motion to buy a computer and laser printer was carried. A division was demanded. The vote was retaken, and the motion to buy a computer and laser printer was lost.

Deadra moved that we lease a computer system from the Zone Corporation, not to exceed the specifications submitted in Proposal A.

Doc moved that when the meeting adjourns, it should adjourn to meet here tomorrow at 3 p.m. The motion carried. Doc moved to postpone the motion to lease a computer system to the adjourned meeting and make it the first item of business. The motion was adopted.

Byron moved to have a float in next year's homecoming parade.

Olivia raised a point of order that the motion to have a float in the homecoming parade was not within the scope of our bylaws. The chair ruled that the point was well taken. Byron appealed from the decision of the chair. The chair ruled that the motion was out of order because the purpose of our organization is to govern, not necessarily to participate in events. The chair's decision was sustained. The motion to have a float in next year's homecoming parade was no longer considered.

Leslie moved to adjourn. The motion was adopted.

Olivia gave notice that at the next meeting she would move to rescind Standing Rule number 5, which states that we give $100 to Goofy Days.

The meeting adjourned at 4:30 p.m.

Jane Jones
Secretary

MINUTES OF AN ADJOURNED MEETING

When an assembly can't complete its business at the present meeting but, nevertheless, must have it completed before the next regular meeting, a member can move to set the time for an adjourned meeting. This is helpful for groups that do not provide for special meetings in their bylaws. An adjourned meeting is a legal continuation of the current meeting. When the adjourned meeting is called to order, the assembly begins where it left off. However, the minutes of the meeting being continued are read and approved before beginning the business portion of the meeting. To set an adjourned meeting is one of the motions that can be made when no quorum is present.

Following are the minutes of the adjourned meeting:

Secretary:　The adjourned meeting of Student Government was called to order April 11, at 3 p.m. by the President. The secretary was present. The minutes of the April 10 meeting were approved as read.

The motion to lease a computer system that was postponed to the adjourned meeting was discussed. During the meeting the Treasurer received a note from the Dean's office that stated that all student activities offices will be getting a computer system by the end of the term. Deadra requested permission to withdraw the motion. Permission was granted by the assembly.

Mark moved that the meeting adjourn at 3:25 p.m. The previous question was ordered on the motion. The motion to adjourn at 3:25 p.m. was adopted.

Keith moved that the time of our meetings be changed to 7 p.m. Byron questioned the assembly's ability to change the time because it had been established by a prior vote to be 3 p.m. The chair ruled that the procedure was proper. It was the motion to "amend something previously adopted." Since no previous notice was given, it will take a two-thirds vote to adopt.

The chair adjourned the meeting at 3:25 p.m.

Jane Jones
Secretary

APPENDIX E

Steps in Making a Motion

1. Rise and address the chair:

> Madam President or Mr. President

or

> Madam Chairman or Mr. Chairman.

2. The presiding officer assigns you the floor by stating your name or by nodding at you.

3. State the motion:

> I move to . . . or I move that . . . . [*Sit down after you make the motion.*]

4. It needs a second.

5. The presiding officer repeats the motion and places it before the assembly by stating:

> It is moved and seconded that . . . . Is there any discussion?

6. Members discuss the motion by rising, addressing the chair, and being assigned the floor.

7. The presiding officer takes a vote by stating:

> All those in favor say "Aye." Those opposed say "No."

8. The presiding officer announces the vote and whether the motion is adopted or defeated. If the motion is adopted, the presiding officer states the name of the person who will carry out the action.

> The ayes have it, and the motion is carried. We will . . . .

or

> The noes have it, and the motion is lost.

APPENDIX F

Ranking of Motions

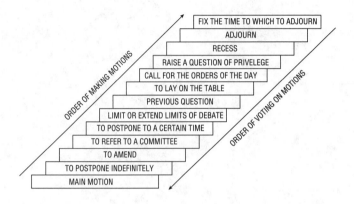

APPENDIX G

Motions That Take a Majority Vote

FIX THE TIME TO WHICH TO ADJOURN
ADJOURN
RECESS
LAY ON THE TABLE
POSTPONE TO A CERTAIN TIME
REFER TO A COMMITTEE
AMEND
POSTPONE INDEFINITELY

MAIN MOTION

TO CREATE A BLANK
TO REQUEST PERMISSION TO WITHDRAW
A QUESTION
TO TAKE FROM THE TABLE
TO RECONSIDER
TO RESCIND
(with previous notice)
TO AMEND SOMETHING ADOPTED
(with previous notice)
TO REOPEN NOMINATIONS OR THE POLLS

APPENDIX H

Motions That Take a Two-Thirds Vote

In general, a two-thirds vote is required for any motion that takes rights away from members. Such rights include the right to be informed of pending action, to conduct business by known and established rules, to debate and to vote. The following motions require a two-thirds vote in all cases:

Previous Question (close debate)

Limit or Extend Debate

Close Nominations or Close the Polls

Object to the Consideration of a Question

Suspend the Rules

In some cases, a majority vote is sufficient when previous notice is given. The following motions take a *two-thirds vote without previous notice* or a *majority vote with previous notice:*

Rescind

Amend Something Previously Adopted

Discharge a Committee

APPENDIX I

A History

The term *parliamentary law* came from the English Parliament where it meant the rules for carrying on the business of the Parliament. These rules evolved through a continuing process of development and precedent, similar to that of common law. They were brought to America with the early settlers who used them in their own legislative assemblies, and where they further evolved. General parliamentary law or common parliamentary law of today has developed out of this legislative tradition.

Parliamentary law is used in *deliberative assemblies,* a term first used by Edmund Burke to refer to the English Parliament. It means a "group of persons meeting to make group decisions, to discuss and to determine a common course of action."

Under parliamentary law, a deliberative assembly can adopt any written rules of procedure. It can also add to or deviate from its own rules of procedure. *Rules of Order* refers to a set of written parliamentary rules adopted by the assembly to conduct its business. These could be an existing set of rules especially composed by the assembly. *Parliamentary procedure* refers to the parliamentary law that a deliberative assembly follows, plus whatever additional rules of order the assembly might have adopted for itself.

The origin of the English parliament is found in the village assemblies of the Anglo-Saxon tribes that migrated to the British Isles in the fifth century A.D. In those days, freemen came together in a "village-moot" to make "bye-laws" for their village and to administer justice. Other larger deliberative assemblies of the day were the "hundred-moot," a kind of district court of appeal, and the "folk-moot" a still higher authority for arbitrating disputes. In Anglo-Saxon times, the "folk-moot" became the "Shire-moot," later called the "Shire-court."

After the Norman Conquest in 1066, the French administration developed a "Great Council" made up of feudal barons who advised the king on such matters as he might wish advice. These were not truly democratic organizations because they were under the thumb of a king and a feudal system, but they formed the beginnings of a democratic parliament.

In the thirteenth century, the "Great Council" gradually evolved into the beginnings of the "parliament" we know today when the barons who attended began to discuss *with each other* the "state of the realm" and the "king's business." Then the parliament began to include representatives of the shires and the boroughs (similar to counties and towns). These representatives were called the "commons." Before long, they were in attendance at every parliament. Then parliament was separated into the "House of Commons" and the "House of Lords."

During the next two centuries, procedures in the parliament developed slowly and eventually were written down and published as part of a larger work by Sir Thomas Smyth in the sixteenth century. The first book about it was *Lex Parliamentaria* by G. Petyt, a pocket manual prepared for members of parliament. This book enumerated some of the most fundamental principles of parliamentary procedure such as:

Take up business one subject at a time.

Alternate between opposite points of view in debate.

Require the chair to call for the negative vote.

Keep personal attacks out of the debate.

Debate only the merits of the question under discussion.

Divide a question into two or more questions if appropriate.

Parliamentary procedure came to America in the seventeenth century when Virginia's House of Burgesses was founded in 1619. Other colonies founded governing assemblies based on their experiences in the old European countries from which they came. Eventually their experiences led to the framing of state constitutions and state legislatures, which have their own rules of order. In the eighteenth century, the restrictive policies of the British Empire caused the American colonists to consider common resistance to the British colonial government. When the First Continental Congress convened in Philadelphia in 1774, its members already had enough parliamentary procedural experience to conduct business expeditiously. The Second Continental Congress framed the Declaration of Independence and declared war on the British colonial government. Existing state constitutions provided the material from which the Constitutional Convention of 1787 framed the U.S. Constitution. Through all of this turmoil, parliamentary procedures and rules were used to expedite business and to help resolve deep disagreements among the delegates. Out of this experience came the U.S. Constitution, which has been used as a model for other independent national constitutions worldwide. The usefulness of parliamentary procedure cannot be over-emphasized in such a process because it enables many different representatives of widely varying points of view to come to a common agreement in the very difficult circumstances of a political revolution.

The first book about parliamentary procedure in America was Thomas Jefferson's *Manual of Parliamentary Practice,* published in 1801. Jefferson was serving as Vice President and Presiding Officer of the Senate. He observed that the Senate did not have a codified set of rules of order but rather allowed the presiding officer a wide discretionary power to make up rules as he went along. Jefferson saw that this power could easily be abused in the future, so he developed a set of parliamentary rules based on English works and documents regarding the procedures of the British Parliament. Jefferson's *Manual* was adopted by the Senate, by state legislatures, by other groups, and by the House of Representatives. (The House later developed its own unique set of procedural rules.)

The next book about parliamentary procedure was *Cushing's Manual,* which was a set of rules of voluntary organizations that had needs different from legislative bodies. The meetings of small organizations were shorter, their delegates unpaid, and their business was less voluminous, so a different set of rules was needed to accommodate such organizations. *Cushing's Manual* basically said that each organization should follow fundamental parliamentary law as outlined in the manual but should adopt its own rules of order appropriate to itself. While this idea was good in theory, it didn't have the practical effect of significantly helping new voluntary organizations. Many of them did not have the time, the expertise, or the will to develop their own set of parliamentary rules. Thus, there was still parliamentary confusion in organizations when Henry Robert arrived on the scene in the 1860s.

APPENDIX J

Who Was Henry Robert?

Henry Robert (1837–1923) was a West Point–educated United States Army officer. He became interested in parliamentary law when he was asked to preside at a meeting and didn't know how. After the meeting, he vowed to learn something about parliamentary law. He soon found that little information about the subject was applicable to small voluntary organizations. While he was stationed as an army officer in different parts of the country, he attended meetings and noticed that each organization was conducting meetings by its own set of "rules." There were no universally accepted rules in existence. He saw that organizations would be better able to function and carry out their purposes if they had a universally recognized and accepted set of parliamentary rules. In researching the question, he obtained a copy of *Cushing's Manual,* Jefferson's *Manual of Parliamentary Practice,* and Barclay's *Digest of Rules and Practices of the House.* Seeing that these three standard works did not agree on the major points of parliamentary law, he began writing his own rules of order, a work he, at first, expected to be short.

In 1874, Robert had a few months to devote to writing his book of procedure. He envisioned a book that would be based on the rules of Congress but would be general enough to be adopted by any society, while still allowing the society the latitude to make up and adopt for itself any special rules of order it might need. He wrote the book during 1874 and 1875. When the manuscript was completed, he couldn't find a publisher, so he published it himself by hiring a printer to make 4,000 copies. The book was titled *Pocket Manual of Rules of Order for Deliberative Assemblies* (176 pages). Then he did find a publisher, S. C. Griggs Co. of Chicago, who retitled the book *Robert's Rules of Order*. The first edition of 3,000 copies (now a rare book) sold out in four months. A second edition, somewhat expanded and revised, came out in 1876, and a third edition was published in 1893. When the Griggs publishing company went out of business in 1896, the publishing rights were taken over by Scott, Foresman & Co., who held the publishing rights for 100 years until 1996.

APPENDIX K

National Organizations

There are two national organizations that provide information on parliamentarians and parliamentary procedures. For those who are interested in becoming a parliamentarian, these organizations provide excellent guidance and also sell instructional materials. Each organization has a different requirement for membership, and both have local chapters that meet regularly. Those interested are welcome to attend as guests. For those needing assistance with parliamentary procedure, these organizations have listings of registered and certified parliamentarians who can be hired in various capacities such as: convention parliamentarian, presiding parliamentarian, bylaws consultant, etc. They can also suggest parliamentarians to give targeted workshops to your organization.

The National Association of Parliamentarians
213 South Main Street
Independence, MO 64050-3850
816-833-3892
e-mail **ffgp00a@prodigy.com**

The American Institute of Parliamentarians
P.O. Box 2173
Wilmington, DE 19899
302-762-1811
e-mail **aip@aipparlipro.org**

Index

Robert McConnell Productions

6018 West Hellis Drive ~ Muncie IN 47304 ~ USA
Phone: 765-282-9845 ~ Fax: 765-282-2171 ~ E-mail: drvideo@netdirect.net
Web site: http://parli.com

VIDEOS FOR PARLIAMENTARIANS
1-800-532-4017

_____**HOW TO CONDUCT A MEETING** (32 min. VIDEO)
World's first video about conducting a meeting from beginning to end according to
Robert's Rules of Order. Covers basic procedures: quorum, agenda, call to order,
minutes, reports, unfinished business, new business, discussion, voting, and
adjournment. Includes an audio cassette, a generic meeting script to help you
perform like a pro, and an agenda planning guide. $74.50 +$5 S & H **$79.50 total.**
_____**Video cassette only** $54.50 +$5 S & H **$59.50 total.**
_____**Audio cassette only** $15 +$5 S & H **$20.00 total.**

_____**COMO CONDUCIR REUNIONES (en Espanol)** (46 min. VIDEO)
World's first video entirely in Spanish about conducting a meeting from beginning to
end according to *Robert's Rules of Order*. Covers basic procedures: quorum, agenda,
call to order, minutes, reports, unfinished business, new business, discussion, voting,
and adjournment. Includes an audio cassette, a generic meeting script to help you
perform like a pro, and an agenda planning guide. $74.50 +$5 S & H **$79.50 total.**
_____**Video cassette only** $54.50 +$5 S & H **$59.50 total.**
_____**Audio cassette only** $15 +$5 S & H **$20.00 total.**

_____**PARLIAMENTARY PROCEDURE MADE SIMPLE** (80 min. VIDEO)
Details how to make motions, amend motions, take minutes, vote, and run meetings
according to *Robert's Rules of Order*. This video is ideal for libraries, schools,
colleges, unions, churches, municipalities, business, individuals, organizations, and
associations. Every group, organization, and association should have a copy. $64.50
+$5 S & H **$69.50 total.**

_____**ALL ABOUT MOTIONS Pts 1 & 2** (140 min. VIDEO)
The second in the series about parliamentary procedures. As a set, the **ALL ABOUT
MOTIONS** videos are a visual encyclopedia of virtually every motion in *Robert's
Rules of Order*. Each individual video cassette comes with a time coded booklet full
of helpful additional information. $114.50 +$5 S & H **$119.50 total**.

FREE OFFER:
**A list of the motions in Robert's Rules of Order entitled *Basic Parliamentary
Information*. You can take this handy quick reference sheet into your meetings,
and use it to make any motion that is appropriate and in order. To receive this
free offer, just call 1-800-532-4017.**

** Prices above exclude shipping and handling, which may apply. All monies payable in U.S.
dollars. Prices subject to change. All videotapes are subject to avaliability.*